THE ADMINISTRATION OF
PUBLIC SAFETY IN HIGHER EDUCATION

THE ADMINISTRATION OF PUBLIC SAFETY IN HIGHER EDUCATION

By

DAVID NICHOLS, Ed.D.

Chief of Police
Jacksonville State University
Jacksonville, Alabama

CHARLES C THOMAS • PUBLISHER
Springfield • Illinois • U.S.A.

Published and Distributed Throughout the World by

CHARLES C THOMAS • PUBLISHER
2600 South First Street
Springfield, Illinois 62794-9265

© *1987 by* CHARLES C THOMAS • PUBLISHER

ISBN 0-398-05330-8

Library of Congress Catalog Card Number: 87-1898

With THOMAS BOOKS *careful attention is given to all details of manufacturing and
design. It is the Publisher's desire to present books that are satisfactory as to their physical
qualities and artistic possibilities and appropriate for their particular use.* THOMAS
BOOKS *will be true to those laws of quality that assure a good name and good will.*

Printed in the United States of America
SC-R-3

Library of Congress Cataloging-in-Publication Data

Nichols, David, Ed. D.
    The administration of public safety in higher education.

    Bibliography: p.
    Includes index.
    1. Universities and colleges—United States—
Safety measures.   2. Universities and colleges—United
States—Security measures.   I. Title.
LB2866.N53   1987   378.73′028′9   87-1898
ISBN 0-398-05330-8

PREFACE

The purpose of this book is to provide a comprehensive study of public safety in higher education with an emphasis on effective management approaches. It is aimed at those responsible for the delivery of public safety services within the campus community to include presidents, vice-presidents, deans, and public safety directors. It is also intended for use as a text by criminal justice teaching programs and as supplemental reading for higher education administration courses. While the few existing books on the subject focus primarily on campus law enforcement and/or security, this text represents an effort to provide an overview of the broad and complex functions which campus public safety performs today. This is done by reviewing historical developments, gleaning current literature and research, and presenting innovative campus public safety programs. This book offers a philosophical and conceptual approach to effective management as well as practical guidelines for administering a public safety operation within an academic setting. Problems and issues facing campus public safety are also addressed in realistic terms. Serious treatment is given to public safety's role within the campus community and its significance to the mission of higher education.

It has been my observation and the consensus of many of my colleagues that campus public safety has been largely overlooked or ignored as an integral part of any professional or associational sphere. Institutions of higher education have generally relegated it to any number of lower-rung organizational levels. Consequently, it has suffered an identity problem. The criminal justice system often fails to consider campus law enforcement's efforts and impact on its processes. Criminal justice academic programs have generally not recognized campus public safety as a potential career opportunity for its students. Consequently, it receives little or no attention in most criminal justice teaching programs. Other public safety agencies, (e.g., fire safety, emergency medical services, civil defense), often exclude campus public safety organizations from their activities, even though the campus public safety operations may be responsible for the communication and/or delivery of these services. Therefore, it is hoped that this book will contribute to the recognition and acceptance of campus public safety by other peer organizations and related professions.

Finally, I wish to enlighten the readers of this text about the remarkable progress and accomplishments which have been made by campus public safety. After years of research on the subject, experience as an administrator, and visits on many campuses, I am convinced that campus public safety has enhanced the quality of life within the campus community and furthered the goals of higher education.

D.N.

CONTENTS

THE ADMINISTRATION OF
PUBLIC SAFETY IN HIGHER EDUCATION

Part I

THE IMPORTANCE OF PUBLIC SAFETY
WITHIN THE CAMPUS COMMUNITY

Expansion, increases in enrollment, and changes in social mores have significantly changed life within the campus community over the past three decades. These changes have not been without their growing pains and resulting problems. Student demonstrations, congested parking and traffic, liability concerns, and crime are among the challenges faced by many campus administrators. In response to these problems, many university officials determined that improved campus public safety efforts were needed. In some cases, public safety programs did not exist. Others were inadequate to meet the accelerated changes taking place within many campus communities. Consequently, what is now called campus police, campus security, or campus public safety emerged with the mission to protect students and make the campus community a safe and peaceful environment. While this mission has, to a large extent, been accomplished, some institutions of higher learning continue to experience a great deal of concern over the proper role of public safety within the campus community. One thing has become clear: An effective campus public safety program is important and, in fact, essential in supporting the broad missions of higher education institutions.

Chapter 1

THE EMERGENCE OF CAMPUS PUBLIC SAFETY IN HIGHER EDUCATION: AN OVERVIEW

3:45 P.M.   ...Officer Smith reports to work at the State University Police Department and punches his time card before beginning his assigned tour of duty from 4:00 P.M. until midnight.

4:30 P.M.   ...While on routine patrol at University fraternity row Officer Smith receives a call from the police radio dispatcher to assist a student motorist at the science building parking lot who has locked her keys in her car.

4:48 P.M.   ...Officer Smith responds to a minor traffic accident call at University Circle and Coliseum Street and writes an accident report on the two-car collision.

6:25 P.M.   ...University Police radio dispatcher sends Officer Smith to a fight incident with injuries in the campus cafeteria involving a football player and two fraternity members. Sergeant Jones responds as a backup and jointly they take the three students into custody for questioning.

7:40 P.M.   ...While issuing parking tickets to illegally parked cars in the library's loading zone, Officer Smith is dispatched to a men's dormitory to write a theft report involving the theft of a stereo and $35 in cash from a student's room.

8:33 P.M.   ...A fire alarm at a female dormitory sends Officer Smith with emergency lights and siren to the scene. A trash can fire on the third floor requires the response of the local fire department who quickly extinguishes the fire and order is restored. Officer Smith writes a report on the incident with following investigation to be done later.

9:52 P.M.   ...A male trespasser is reported in the hallway of a female dormitory. Upon his arrival, Officer Smith finds an intoxicated non-student wandering in a hallway and places him under arrest and transports him to the local city jail.

11:36 P.M.   ...Officer Smith is called to assist a dormitory director with a female resident who reports having been raped by a "friend" while parked in a remote campus parking lot.

2:20 A.M.   . . . Officer Smith "clocks out" on his time card after completing his investigation of the rape incident, finishing other incident report writing and completing routine shift reports.

Such is a typical shift for a campus public safety officer on a medium to large campus. This example serves to illustrate the kinds of occurrences and incidents which are common in most campus communities today. As one might observe, these incidents differ little from those in many municipalities and require the same responses by the campus public safety officer as would be expected from the city police officer.

The campus community, in a sense, is a city of its own with most of the same problems that exist in a municipality to include traffic congestion, fire protection, medical emergencies, and crime. Yet, it is different and unique, in that its institution is in the sole business of higher education. This business of teaching, research, service, and subsequent support efforts for the most part occur within the campus community setting. These communities vary in terms of type, size, and location from public to private, rural to urban, small to large, commuter to residential, two-year to four-year programs, technical to liberal arts, and other variations. In order to better view the role and administration of campus public safety, it is important to take a close look at the unique environment of today's campus community.

CHARACTERISTICS OF THE CAMPUS COMMUNITY

Most colleges and universities across the country share and exhibit common characteristics. These characteristics provide the uniqueness of the campus community in contrast with municipalities and other communities.

The first of these is the overall homogeneous population which consists primarily of students in pursuit of higher education and employees who work either directly or supportively in the educational process. This is somewhat of a paradox, since the complexion of the student population is also heterogeneous in terms of the backgrounds, races, and cultures represented. A related characteristic is the "student citizen" of the campus community.[1] Nowhere else is found such a concentrated population made up of individuals, for the most part between the ages of

18 and 22, with an educational level higher than that of our society at large. Most of these "student citizens" are single and many are experiencing freedom from home and parental control for the first time. In recognizing the uniqueness of the student population, Florida State University's Public Safety Department's philosophy states, "The Department recognizes the unique nature of a community composed of mainly youthful, highly educated, impressionable, vocal, and too often anti-authoritarian citizens."[2] Another characteristic shared by residential campuses is the predominate social life. Fraternities, sororities, dormitory life, parties, athletics, rock concerts, and other activities create a most unique social atmosphere, often resulting in problems related to alcohol abuse, misconduct and criminal activity. The influence that social aspects of campus life have on students' behavior and long-term social and personal development is tremendous. Another common characteristic is the denseness of the population within relatively small geographical boundaries. Often, there are 8,000 to 10,000 residents within one square mile, thus creating congested traffic, close living conditions, and other environmental and societal problems.

One characteristic which has recently emerged and is important to recognize is the open-campus concept. Traditionally, the campus was considered to be a closed community immune to the outside influences of crime, environmental hazards, and "locals." While some few campuses are able to lock their gates, there is a predominance of the open campus with no gates, no curfews, and little or no restrictions to many outside influences. Often, it is difficult to ascertain where the campus boundaries begin and end.

Perhaps the characteristic which has had the greatest impact is the adult status of the student. This resulted from the U.S. Supreme Court's decision in *Dixon* v. *the Alabama Board of Education* (1961) that struck down the doctrine of *in loco parentis* under which educational institutions had operated for many years. Students were no longer subject to many traditional institutional disciplinary rules and procedures but were afforded the same rights as any citizen.

While these characteristics are not intended to be all inclusive, they afford a perspective with which to view the uniqueness of the campus community. It is within this environment and special circumstances thereof that campus public safety has emerged to meet the changing needs of its constituents. While college campuses have existed for over two centuries in this country, campus police/security is relatively young and, in fact, is still developing.

THE EVOLUTION OF CAMPUS PUBLIC SAFETY

The beginning of the modern campus police force can be traced back to the school maintenance staff or faculty chairman of the school grounds. Their major attention was focused on physical needs such as building construction, the provision of heat, waste disposal, fire prevention, and protecting property from trespassers or straying animals. Neal states, "In different eras and on different campuses his forerunner was the janitor, or the watchmen, or the faculty chairman of the grounds committee, or in some cases the lineage can be traced directly to the president of the institution."[3]

In all probability, campus safety/security had its formal beginning in 1894 when the Yale Campus Police was established. Because of frequent conflicts between Yale students and townspeople that often developed into full-scale riots, two New Haven police officers were hired by Yale as campus police officers. These officers retained their sworn authority as city officers, a situation that has existed for Yale officers to this day. One of these first officers, William Weiser, was appointed chief. Chief Weiser wrote a book in 1914, entitled *Yale Memories,* in which he stated that his department's most important function was to "protect the students, their property, and University property."[4] While Yale established a police department in 1894, this was the exception rather than the rule.

During the early 1900s there was little need for a campus police or security forces, and most colleges and universities depended entirely upon the local police to handle any criminal violations and campus disruptions. Most matters involving student misbehavior were handled "internally" through the dean of students' office.

During the 1920s the watchman or guard appeared as the prominent approach to campus safety. Historically, these watchmen, who were usually older retired men and employed only at night and on weekends, were attached to the maintenance or physical plant department. Their main concern was with the protection of college property. These watchmen were given no training as law enforcement officers and were not expected to perform as such. Their chief functions were to determine the security of buildings at night and on weekends (e.g. closing windows, locking and unlocking doors, and other duties to protect property) and "patrol" the campus in order to detect fire hazards, check boilers, detect leaky pipes and otherwise perform preventive maintenance duties. With the repeal of Prohibition in the early 1930s the watchman-guard gradually began to take on other functions dealing with the enforcement of rules and regulations governing student conduct.[5]

While the watchman-guard type approach was predominant until the 1950s, there were a few colleges and universities that established police oriented safety/security departments. One such institution was the University of Maryland. In 1936, after the rotation of many Maryland State Troopers temporarily assigned to the campus at College Park, two volunteered for permanent duty at the university and subsequently were hired by the university as campus police officers.[6]

It was during the decade of the fifties that university administrators began to recognize the need for a more organized protective force on campus. This was brought on by the problems created by increasing growth and consequent complexities of the campus. Increases in enrollment, potential increases in behavioral incidents, expansion of the physical plant, increases in motor traffic, and problems incident to parking led to an awareness for some semblance of police presence on campus. Consequently, at the beginning of the 1950s retired law enforcement officials were hired as campus "cops" and often patterned campus safety departments after models used in municipal settings. Usually, the "police" authority was still limited to detection of crime, physical security functions, and notification of local police authorities in the event of necessary arrests or other formal police action.[7]

In 1953 the Northeastern College and University Security Association was formed by a group of campus security administrators in the Northeast to foster professionalism and the exchange of information. Soon to follow this effort was the formation of the National Association of College and University Traffic and Security Directors in 1958 which is now the International Association of College and University Law Enforcement Administrators. This association presently has over 800 institutional members. These associations were clear indications that the once campus watchmen-guards were becoming organized and developed into more professionally oriented safety officers.

However, it was not until the tumultuous sixties when disorder and crime were introduced to the academic community that college administrators realized the inadequacy of their campus "law" and, at the same time, became dissatisfied with the local police attitude and methods.

Subsequently, administrators concerned not only with students' needs, peace and safety, but also with more autonomy of law enforcement responsibilities on campus, recognized the time for a change of priorities and the need for a new direction which would create a more professional police/security department on campus. The concept of hiring former municipal and county police officers began to be less popular.

Bordner and Petersen state:

> With the advent of the era of student dissent, campus protest demonstrations, disruptive student activities, violence and increases in reported crime and fear of crime, an increasing number of educational institutions began replacing their line security officers with more educated and better trained police officers with police powers of arrest and duties to enforce state statutes on campus. The decision to professionalize the campus police was, in part, a direct result of the negative experiences with intervention of local police and National Guardsmen on campus. During the era of student dissent, Kent State offers a vivid example. It was also recognized that if the university did not govern itself it would be governed by others who might be less responsive to the campus community. Thus, professional police departments began to emerge on college campuses during the 1960s and early 1970s, and law enforcement activities became part of the ever-expanding role of the university officer.[8]

During the 1970s campus security began to be programmed to meet student problems and needs. It emphasized a low-key but highly professional approach utilizing well-trained young officers who were either enrolled in college-degree programs or who had already achieved a degree. These officers were often attired in blazer-slacks outfits bearing the college seal and department name instead of the police-type uniforms of the former watchmen-guards. Professional degree-holding safety and security administrators were very much in demand to head these departments. Security directors, who once answered to the head of the physical plant, were now often reporting to the president and vice-president. In a 1968 survey of 120 campus safety and security directors, Nielson reported that less than one-half of all respondents still reported to the physical plant director. Among this group, from 28 percent to 60 percent, depending on the category, advocated a change to reporting to a vice-president. This trend would suggest that the role of watchman-guard with its property-protection orientation is changing to one of a more professional police and "people" orientation.[9]

To conclude, campus safety/security was slow to develop. As college enrollments increased, however, the need for campus safety became an important administrative concern. This review of campus safety history points out that growth in the universities coupled with a parallel growth in crime and safety problems prompted a change in campus safety operations and role.

HIGHER EDUCATION AND THE
ROLE OF CAMPUS PUBLIC SAFETY

Before undertaking a discussion of the administration of campus public safety, it is important to briefly examine the philosophy and mission of higher education. It is within this context that the role of campus public safety can be viewed and, thus, afford a better perspective of its mission, objectives, and operation.

What is higher education? For the sake of simplicity, the phrase "higher education" will be used inclusively and genericly to encompass education ranging from higher learning, which often refers to graduate education, down to postsecondary education, which generally refers to the several years immediately following secondary school. College usually refers to the first two to four years beyond high school, and a college may or may not be a part of a university. The university is the institution of most inclusive scope in its academic offerings.

Brubacher (1978), a noted scholar and author on higher education, states that there are at least two different philosophies legitimating the institutions of higher education: epistemological and political. Each has been dominant at one time or another on American campuses. Simply put, the epistemological view espouses the seeking of knowledge for knowledge's sake quite apart from any bearing it might have on the world or the good of man. With the founding of Johns Hopkins University in 1876, the epistemological justification of higher education became predominate.[10]

During most of the remainder of the nineteenth century, higher education was not an important influence in American life. This was soon to change, however. What happened was that the accelerating forces of the Industrial Revolution throughout the nineteenth century gave the expertise to be found in the colleges and universities increasing practical significance. As a result, the political philosophy of higher education came abreast of, and even overtook, the epistemological. The political philosophy views knowledge learned at colleges and universities as having practical application toward solving the intricate problems of our complex society. Problems of government, industry, agriculture, labor, raw materials, international relations, education, health, and the like can be solved by the expertise and people trained in institutions of higher education. Since the turn of the century the political philosophy has been predominate. With this philosophy came more students seeking an education/vocation to prepare them for their future in a growing society.

Institutions of higher education serve three principal functions: to transmit the higher learning, to expand its limits and to put its results at the service of the public.[11] In general, the mission of higher education is to provide education, research, and resources for society. In a sense, higher education institutions are industries competing for and marketing for the student consumer.[12] They must gear their programs and products (graduates) to society's needs and demands.

It is within this broad mission and goals of higher education that campus public safety must adapt its role and provide its services. Campus public safety, to include law enforcement, security, fire safety, emergency medical services, and other service-related responsibilities, is clearly a support function to the broader mission and goals of the higher education institution.

Today, the public safety function has become an integral and essential component of higher education administration in most colleges and universities. There has been a propensity for its emergence parallel to the proliferation of colleges and growth in enrollments during the 1960s and 1970s. There are over 3,000 colleges, universities, and branch campuses in the United States today. They serve approximately 11.5 million students, employ approximately two million people, and represent more than 78 billion dollars of investment in property, facilities, and equipment.[13] Even though the 1980s have seen a modest decline in college enrollments, the need for effective law enforcement/security and other public safety services continues to be great.

College and university presidents and top administrators are concerned with every area of the campus community and are committed to quality in both academic and support divisions. The assiduous top administrator is becoming more aware of the importance of effective public safety efforts on campus. While the primary mission of the institution should be that of facilitating academic development, the assurance of a safe environment conducive to the pursuit of educational goals is also essential. This is the primary role of campus public safety.

Personal safety and property security are major areas for which public safety services must be provided. The increasing liability awareness of the past few years has been a major concern of administrators when making public safety decisions.

During the past two decades, significant strides have been made in campus public safety. Innovative programs, as well as a new professionalism, have been achieved through supportive administrative efforts emanating from a cognizance and concern for the total environment of the institution. Public safety on campus includes law enforcement/security, fire safety, emergency medical services, and civil defense procedures. These services are particularly important for the residential campus community. College communities have the same public safety responsibilities as do the municipalities in which they are located and often share services through cooperative arrangements with the local government. However, the chief administrator knows that the ultimate responsibility for safety and security rests with the institution. Therefore, the best services feasible within budgetary constraints must be afforded.

SPECIAL PROBLEMS AND ISSUES
FACING CAMPUS PUBLIC SAFETY

While it is true that campus public safety has made great strides and progressed to a high level of service, there are still problems and issues facing campus safety officials. A brief treatment of a few of these will provide a better perspective of the role of campus safety with its special concerns.

The 1960s and 1970s were marked with social and political unrest and subsequent disturbance on college campuses. While these conditions were of great concern to college and university administrators, they did not seriously threaten the safety of the campus population. As campus unrest waned, it appeared to be replaced by a new problem—namely, increased crime in the form of thefts, assaults, robberies, rapes, and the illegal use and selling of drugs.* College and university campuses became prime targets for outside criminals who realized that a campus population was made up of mostly young people who had little concern

---

*While it is appropriate here to include crime as one of the problems facing campus safety, the crime problem will be dealt with in depth in the next chapter.—ED.

for security or crime and administrators whose main interest was education, not protection or enforcing the law.

Bordner and Peterson state: "The university is like a city as far as crime is concerned. It experiences many of the problems of the city. Stated differently, campus police are confronted with many of the same problems as municipal agencies."[14]

A particular problem related to crime on campus is safety for female students. The State University of New York at Albany established a task force to identify safety problems encountered by women and make recommendations for improved safety and security efforts. Shortly after the formation of the Task Force, a series of serious sexual attacks occurred. These events prompted immediate attention by the Task Force and resulted in a number of projects to ensure the safety of women on campus.

Parking on campus continues to be a problem. It seems that more students bring cars to campus each year. Several campus officials have reported that their number one problem is parking. The University of Wisconsin at Parkside experienced this problem and implemented an innovative program to relieve the congested situation. The campus security department solved the problem by increasing the number of parking spaces by reducing the size of many parking spaces to accommodate small cars.[15]

There are several other problems facing campus safety. The use and abuse of alcohol by students presents several consequent problems for campus safety officers. Powell states: "A rather alarming return to the heavy use of alcohol has occurred in the past few years. Most campus security administrators have expressed to me that alcohol is getting to be a major problem and contributes to increased acts of vandalism, personal injuries, and disorder."[16]

The federal government has taken measures to encourage states to pass laws raising the legal drinking age to 21 years. This will present special problems of enforcement for campus public safety officials.

A recent issue confronting many colleges and universities is whether or not campus safety officers should be armed with a weapon. Powell points out that: "The arming of campus police or security forces is an extremely sensitive issue and must be treated with the utmost care."[17] He further states:

> During the past few years a marked softening of the attitude regarding weapons on campus has occurred, undoubtedly because of increas-

ing crime—particularly crime against the person. Today the great majority of students not only accept the fact that their campus officers are armed, they expect them to be armed.[18]

The State University of New York at Oswego first allowed its security officers to be armed in 1929 after several incidents involving armed assaults on students by intruders to the campus. While the transition from unarmed officers to armed was met with some opposition, the institution's president justified the need for better trained and equipped safety officers.[19]

Iannarelli supports the policy of armed officers because, he contends, it acts as a deterrent to the potential criminal.[20]

Another current issue involves the question of whether to allow full police authority for campus safety officers. Findings from a study conducted by Milliron (1980) revealed that deans of students did not support full police authority for campus safety officers.[21] However, according to Powell (1981), "Over forty states have passed legislation to provide police authority to campus security personnel."[22] Campus safety officers who do not possess full police authority are placed in a tenuous position when they must justify the use of force in apprehending law violators. This issue will receive further treatment in a later section of this volume.

Hazardous waste and dangerous chemical storage often falls under the responsibility of the campus safety department. Increased vehicular traffic on and adjacent to the campuses is a common problem in terms of traffic congestion, traffic flow, speed, and accidents which result in property and personal injuries.

Destructive cults on campus is an issue confronting university officials and, often, campus public safety personnel. These quasi-religious groups may create problems for students who, in turn, may demonstrate abnormal and/or disruptive behavior.

There has been a resurgence of student protests and demonstrations since 1985, causing considerable problems for campus public safety officials resembling those of the 1960s. This will be discussed further in a later chapter.

Hazing continues to be a problem on many college campuses. Often, these fraternity-related rituals result in assaults and injuries. Many college administrations have taken a strong position in opposition to hazing. For example, two students at the State University of New York's Old Westbury campus were expelled from the university after being involved in a hazing incident in which a fraternity pledge was dropped on his head on concrete, knocking him unconcious and causing a severe concussion. Both expelled students were also arrested and charged with assault.[23]

This list of current issues and problems is certainly not all inclusive but represents a few of the more popular issues today. There are a variety of problems which face campus public safety directors and other university administrators. While some of these occur with less frequency than other more traditional problems, their very existence presents serious difficulties which must be addressed by public safety officials.

DEFINITION OF TERMS

Before undertaking an in-depth discussion of the administration of campus public safety, it is beneficial to set forth some often confusing terms and clearly define them. It is important to note that some of these terms are used interchangeably depending on the context and author(s).

Campus Public Safety Department. A subdivision of the college or university that has as its responsibility the safety and welfare of the faculty, staff, students, and others who have an interest on the campus, as well as the protection of the physical properties of the school. The areas of responsibilities may include law enforcement, building security, fire safety, parking and traffic control, emergency medical operations, civil defense procedures, and public service activities.

Director of Campus Public Safety. The manager/administrator who is directly responsible for the operation of the institution's department of public safety, police department, or security department. He/she is responsible for all personnel, operations, and functions of the public safety department. Other titles may include "Chief of Police," "Chief of Security," and "Director of Safety and Security."

Campus Public Safety Officer. All full-time employees of the campus safety department who are commissioned as peace officers, either by the state or other agency of authority, who have arrest powers and who are assigned to carry out the responsibilities of the campus safety department.

Municipal Police Officer. A sworn public law enforcement officer who is employed by a municipality to keep the peace, enforce federal, state, and local laws, and provide other non-police functions. This individual generally represents the traditional law enforcement role and image.

Security Guard/Watchman. An individual employed by an institution to provide physical security functions to include locking and shaking doors and guarding the premises. This individual has no police authority and is usually concerned with the prevention of crime rather than apprehension of violators.

Law Enforcement Role. A strict law-and-order approach to carrying out the duties of a campus safety officer. When the campus safety officer invokes criminal statutes (including traffic violations), when violations or offenses have occurred, and the result is arrest or detention of the offending party, a law enforcement orientation prevails. With this orientation, campus safety officers may be responding to incidents and act in a similar manner to municipal police officers.

Service Role. The handling of a wide variety of situations in which the law may have been violated employing some alternative to invoking the criminal process. Arbitrating quarrels, pacifying the unruly, and aiding people in trouble are examples of service. Providing building security functions, student escorts, and assisting motorists are also activities which illustrate a service orientation. Officers with this orientation will tend to take a non-police approach to most situations when possible.

SUMMARY

Campus public safety is now an integral part of almost every campus community in our country. Its emergence has been a responsive one. Campus public safety has responded to the growth, changes, and problems that have occurred in higher education over the past three decades. While some college administrators have been reluctant to accept the law enforcement role and give due support to other areas of campus public safety, strides have been made on the great majority of our nation's campuses. Campus public safety departments have become well established and, in fact, emerged as innovative leaders in the law enforcement community. Certainly, many old problems still exist and new ones are on the horizon, but one thing is evident: campus public safety has earned its place and rightful role within higher education and is now looked to for answers in solving many current problems facing the campus community.

NOTES

1. John W. Powell, *Campus Security and Law Enforcement* (Boston, Massachusetts: Butterworth, Inc., 1971), p. 55.

2. Florida State University Department of Public Safety, Departmental Philosophy, General Order 85-1, 1985.

3. Robert E. Neal, "A History of Campus Security: Early Origins," *Campus Law Enforcement Journal* 10 (1980):28.

4. Powell, *Campus Security,* p. 4.

5. Diane C. Bordner and David M. Petersen, *Campus Policing: The Nature of University Police Work* (New York, New York: University Press of America, 1983), p. 34.

6. Eugene Sides, "Policing the Campus: Responsibilities of A University Police Department." *The Police Chief,* 50, (1983):69–70.

7. Bordner and Petersen, *Campus Policing,* p. 38.

8. Ibid., p. xi.

9. Swen C. Nielson, *General Organizational and Administrative Concepts for University Police* (Springfield, Illinois: Charles C Thomas, 1971).

10. John S. Brubacher, *On the Philosophy of Higher Education* (San Francisco: Josey-Bass Publishers, 1978).

11. Ibid., p. 63.

12. David Reisman, *On Higher Education* (San Francisco: Josey-Bass Publishers, 1980), p. 105.

13. National Center for Educational Statistics.

14. Bordner and Petersen, *Campus Policing,* p. 181.

15. Richard Brinkmann, "Mini-car Parking: An Alternative." *Campus Law Enforcement Journal,* 11, (1981):26–27.

16. Bordner and Petersen, *Campus Policing,* p. 15.

17. Ibid., p. 92.

18. Ibid.

19. Ross Aldrich, "Should Your Campus Police Carry Guns?" *Campus Law Enforcement Journal,* May/April 1983, Vol. 13, No: 2, pp. 36–38.

20. Alfred V. Iannarelli, *The Campus Police* (Precision Photoform, 1968), p. 2.

21. George W. Milliron "Attitudes of Chiefs of Police, Deans of Students, and Directors of Campus Security Toward Violators of Law by College Students" (Doctoral Dissertation, University of Northern Colorado, 1970), Dissertation Abstracts International, 31, 6311 A. (University Microfilms No. 71–74, 533) 1970.

22. Powell, *Campus Security,* p. 81.

23. Chronicle of Higher Education, "Two Charged in Hazing Incident at Old Westbury Campus," May 21, 1986, Vol. 32, No. 12, p. 30.

Chapter 2

CRIME ON CAMPUS

Campus Crime Alert...

...A female student is raped at gunpoint in the science building of Huntingdon College, Montgomery, Alabama on a spring evening.

...A professor is shot to death by one of his graduate students at Florida State University, who, in turn, turned the pistol on himself and committed suicide.

...A science building is burglarized and approximately $1,000 worth of equipment stolen on the campus of Jacksonville State University, Jacksonville, Alabama.

...A student selling illegal drugs is arrested for a large quantity of drugs located in his automobile on the campus of Middle Tennessee State University.

...A female student is raped in her dormitory room at the State University of New York at Stony Brook.

...Two non-student males are arrested for criminal trespassing and assault on a female student at the University of Montevallo, Montevallo, Alabama.

...An armed robber took approximately $10,000 from an unsuspecting bursar's office employee at Seton Hall University.

These incidents represent but a few of the many types of crimes which occur on our nation's campuses every day. The 1985 *Uniform Crime Reports* (UCR) issued by the FBI includes crime reports from 359 colleges and universities.[1] These reports indicate that virtually every category of crime is represented among these reports to include murder, rape, assault, robbery, burglary, theft, and arson. While these figures represent only about 10 percent of the approximately 3,000 colleges and universities in the U.S., it is clear that crime on campus is a reality. To say that the campus is a closed community immune to the crime problem is to ignore the facts. According to the FBI's 1985 UCR there were over

19

2,000 violent crimes reported by these 335 institutions. Violent crimes include murder and non-negligence manslaughter, forcible rape, robbery, and aggravated assault. One midwestern university reported 45 violent crimes and over 2,000 property crimes (burglary, larceny theft, auto theft, and arson) in 1985.[2]

The following article appeared in a campus student newspaper at a southern university. It serves to illustrate the reality of crime on campus.

CAMPUS EXPERIENCES VARIETY OF CRIMES

Certain crimes do occur on campus that students either hear through the "grapevine" or do not hear at all. These crimes or incidents are sometimes unusual, sad or ordinary but they do happen—and here on the JSU campus. The following are examples:

Police Truck Smashes Into Tree

University Police Chief Smith said when a police truck driven by Officer Johnston crashed into a tree behind the Campus Library, it was not the result of brake failure nor criminal mischief, but the gear had been left in DRIVE.

On Oct. 14 at approximately 7 P.M., Smith said Johnston answered a burglary alarm at the School of Nursing.

After approximately 10 minutes, Johnston came back to find the truck had rolled across Bennett Drive and hit a tree in a grassy area behind the Campus Library.

Smith said an investigation determined that the truck's gear was in DRIVE when it rolled approximately 100 yards from the nursing building. He said repairs will run over $1000 to fix the truck.

Student Arrested On Marijuana Charges

After following an anonymous tip, a dormitory resident was arrested in her dorm room Oct. 14 at approximately 9:50 P.M. on possession of marijuana charges, said Smith.

He said an informant called the department with the tip and Officer King responded to the call.

Smith said the suspect permitted King to enter her residence where he found a small amount of marijuana.

The female was released after she signed a signature bond, Smith said. "The case is still under investigation until it goes to court," he concluded.

Reported Rape on Campus

A non-student male was recently arrested on Oct 21 in his hometown and charged with first-degree rape after a female student filed charges and signed a warrant for his arrest Oct. 14 at 2 P.M.

Smith said the incident occurred Oct. 5 between 8–11 P.M. in the parking lot of Rowan Hall.

King was the arresting officer; Officer Jackson filed the report.

Bond was set at $500 and the suspect was put into the Calhoun County Jail, Smith said.

At this time, Smith did not know what other action has followed.

Shooting Incident

University police report that they may have a suspect in a shooting incident which occurred Friday, Oct. 25 between 10 and 10:30 P.M. in the area between Snow Stadium and Jacksonville High School.

Smith said two shots were fired during the high school football games and Sgt. Jones, Officer Green and several city police officers answered the call.

Smith said the suspect was not located that night, but through investigative measures, they now have a possible suspect in the case.

The fact is that crime in the campus community has paralleled the increase in the national crime rate since the 1960s. While the crime rate dropped slightly during the early 1980s, the FBI's UCR reported that the number of crimes reported to police went up 4 percent in 1985.[3] A comparison done by the International Association of Campus Law Enforcement Administrators in 1985 indicated a similar trend in the campus crime rate. The increase in crime on campus may be related to the more open, accessible campus since the demise of *in loco parentis*. It may be the increased amount of cash, goods, and new cars brought to campus by today's student. Perhaps it is related to the change in values, morality, and increased freedom among many college students which has occurred since the student revolution of the 1960s. Whatever the reasons, crime has increased on campuses across the country.

Newspaper headliners frequently read "Student Files $2 million Lawsuit Against University" and "University Loses: Student Wins $5 Million Case." Such legal actions have often been the resulting "fallout" of crime on campus. Perhaps no other single factor has been responsible for getting the attention of college and university administrators. Just when many institutions were loosening their controls and adjusting their policies to a more liberal approach in keeping with the *Dixon* decision, they found themselves faced with increased liability regarding the safety of their students. Colleges and universities now find themselves in a "catch 22" situation in which they must afford students the same rights and privileges as any other citizens; yet, they are responsible and liable for their safety and welfare. Rules, regulations, and traditional discipline policies designed to protect students have been relaxed and, consequently, lead to increased safety and security problems for institutions of higher education. Rape is one crime which has been the focus of increased litigation. Let's consider the following examples as cases in point:

1. A woman law student was sexually assaulted in the women's restrooms at Hastings Law Center at the University of California. She sued Hastings Law Center, the State of California and the governing board of regents for the University. In 1980, a jury awarded the plaintiff $215,000.
2. In 1979 female student at Huntingdon College in Montgomery, Alabama was awarded $25,000 because she was raped at gunpoint in the science building on that campus. The original suit filed against the college included punitive damages totaling $2.5 million.
3. In July 1976 the U.S. District Court for the District of Columbia awarded $20,000 to a plaintiff who was raped in the gymnasium at the Catholic University of America. The plaintiff sued the defendant university for actual and punitive damages.

When the crime problem on campus is viewed in this light, it becomes apparent that institutions must be concerned and take formidable action to protect their students as well as the institution's interests.

In order to understand the impact of crime on campus and to keep the crime problem in a proper perspective, it is important to consider the various factors that can affect the type and amount of crime of a particular campus community. These include: the characteristics of the campus physical plant, demographic characteristics of the surrounding community, ratio of male to female students, number of on-campus residents, accessibility of outside visitors, size of enrollment, security measures, etc. For instance, while personal assault may be more prevalent on the large urban campus than on the small rural residential campus, the rate of petty theft may be greater on the small rural residential campus than on the suburban commuter campus. Caution should be exercised in making comparisons of crime statistics between campuses. This discussion attempts to present an overview of campus crime and offer some general conclusions.

There are essentially three major categories of crimes on most campuses even though other kinds of crime may occur infrequently: crimes against persons, crimes against property, and public order crime.

CRIMES AGAINST PERSONS

Crimes against persons or violent crime include murder, sex offenses, robbery, and aggravated assault. The 1984 FBI UCR statistics for college and universities include seven murders from the 335 reporting institutions.[4] While murders do not occur with great frequency on campus, the possibility exists. A stabbing death marred Auburn University's homecoming celebration during the 1985 football season. According to Auburn's university police, the incident stemmed from an altercation near the campus's fraternity row and appeared to be alcohol related. Florida State University experienced the shooting murder of one of its professors, committed by a graduate student who, in turn, committed suicide. Every year across the nation murders occur on our college campuses.

Forcible rape usually receives the most attention among campus crimes. And well it should! Rape is a major problem on campus, with a majority of rapes going unreported. Acquaintance rape is the most common and the most frequent.

Acquaintance rape, sometimes called date rape, has recently emerged as a widespread phenomenon. Within the past two or three years, several articles concerning acquaintance rape have appeared in such popular magazines as *Ms.* (September, 1982), *Newsweek* (April 9, 1984), *Glamor* (April, 1981), and *Redbook*. Radio and television talk shows have featured the topic of acquaintance rape, and even such popular television shows as "Cagney and Lacey" have dealt with the problem.

According to Doctor Andrea Parrot, a noted sex educator at Cornell University, acquaintance rape is defined as forced intercourse by someone the victim knows.[5] An estimated 84,233 forcible rapes were reported to law enforcement agencies in 1984 according to the FBI's *Uniform Crime Reports*.[6] This represents a 7 percent increase over reported rapes in 1983. Rape is still recognized as one of the most underreported of all the UCR's index crimes. Victims' fear of their assailants and their embarrassment over the incidents are merely two factors which can affect their decisions to contact law enforcement authorities. Doctor Barry Burkhart, Associate Professor of Psychology at Auburn University, has conducted significant research in the area of acquaintance rape on campus. His findings supports the UCR's conclusion. Doctor Burkhart interviewed 600 women who acknowledged being the victims of acquaintance rape. Of this number, only four had reported it to the police![7]

Doctor Mary Koss, Department of Psychology, Kent State University, has conducted extensive research on acquaintance rape on campus. In her studies, Doctor Koss found that more than half the women students she surveyed had experienced at some time in their lives sexual aggression in the form of verbal threats, physical coercion, or violence. One in eight of these women had been raped, although many did not use that word to label the experience. On the basis of a survey of 2,016 women students at a midwestern state university, it was determined that 37 percent of the women were victims of rape or attempted rape at some time in their lives.[8]

The legal definition of rape varies by jurisdiction, but the basic dimensions are relatively constant and include three major elements: (a) carnal knowledge of a woman, defined as sexual penetration, (b) lack of consent to this carnal knowledge, and (c) use of force or threat of force to accomplish the act. The legal definition, despite its simplicity, is not always perceived the same as the social definitions of rape on the part of victims, offenders, jurists, and citizens.

The victim of an acquaintance rape may not recognize it as a crime or define the incident as "rape." Usually, she will not talk to anyone else about the incident nor seek professional assistance or support. Her sense of trust and friendship is destroyed. Consequently, she may not report the assailant for fear that she may be blamed. In fact, particularly on a college campus, the victim of an acquaintance rape may again have to face and meet her assailant in a class, in a dorm, or elsewhere on campus.

Most acquaintance rapes on campus can be categorized as "date rapes," since such a personal/social setting provides the best opportunities. Date rape is more likely to occur on the second or third date, since social defenses are higher on the first date. And the woman is less likely to invite him into her room/apartment or go to his on a first date. For example, a female student was raped in the front seat of a "friend's" car while parked in the campus coliseum parking lot. This was their second date and they had mutually progressed to kissing and heavy petting. When he began to remove her clothes, she protested verbally and resisted physically to no avail. While she felt violated, he didn't perceive what he did to be rape. Another example on the same campus involved the rape of a coed by her friend in his dormitory room. She had visited him at his invitation given during class earlier the same day. In many such cases a woman's acceptance to visit a man's room or apartment is perceived by the man as an indication that she really wants to engage in intercourse despite her pleas for restraint.

Forced rape by strangers is also a crime problem on campus. The campus is often viewed as "easy pickins" for the would-be rapist. Stranger rapes are committed by transient workers, "locals" from a surrounding town, and/or serial rapists. They may occur in female dormitories, outdoors on campus, in campus classroom buildings, in isolated areas of campus, and in buildings or areas near the campus. They may take place at night or in broad daylight. These kinds of rapes more likely involve the use of violence and weapons than do acquaintance rapes.

It was 1:30 P.M. on a beautiful fall afternoon in November 1978 in Montevallo, Alabama. Montevallo is a small town with a population of approximately 4,500 and boasts a state-supported university, the University of Montevallo, with a student enrollment of 2,800. On this particular afternoon, Diane, a sophomore at UM, was walking the usual two-block route from campus to Montevallo's mainstreet when she was called to by a young white male from the steps of the Presbyterian student center located adjacent to the campus. He requested that she assist him in cleaning and straightening the inside because he was late for a dental appointment. Since Diane had frequented the student center on several occasions, she, though hesitantly, agreed to go in and help the young man. He appeared to her to be a janitor or handyman. Once inside he pulled out a small-caliber revolver, raped her at gunpoint, and left her tied up bound hand and foot. The assailant was seen by four other people, but no one could identify him. He was never apprehended despite extensive investigative efforts by campus, city, and county law enforcement officials.

Similar incidents occur on many college campuses. Few are immune from this crime problem.

Robbery, as with murder, does not occur with great frequency on campus. According to the 1985 FBI UCR statistics, robbery occurred on over half of the 335 reporting campuses, yet, in small numbers on most. One major midwestern university reported the largest number of robberies with 29. Otherwise, the majority of reporting institutions experienced less than a half dozen robberies for 1985. The campus as a "city within a city" provides the criminal element with the same type of opportunities as does the city. A typical college or university has a bursar's office, bookstore, cafe, and people with cash. Many robberies are committed by non-students and "locals" from the nearby community who prey on unsuspecting coeds, cashiers, and vendors on campus. Since the advent of fast-food delivery to campus, i.e., pizza, burgers, etc., robbery of the delivery clerks has posed a new problem for campus police safety officials.

Another frequent crime against persons found on campus is assault. Most assaults do not involve weapons. Usually, these incidents are fights in dormitories, at fraternity parties, or at athletic events on campus. Often, these simple assaults result from lovers' quarrels and disputes between roommates. While not as frequent, more serious aggravated assaults do occur on campus. Handguns, shotguns, knifes, and baseball bats are among the most common weapons known to be used by students and non-students on campus.

Perhaps the most common incidents of violence and crime against persons occur at athletic events. Brawls at basketball games in 1986 prompted several colleges and conferences to cancel games, reprimand players and coaches, threaten to punish them if they continued to misbehave, and seek ways to avoid future incidents. Several games were interrupted by on-court fights among players, and others were delayed or ended prematurely by unruly fans. In some cases, fans became involved in fights resulting in injuries and arrests by campus police. Football games also provide the ingredients for violence to include alcohol, intoxicated fans, overzealous fans, and crowded seating arrangements. While most universities attempt to control alcoholic beverages at these events, alcohol-related problems frequently occur resulting in personal injury.

Crime against persons on the college campus is a reality. It is a fact that must be recognized, taken seriously, and responded to by university administrators. The attitude and response that "we don't have a crime problem on our campus" won't afford students adequate protection nor the university sufficient liability coverage. The campus community is not immune to violent crime against its citizens and must take necessary measures to ensure their safety.

CRIMES AGAINST PROPERTY

The second broad category of crime to be discussed is crime against property. This category includes burglary, larceny-theft, auto theft, arson, and destruction of property. The FBI's UCR includes all of these categories, with the exception of destruction of property. In the UCR's 1984 issue, the majority of reporting institutions experienced criminal incidents in all four categories. The larceny-theft category by far contain the greatest number of reported crimes. This was followed by burglary, auto theft and arson, in that order.

The larceny-theft crime problem on campus consists primarily of petty thefts such as small amounts of cash, personal items, and equipment usually valued at less than $100. There are some incidents involving expensive personal items such as stereos, computers, guns, etc. Many of these thefts occur in dormitories where the offender and victim may be acquainted. Such a communal setting makes for convenient opportunities for the taking of personal property. It also makes it difficult to pinpoint a suspect. While stolen institutional equipment may be valued in excess of $1,000 (i.e. typewriters, computers, musical instruments), an even larger number of thefts of institutional property involve much less property value such as bookstore items, library books, trash cans, fire extinguishers, etc. Often, these items are taken in broad daylight without arousing any suspicion of peer students and busy faculty and staff. A study conducted by Bordner and Petersen revealed that approximately 21 percent of all criminal incidents on a major college campus occurred in the library. No other single building even approached this figure.[9]

Burglary does not occur as frequently as larceny-thefts on most college and university campuses. However, it was reported by most institutions in the FBI's 1984 UCR. As mentioned earlier, this crime varies from institution to institution. A sampling from these reporting institutions which illustrates this variety is as follows:

Institution	Enrollment	No. of Burglaries
University of Alabama	17,085	30
University of California at Los Angeles	33,388	419
Yale University	10,190	428
Florida A & M	4,593	31
Joliet Junior College	5,310	7
University of Minnesota	47,387	44
East Tennessee State University	8,318	4

Most burglaries on campus tend to occur in non-resident buildings such as academic buildings and athletic complexes. Usually, they occur at nighttime when these buildings are unoccupied. It is surprising to consider that many burglaries on campus are committed by students with keys to the building obtained fraudulently. Buildings are entered through doors found ajar, unlocked windows and by breaking and entering.

The targets of these student-burglars include athletic equipment, professors' tests, audiovisual equipment, typewriter, etc. This is not to say that only students commit burglaries on campus. Often, off-campus perpetrators come on campus for what they consider "easy pickins." These off-campus burglars are frequently juveniles from the surrounding town or city and usually travel by foot. For the most part, burglaries on campus are committed by amateur criminals who are not usually armed.

Arson does occur on campus. In 1978 a series of arsons occurred on the campus of a small southern liberal arts college. All of these trash-can fires occurred in female dormitories at nighttime. There were seventeen such fires within a two-month period. While only two of these fires resulted in substantial property damage, all created a lot of smoke in hallways and subsequent fear among the female students throughout the campus community. It was difficult to identify a suspect, since it was believed that the arsonist was a female student with access to all of the female dormitories on campus.

Arson takes on different forms with different motives and perpetrators. Arson is generally one of the most difficult of all crimes to solve. There is little information with which to approach this problem. It is important that adequate fire safety devices and procedures be in place to prevent serious injury.

Destruction of property or vandalism is a common crime on campus. Frequently, it is difficult to determine whether such an incident involves criminal intent or was done accidently during mischievous activity. This crime ranges from defacing a prominent school official's portrait to breaking windows in the administration building to slashing a fellow student's car tires. This amounts to thousands of dollars in property value loss each year on most campuses. Usually, this crime is committed by students against other students, fraternities, and/or administration officials. Many times this is viewed as a tradition or prank between rival fraternities. In other instances such acts are deliberate and intentionally destructive. A common target of these acts of destruction has been the campus police. Campus police patrol cars have been egged, had sugar put in the gas tanks, had tires slashed, had antennas bent, etc. In one instance a complete set of blue lights and siren was removed from a campus police patrol car! Another common target of vandalism is the fire extinguisher which is often emptied by dormitory students for various reasons.

Whatever the reasons and motives, destruction of property/vandalism continues to plague our campuses. The victims may be the institution, faculty/staff, or students. They are defenseless to the perpetrator in most cases. It is a crime that frustrates the police/security officials, in that the perpetrators are often difficult to identify and, in many instances, difficult to prosecute.

Crimes against property constitute a significant problem which requires the attention of all college and university administrators and demands a meaningful response on their part. These crimes can be costly in terms of property and financial losses. One successful arson incident can cost a university millions of dollars. Burglaries, thefts, and vandalism can also take their toll, both on the institution and its clientele.

PUBLIC ORDER CRIME

The third category of campus crime is public order crime. Crimes in this category include public intoxication, disorderly conduct, drinking in public, criminal trespassing, public lewdness, loitering, and violations of public order and decency. These are considered less serious crimes and are often covered by local ordinances. These crimes comprise a large portion of all complaint calls to campus police and security departments. The complexion of the campus community lends itself to activities that tend to generate many of these crimes. The traditional college age of young, single adults, the kinds of special activities usually mixed with alcoholic beverages, frequent social activities, concentrated housing arrangements, and open access by outsiders are factors which provide the opportunity for misconduct and violation of the law. Fraternity parties, major intercollegiate athletic events, rock concerts, and campus pubs are common sites for disruptive behavior and criminal incidents. Dormitories and apartment complexes are often the locations for fights, disorderly conduct, intoxicated students, and off-campus trespassers.

The following scenario is a hypothetical illustration of what may commonly occur on a college campus. This situation involves several crimes against public order. The author is familiar with several very similar incidents which actually occurred.

On the first hot afternoon of spring, several dozen students
and some "locals" gathered on the campus commons square
to welcome warm weather. Loud voices and music filled the
air. Alcohol, and perhaps marijuana, was being consumed.
Campus police officers were summoned to the scene. Several
fully clothed male and female students plunged into the two-
foot deep pool, maintaining a tight grip on their beer cans.
More students joined them followed by several non-student
"locals" who were known troublemakers. Realizing the potentially dangerous situation that could develop, the officers
ordered the crowd out of the pool. This directive was met with
a shower of derogatory and obscene remarks. The officers
persisted to no avail. One female stripped to the waist as she
splashed in the water. Encouraged by the cheers of fellow
students, several others in the pool removed all of their clothes.
The police officers began dispersing the students and ordered
the "locals" to leave the campus. Some of the participants
refused to get out of the pool. Beverage cans began flying at
the officers. Three students were pulled from the pool, covered with blankets, arrested and taken into custody. The crowd
attempted to free fellow students and knocked one officer to
the ground. The officers began using their mace and batons
to disperse the crowd. Finally, the crowd left the area and an
uneasy calm prevailed on campus.

Many, and perhaps most, public order crimes on campus are alcohol
related. Frequently, the activity itself could be viewed as misconduct and
dealt with through non-police procedures (i.e. student affairs, campus
housing officials, etc.). However, intoxicated participants are often difficult to reason with and precipitate the incident to require custodial
measures by police. Alcohol consumption and abuse and the resulting
behavior is a real problem on most campuses. Not only is alcohol usually
associated with disorderly conduct, public intoxication, and trespassing,
it is very often a factor in rapes, destruction of property and aggravated
assaults.

Recent federal legislation aimed at raising the minimum drinking age
to twenty-one will have an impact on college campuses. This effort is
intended to save lives by reducing the number of drunk drivers and,

subsequently, traffic deaths. Most states have complied, since non-compliance will mean less federal dollars. On the surface it would appear that this trend will reduce alcohol consumption by college students, since the majority are under twenty-one years of age. However, many college officials disagree and argue that a higher drinking age does not prevent students from drinking but only changes where and how they drink—usually for the worse. Most students begin drinking in high school, they say, and by the time they get to college they see drinking as a right. The new laws make it difficult for colleges to provide controlled settings, such as campus pubs, where bartenders are trained to check ID's, not to serve intoxicated people, keep the noise level down, and generally keep the atmosphere quiet and controlled. Others say a higher drinking age forces drinking underground and may cause students to drive to isolated spots off campus, subsequently, driving while intoxicated or demonstrating unruly behavior in an uncontrolled environment.

It is important to note that distinguishing public order crime from student misconduct is often difficult. A fine line often exists. A lot of student behavior (i.e. panty raids, fraternity initiation activities, student pranks, etc.) may be viewed as violations of the law in a typical city. However, due to the nature and intent of such activity, campus authorities may treat it as student misconduct and either permit it or deal with it through campus administrative disciplinary channels. This approach places a good deal of responsibility on campus police/security officers who must exercise discretion on a case-by-case basis.

ILLEGAL DRUGS

Illegal drugs on campus present problems both as a crime and their effect on other crimes. Drugs first appeared on campus in a significant way during the turbulent sixties when students were experimenting with whatever was "in," seeking new freedoms and defying authority. They were popular at rock concerts, at parties, and in dorm rooms. Drugs were associated with hippies, faded jeans, long hair, and "pot" parties. Today, those drug culture symbols no longer exist on campus. Students are different and so are their behavior and attitudes. The rebellious, non-conforming attitudes have been replaced with more serious-minded, academic-oriented interests. The "drug scene" is no longer as popular on campus as it was two decades ago. The pendulum has swung back to alcohol and the more traditional, acceptable social usages.

This is not to suggest that illegal drugs no longer present a problem on campus. While the numbers of students using drugs may have dwindled and the associated subculture has changed, the possession, use, and sale of illegal drugs and narcotics still exists and poses some real problems. Marijuana continues, as during the sixties and seventies, to be the dominant illegal drug. Marijuana aroma is common in dormitory hallways as it seeps from residents' rooms. Such reports are frequent to campus police/security departments. Many campus police agencies report dozen of drug-related arrests each year—usually marijuana possession and/or sale. Cocaine, "downers," "uppers," heroin, and other narcotics are often used and sold on campuses. A trend toward increased popularity of cocaine usage is evident across our nation's campuses.

A significant number of drug-related crimes occur on campuses (i.e. burglary, theft, disorderly conduct, public intoxication, and personal violence). Several campuses have reported the presence of drugs in rape victims, indicating drugs as a factor in their vulnerability and mental capability. In 1983 on a medium-sized southern campus, five vehicle burglaries were committed by a student who was seeking items of value to support his drug addiction. Many thefts are committed by drug users in a effort to obtain money to buy drugs. Crimes of violence (e.g. fighting, stabbings, shootings) are the consequences of drug usage. Self-inflicted injuries and accidents by students intoxicated on drugs are common and represent another result of the illegal drug problem.

The law enforcement efforts by campus police/security departments is sometimes frustrating. The attitudes of many university administrations is to pretend there is no drug problem, ignore drug possession, and, when it is blatant, handle it administratively. This places sworn police officers in a difficult position when they are aware that drug violations exist. Another problem facing campus law enforcement agencies is the difficulties in investigating and apprehending drug users and, particularly, drug pushers. Since the vast majority of campus police/security departments are relatively small, few have specially trained investigators, surveillance equipment, and the manpower to focus on the drug problem on campus. Subsequently, they approach the problem in a reactionary manner, only responding to complaint calls and information brought to their attention. Many students recognize this and feel comfortable using drugs in the privacy of their rooms, only to take the results beyond their rooms to the streets, classrooms, and public places.

There is some indication that leaders in higher education are tired of drug users diminishing the quality of life on our nation's college campuses. Hopefully, this attitude will become prevelant among college administrators. Speaking before the Association of Governing Boards of Universities and Colleges in San Diego in March 1985, Secretary of Education William J. Bennett urged college trustees and presidents to rid their campuses of drug pushers, drug users, cheats, and exploiters. He called for colleges to direct the minds and sensibilities of these young men and women to what is better and not to what is worse, to good things, to even noble things, to exemplary things.[10] Mr. Bennett noted that some campuses have serious problems and should directly address the problems on a regular basis.

CAMPUS DISORDER: THE SIXTIES REVISITED

Just when the tumultuous sixties with all their campus riots, sit-ins, demonstrations, and violence seemed to be almost forgotten, a new wave of student protest emerged in the mid-1980s. The issue: Apartheid in South Africa. Students on campuses across the country demonstrated their opposition to university investments in companies that do business in South Africa. The issue is a moral one directed against segregation and unfair treatment of blacks in South Africa by the minority-controlled white government. These demonstrations resulted in civil disobedience, violence, and property destruction. Campus public safety officials had to respond to these disorder, often by arresting students.

In April 1985, Yale campus police and New Haven, Connecticut police arrested more than 150 anti-apartheid demonstrators during three days of protest at Yale University. The protests followed a standoff between university officials and students who erected wooden shanties and tents on the campus to protest Yale's investments in companies doing business with South Africa. Students were arrested for refusing to abandon the symbolic structures and for disorderly conduct.[12]

Fifty-three students were arrested during a protest at a meeting of a trustees committee at the University of Illinois's Urbana-Champaign campus. The protestors were charged with interfering with a public institution of higher education and criminal trespassing.

Police at the University of Texas at Austin arrested 42 people (including 35 students) after they refused to disperse an anti-apartheid rally or move the protest to one of the university's "free-speech areas."[13]

Similar protests occurred at the Johns Hopkins University, Utah State University, Dartmouth College, and the University of California at Berkeley in early 1986. The Dartmouth protest resulted in 18 student arrests. An anti-apartheid demonstration at the University of California at Berkeley campus resulted in 150 arrests in which 18 police officers and 11 protestors were injured.[14]

Such disorder and violence on campus serves to illustrate that serious crime can and does occur within the campus community. Public safety officials must be prepared to deal with all kinds of crime and problems.

WHO, WHEN, AND WHERE

There is no valid research to indicate who is committing crime on campus. One study undertaken in 1982 (Bordner & Petersen, 1983) attempted to determine who committed crimes on campus—insiders or outsiders ("locals"). No conclusive data was obtained. It was found that both insiders and outsiders commit crime on campus. Yale University Police Chief Louis Cappiello points out that most crimes committed on his campus are committed by teenagers who pass for students and enter university buildings. There are also indications that most serious crimes (i.e. burglaries, rapes, robberies) are committed by outsiders and less serious crimes (i.e. thefts, disorderly conduct) are committed by insiders. Most of these insiders are students, with the remainder being staff and faculty employees. Trespassing would be the exception, since most trespassers are outsiders. These indications are generally consistent on other campuses. However, caution must be exercised when drawing conclusions and making comparisons among institutions, since there are a number of variables which affect such statistics. These variable factors include: demographic characteristics of the surrounding community, ratio of male-to-female students, number of on-campus residents, accessibility of outsiders, size of enrollment, etc. These factors should also be considered when discussing when and where crime is committed.

In the same study done by Bordner and Petersen (1983), it was discovered that most crimes occurred between 7 A.M. and 11 P.M.[11] Again, this will vary by institution but generally this will be the case, since the campus is more accessible during these hours and more people are up and out on campus. Generally, more serious crimes (i.e. crimes of violence, burglaries) occur during evening and nighttime hours—usually between 6 P.M. and 2 A.M. Also, public order crimes (i.e. disorderly conduct, public intoxication) tend to occur after dark on campus with more frequency than during daytime hours. The cover of darkness provides the setting, and people usually are off work and out of classes. Alcohol consumption is normally increased during these hours. Theft, which usually represents the largest number of reported criminal incidents, accounts for the volume of daytime crimes. Thefts of books, items from vehicles, purses, cash, and equipment occur frequently during the day when such items are in plain view and unattended by busy students and careless staff employees.

There is virtually no area on campus immune from crime—offices, classrooms, restrooms, study areas, libraries, student centers, dormitories, TV rooms, laundry rooms, parking lots, cafeterias, and so forth. But perhaps the most commonly reported single location for crime is the campus library. There such crimes as sexual offenses and petty thefts are common. Females studying alone or standing among poorly lighted bookshelves make perfect targets for would-be sex offenders and "Peeping Toms." Books, purses, and other items left lying on tables are "easy pickings" for thieves. Of course, books, records, and magazines are common items stolen from libraries. Dormitories also rank high among locations for crime. Whether coed or single-sex residence halls, these living quarters house young, single adults, many of whom are irresponsible and careless. "In-house" theft is a major problem and one difficult to solve, since the culprit lives there and would be noticed roaming the hall as would a stranger. It is analogous to determining which member of a family ate all the cookies! There is a strong indication that campuses with large resident populations generally have more property crime than commuter campuses.

SUMMARY

Certainly, few campuses can be considered high crime districts. The majority of campuses have no serious crime problems. Yet, crime poses a problem on all campuses and can be detrimental to the students, the employees, and the institution's programs. One rape can cause panic among female students, unsettle parents, and influence recruiting efforts. Excessive thefts of students' property or vandalism of the institution's property can create an unhealthy atmosphere and spoil the traditional campus life. Crime on campus is a reality. To that end, it is important to understand its impact, assess the problem, and recognize the importance and role of public safety on campus.

NOTES

1. Uniform Crime Reports for 1985, U.S. Department of Justice (U.S. Government Printing Office, Washington, D.C., 1985), pp. 110–117.

2. Ibid., p. 112.

3. Uniform Crime Reports for 1985, U.S. Department of Justice, (U.S. Government Printing Office, Washington D.C., 1986).

4. Uniform Crime Reports for 1985, pp. 110–117.

5. "The Problem of Rape on Campus," Campus Crime Prevention Program Handout, Goshen, Kentucky, 1985, p. 1.

6. Uniform Crime Reports for 1985, pp. 110–117.

7. The Problem of Rape, p. 15.

8. Ibid., p. 10.

9. Uniform Crime Reports for 1985, pp. 110–117.

10. Ibid., pp. 110–117.

11. David C. Bordner and D. M. Petersen, *Campus Policing: The Nature of University Police Work* (New York, New York: University Press of America, 1983), p. 108.

12. Uniform Crime Reports for 1985, pp. 110–117.

13. Chronicle of Higher Education, "Bennett Urges Leaders to Rid Campuses of Cheats, Exploiters, and Drug Users," March 26, 1986, Vol. 32, No. 4, p. 2.

14. Chronicle of Higher Education, "Campus Apartheid Protests Continue; 150 Arrested at Yale," April 23, 1986, Vol. 32, No. 8, p. 34.

15. Ibid.

16. Chronicle of Higher Education, "150 Arrested in Anti-Apartheid Demonstrations at Berkeley," April 9, 1986, Vol. 32, No. 6, p. 2.

17. Bordner and Petersen, Campus Policing, p. 192.

Chapter 3

TOWARD A PROPER PERSPECTIVE:
LAW ENFORCEMENT VS. SERVICE

THE ISSUE

Since the emergence of law enforcement capabilities on some campuses, there has been the controversy of whether or not campus officers should be "real police" like their municipal counterparts or more resemble security guards/watchmen with only service responsibilities. The issue has been raised from campus to campus across the country and caused considerable frustration and debate within some institutions. The issue is still not settled on many campuses for various reasons. As was mentioned in a preceding chapter, due to certain crises on campus some administrators felt it necessary and actually beneficial to their institution to control the law enforcement function on their campus, thus supporting the "real police" concept. Yet, others have been reluctant to allow campus officers such police authority. On some campuses, vestiges of *in loco parentis* still remain in spirit and, subsequently, a parental approach is often preferred in minor criminal violations. In such situations when police help is needed, college administrators prefer the local police (i.e. municipal or county) to be the "bad guys." The question is "should campus police/security's role be more law enforcement oriented or more service oriented?"

It is more important to note here that in many states there is legislation which empowers campus police/security officers with sworn police authority similar to municipal, county and state law enforcement officers. In a study conducted by George Eastman in 1980, the majority (62%) of the 543 responding institutions of higher education reported that their public safety officers were commissioned as police officers by state law.[1] In some states this authority extends only to public institutions, while others also make provisions for private institutions. In most cases the police authority afforded campus police/security officers is intended to be exercised primarily on the institution's property or, sometimes, contiguous streets. Other states still have no such legislative provision for their campus officers, and, in some cases, campus police rely on local municipal police agencies or county sheriffs to grant them such sworn authority under their auspices. Still, there are those states in which campus police/security officers have no sworn authority and are limited in their actions.

As an example, Alabama's law providing for authority for public campus police officers is presented below.[2] Note that this includes only public institutions. Private colleges and universities in Alabama have no such authority afforded to their security officers and must rely on local law enforcement agencies for police action.

POLICE OFFICERS AT STATE COLLEGES AND UNIVERSITIES OR INSTITUTE FOR DEAF AND BLIND— EMPLOYMENT; POWERS AND DUTIES GENERALLY

The president or chief executive officer of any state college or university or of the Alabama Institute for Deaf and Blind shall have authority to appoint and employ one or more suitable persons to act as police officers to keep off intruders and prevent trespass upon and damage to the property of the college or university or of the said institute. Such person shall be charged with all the duties and invested with all the powers of police officers.

EXTENSION OF JURISDICTION

(a) Any police officer appointed pursuant to the provisions of section 16-47-10 or 16-22-1 is a peace officer whose authority extends to any place in the state; provided that the primary duty of any such police or peace officer shall be the enforcement of the law on property owned or leased by the institution of higher education employing said peace officers; provided further that he shall not otherwise act as a peace officer in enforcing the law except: (1) When in pursuit of any offender or suspected offender who is charged with the commission of a crime while on the premises of said institution; or (2) To make arrests otherwise lawfully for crimes committed, or for which there is probable cause to believe have been committed, within his presence or within the boundaries of said property of this section (b) The provisions of this section granting authority to police officers at institutions of higher learning in the state of Alabama are not intended to limit or abridge any powers heretofore granted to said officers by law, and the provisions of this section are, therefore, to be considered cumulative. (c) Nothing in this section shall grant authority to any persons appointed under the provisions of this section to enter a classroom for the purpose of enforcing traffic or parking citations.

This kind of legislative act enhances the campus public safety officers' roles by providing them with the necessary authority to respond effectively to a wide variety of situations. This is particularly important during exigent circumstances which often demand immediate decisions and subsequent forceful actions by campus officers. Such a law also provides more autonomy for the institution's administration in developing policies and procedures for law enforcement services on its own property. Most states now have similar laws for public campus police/security officers. It is interesting to note that even on those campuses where public safety officers are not duly sworn law enforcement officers, they are often required to provide police action until authorized assistance arrives. These "first responders" could better serve their institutions if they were afforded sworn police authority.

THE DUAL ROLES: LAW ENFORCEMENT AND SERVICE

Campus safety department, like their municipal counterparts, have two broad roles to fulfill: service and law enforcement. Evidence suggests that public police spend approximately 80 to 90 percent of their time in service duties. Wilson states:

> The vast majority of police actions taken in response to citizen calls involve either providing a service (getting a cat out of a tree or taking a person to the hospital) or managing real or alleged conditions of disorder (quarreling families, public drunks, bothersome teenagers, noisy cars, tavern fights). Only a small fraction of these calls involve law enforcement such as checking a prowler, catching a burglar in the act, or preventing a street robbery.[3]

In this respect, campus safety is a little different from the municipal police. Bordner and Petersen (1983) point out:

> Law enforcement agencies of all types share the broad and vague mandate to enforce the laws and keep the peace. Therefore, the role of university police in many respects is the same as the role of municipal police—preventer, protector, and law enforcer. Yet the role of campus police remains unclear. Lack of clarity in definition can be attributed

to many causes including the varied historical origins of the campus police departments. The changing attitudes and actions of students over time, the lack of recognition by college administrators until a few years ago of the need for an efficient police operation on campus, and the fact the growth of the campus police field in recent years has been so rapid that the role of campus officers is constantly shifting.[4]

While many campus safety departments now resemble municipal police agencies in organizations, uniforms, procedures, and image, there exists a marked difference in terms of the approach and functions of campus safety within the academic community. Powell (1981) states: "Defining the proper role and functions of a campus security department is difficult because the operation must be programmed to meet the needs and general attitudes of the campus it will serve. However, any campus department must direct its efforts primarily at prevention and service to be successful."[5]

There is a philosophy and common approach within some institutions that provides a more clear distinction between the service role and law enforcement role. Some universities operate on the assumption that "security" is synonymous with service, and "police" is synonymous with law enforcement. Subsequently, in an effort to fulfill both roles effectively, these institutions have created two divisions within the campus safety department: security and police. Abramson (1974) supports the existence of "two well-managed organizations that have common ends but necessarily different means."[6] He contends that security and police each differ in their tasks, yet must coexist in order to serve the campus community. This same arrangement exists at the University of Alabama in Birmingham, where, in addition to a sworn police staff of some forty officers, a fifteen-member security guard force operates to handle physical security functions and many non-criminal service activities.

The service role of campus safety departments is somewhat different in philosophy from that of most public law enforcement agencies. Among the major missions and traditions of higher education is service. If a primary objective of higher education is the provision of services, campus safety must reflect that role. This philosophy is stated well in Florida State's University Public Safety Department's departmental philosophy: "While the principal objective of the Department is the maintenance of a safe and secure physical environment, it is necessary to recognize that, particularly with service as its main product, the goals of a public safety organization must continuously be responsive to the needs and problems of the community it serves."[7] Safety forces oriented toward service may also indirectly assist the university in student retention and recruitment.

The service role of campus safety is fulfilled in many ways. There are the traditional watchmen-type functions that necessarily still exist. In addition to these functions, other service functions have been steadily added to campus safety departments and, in so doing, have significantly changed their image and increased their credibility. North Carolina State University made such a transformation in 1978. According to Cunningham and Jenkins (1981), "The primary function was making certain that buildings were locked at night with little, if any, law enforcement or service orientation."[8] In an effort to better provide services, this institution implemented a number of new changes to include:

1. Redefining the role of the Security Division to stress the concept of a professional law enforcement group designed to be a service organization to the university community.
2. Expand the size and role of the student auxiliary patrol.
3. Establish minimum standards for the selection and employment of sworn officers.
4. Study existing building security systems and develop proposals and plans for improvement.
5. Study high crime areas and make appropriate recommendations relative to improving lighting conditions, installing emergency phones, etc.
6. Cooperate with the Transportation Division and make studies and recommendations relative to eliminating parking problems.

The University of Maryland is another university that exemplifies the service-oriented role of campus safety. Sides (1983) states:

> The central objectives of the University of Maryland are academic, research, and community service. To achieve these goals, there must be a safe, secure, and attractive environment with a positive social atmosphere—and the University Police play a significant role in providing service, protection, and resolution of conflict.[9]

While the service role appears to be predominant among campus safety departments, the role of law enforcement has emerged within the past two decades. The trend has been to "professionalize" campus safety departments in keeping with the public law enforcement model. A study done by Stevens (1972) revealed that a substantial majority of institutions in this study avoided use of the word "police" in the official designation of the campus agency, as the officers often surpassed municipal police officers in experience and education.[10] Milliron (1970) found that many institutions have seen fit to improve campus security/police staffs to enhance the capability of safety officers in dealing with law violations on campus.

Mayer (1983) reports on the Indiana University at Bloomington Police Department's efforts within the past ten years to upgrade its personnel from that of security guards to well-trained, educated police officers capable of responding to the diverse needs of the campus community. He states: "Campus security, as accomplished at Indiana University Campus Police Department, is little different than law enforcement needed for any community with a population of over 30,000. It is around-the-clock, full-time work for uniformed, armed, well-trained professionals."[12]

Referring to a bona fide police agency on campus, Nielsen (1971) states: "It functions within the university as does a municipal police department within a city. It performs all police services performed by local governments plus those functions inherent to the particular institution it was created to serve."[13]

Campus safety officers themselves often prefer to identify with the law enforcement role. Studies conducted by Telb (1980) and Meadows (1982) revealed that campus safety officers know their role expectations were service oriented but preferred to play the law enforcement role on campus.[14-15] This study also found that campus safety officers perceived their role to be similar to the role of municipal police officers. However, in Milliron's study the findings suggested that some university officials preferred campus police to take a different approach than their municipal counterparts when dealing with student violators.[16]

While both service and law enforcement roles are incumbent on public campus safety departments, the service role is predominant. Campus safety's goals will be more compatible with those of the institution if a service orientation is adopted.

THE ROLE-PERCEPTION CONFLICT OF CAMPUS PUBLIC SAFETY DEPARTMENTS

While campus safety officers' functions and images have become more similar to those of municipal police officers', there still exist some significant differences. The academic institutional environment, physical security responsibilities, societal norms, traditional philosophies and administrative constraints inhibit police autonomy and keep the role of campus public safety distinctly different from any other police agency.

As stated previously, college administrations are often reluctant to accept the strict police orientation with its inherent police autonomy. They may prefer the traditional campus security guard/watchman role with its service orientation. It is within this context that the director of the campus public safety department must manage and direct the operations of the organization. He has the task of providing expected traditional services, as well as necessary law enforcement functions, while attempting to adhere to what he perceives to be the wishes of the administration.

In 1985 the author conducted a study to determine if there is a role-perception conflict between campus public safety directors and their immediate supervisors regarding the role and functions of the campus safety division.[17]

In the last two decades, campus safety officers (police or security officers) in most public universities have been empowered with the same sworn police authority as any other peace officer (i.e. municipal, county, state). Subsequently, these safety officers may perceive themselves as law enforcement oriented and function accordingly. The director of campus public safety, who is usually a veteran safety officer, may tend to support this orientation. Often, this law enforcement orientation conflicts with the expectations of the central administration, since many college presidents and their administrative subordinates perceive the role of the campus public safety division to be more service and security oriented.

Such a conflict in perceptions of the role of the campus public safety department could have significance in several ways. It could result in the campus public safety department failing to meet the objectives of the institution's mission and goals. It could result in a lack of harmony and understanding between the director and his/her direct supervisor. It could result in administration's lack of support for the public safety department's efforts. It could determine what kinds of programs, personnel, training and procedures the public safety department requires. Also, with no clear university-wide philosophy and policy on the role of campus public safety personnel embraced by the director, the safety officers could experience frustration. Finally, the kind of service that the academic community receives from the campus public safety department could be affected.

A review was conducted of current literature related to the history of the development of campus public safety, current policies and operations of campus public safety departments, and methodologies and findings of other studies on the role of campus public safety departments. This review provided direction for the development of the study and, specifically, of the questionnaire.

The subjects of the study were directors of campus public safety departments (all IACLEA members) and supervisors of campus public safety directors from four-year, public colleges and universities. A total of 192 institutions responded. A validated questionnaire was used and collected data were treated statistically.

Demographic data from questionnaire responses indicated that the title "chief of campus police" was used more than any other title for the director. The second most frequently used title was "director of public safety." Table I illustrates the frequency distribution and percentages of titles of positions for campus public safety directors. A majority of campus public safety directors reported to a vice-president.

TABLE I
FREQUENCY DISTRIBUTION AND PERCENTAGES OF TITLES
OF POSITIONS FOR CAMPUS PUBLIC SAFETY DIRECTORS

Title		*N*	*Percent*
Director of Campus Safety and Security		29	18.4
Chief of Campus Police		65	41.1
Chief of Campus Security		16	10.1
Director of Public Safety		47	29.7
Other		2	0.6
	Total	158	100.0

The percentages and frequency distributions of the two sample groups indicated general agreement among campus public safety directors and immediate supervisors regarding the predominance of the service role for the campus public safety department. The responses indicated that supervisors were slightly more service oriented than directors.

On the issue of the similarity of the campus public safety officer's role to that of the municipal police officer's, both directors and supervisors agreed that there was very little similarity. However, a greater percentage of the directors perceived the roles to be similar. The majority of campus public safety directors preferred that campus public safety officers be called "police officers" rather than "security officers." Once again, while campus public safety directors perceived the role of the campus public safety department to be service oriented, their responses indicated they are more law enforcement or "police" oriented than their supervisors. A majority of both directors and supervisors strongly supported that the same training be required for campus public safety officers as is required for municipal police.

The findings of the study, within the delimitations set, support the following conclusions:

1. There are differences in the perceptions of campus public safety directors and the supervisors of campus public safety directors regarding the role of campus safety as to a service orientation or a law enforcement orientation.

2. There are differences in the perceptions of campus public safety directors and supervisors regarding the similarity of the campus safety functions to municipal police functions.

3. There are differences in the perceptions of campus public safety directors and supervisors regarding the similarity of campus safety functions to security guard/watchman functions.

4. The campus public safety directors were more supportive of the law enforcement role and a "police" image than were the supervisors of campus public safety directors.

5. While there were statistically significant differences in perceptions among the two groups, both campus public safety directors and supervisors were in general agreement that:

    a. The role of the campus public safety department is one of service, with less emphasis on law enforcement.

    b. Campus public safety officers should be as well trained as municipal police officers, even though campus officers should fulfill a different role than do municipal police.

RECOMMENDATIONS

In an effort to resolve this role conflict and reach a mutually acceptable perspective, it is important for college administrators to recognize the need for such a perspective and exert the necessary efforts to that end. Certainly, each institution must consider its own unique situation and needs. But institutions of higher education have floundered long enough in this area and it is time for some sound and purposeful direction, philosophy and policies for public safety programs. The author makes the following recommendations for establishing a proper perspective for campus public safety's role.

1. A needs-assessment study should be conducted by colleges with participation by administrators, faculty and students to determine what public safety services are needed and what image they perceive the safety department to need.

2. Philosophy, policies and procedures should be developed jointly by the administration and the campus public safety department in keeping with the results of a campus-wide needs-assessment study regarding the role of the campus public safety department.

3. The educational level of campus public safety officers should be raised, based on results from other relevant studies found in the literature review, which indicated that the higher the level of education, the more service oriented officers were.

4. A clear and structured process of communication should be established for the campus public safety director and his/her immediate supervisor for the purpose of clarifying philosophies, policies, procedures and objectives of the campus safety department.

5. A survey should be conducted by the institution to find out how other colleges and universities deal with criminal and misconduct incidents and what kinds of services their safety/security department provides.

6. The institution should conduct a study on the nature and scope of crime on campus to help determine how significant the law enforcement role should be for the campus public safety department.

7. A study should be conducted to determine which, if any, law enforcement functions should be performed by higher education institutions as opposed to local law enforcement agencies providing the function.

8. Attention should be focused on campus safety leadership to include personal characteristics that might be significant in affecting the role of the campus public safety department.

SUMMARY

Crime on campus will continue to plague university and college administrators. It simply cannot be ignored. Some law enforcement response will be needed to deal effectively with crime and afford liability protection for the institution. It is the wise top administrator who will recognize the benefits of providing a comprehensive and quality public safety program which can fulfill the predominate service role and also be equipped to handle law enforcement needs. A positive, service-oriented approach should be adopted by campus public safety officials. Yet, each police/security officer must be well trained and prepared to respond effectively to emergency situations as might occur in any municipality or county. Both roles—law enforcement and service—can and must coexist to reasonably and responsibly serve the campus community.

NOTES

1. George Eastman, "The Campus Law Enforcement Administrator," *Campus Law Enforcement Journal,* Vol. 12, (May–June 1982), pp. 8–13.

2. Code of Alabama, 1975, Section 16, Paragraph 22, p. 10.

3. James Q. Wilson, *Varieties of Police Behavior* (Cambridge: Massachusetts Press, 1968), p. 9.

4. David C. Bordner and D. M. Petersen, *Campus Policing: The Nature of University Police Work* (New York, New York: University Press of America, 1983), p. 115.

5. John W. Powell, *Campus Security and Law Enforcement* (Boston, Massachusetts: Butterworth, Inc., 1971), p. 29.

6. S. A. Abramson, "A Survey of Campus Police Departments; Screening and Selection Practices." *The Police Chief,* Vol. 41, October 1974, pp. 54–64.

7. Florida State University Department of Public Safety, Departmental Philosophy. General Order 85–1, 1985.

8. J. W. Cunningham and W.A. Jenkins, "Evolution of a Campus Security Division." *Campus Law Enforcement Journal,* Vol. 11, Sept./Oct. 1981, No. 7, pp. 8–13.

9. Eugene Sides, "Policing the Campus: Responsibilities of a University Police Department." *The Police Chief,* Vol. 50, November, 1983, pp. 69–70.

10. Robert R. Stephens, "The Necessary Higher Education of Line Campus Officers at Large Four-Year Colleges and Universities," (Doctoral Dissertation, Arizona State University, 1972), 33, 3332A. (University Microfilms No. 72-32, 831), 1972.

11. George W. Milliron, "Attitudes of Chief of Police, Deans of Students, and Directors of Campus Security Toward Violations of Law By College Students," (Doctoral Dissertation, University of Northern Colorado, 1970). Dissertation Abstracts International, 31, 6311A. (University Microfilms No. 71-14, 533), 1972.

12. Robert E. Mayer, "Campus Security Means Law Enforcement." *Campus Law Enforcement Journal,* Vol. 12, Jan 1983, p. 25.

13. Swen C. Nielsen, *General Organizational and Administrative Concepts for University Police* (Springfield, Illinois: Charles C Thomas, 1971), p. 3.

14. James A. Telb, "The Relationship Between Personal Characteristics of Campus Security Officers and Their Role Orientation, (Doctoral Dissertation, The University of Toledo, 1980). Dissertation Abstracts International, 40, 1337A. (University Microfilms No. 80-21, 991), 1980.

15. Robert J. Meadows, "A Study on Relationships Between Demographic Characteristics of College and University Safety Officers and Their Role Orientation Toward Service or Law Enforcement." Unpublished Doctoral Dissertation, Pepperdine University, 1982.

16. Milliron, "Attitudes of Chiefs of Police."

17. David Nichols, "Perceptions of the Role of Campus Public Safety Departments by Public Safety Directors and Their Immediate Supervisors," (Doctoral Dissertation, The University of Alabama, 1985). Dissertation Abstracts International, 46, 1848A. (University Microfilms No. 85-19, 408) 1986.

Part II

ORGANIZATION AND MANAGEMENT

S ince campus public safety is still a relatively young and developing field, many campus police/security directors continue to experience frustration and difficulty in effectively accomplishing the goals and objectives of their department. This may be due, in part, to the department's organizational position within the institution or the department's own organizational configuration. On the other hand, many problems hindering the effective delivery of services may be attributed to inept management. A proper organizational structure and competent management are cornerstones for directing an organization toward its goals. With lean years in the forecast for higher education's economy, more accountability will be demanded for campus public safety directors. Assiduous leadership coupled with sound management practices are needed to effectively and efficiently provide a multiplicity of public safety services to the campus community. A campus public safety director must be more than a manager of operations. He/she must be a leader who instills the proper philosophy and attitude within all public safety personnel. The trend in campus public safety today is to select highly competent leaders who demonstrate the ability to communicate well to a diverse campus population. At the same time this individual is expected to effectively manage a budget and records systems while delivering high quality public safety services. Such leadership has already changed the image and enhanced the credibility of campus public safety within the campus community and among other public safety professionals.

Chapter 4

ORGANIZATIONAL CONSIDERATIONS

THE ORGANIZATIONAL HIERARCHY
WITHIN THE INSTITUTION

As Director of Safety and Security, John Smith has, for some time, been aware of the high-speed traffic problem on campus. Several accidents have occurred, with a few resulting in personal injuries. Mr. Smith has discussed this problem on several occasions with his direct supervisor, the Director of the Physical Plant, and made recommendations for reducing these occurrences through increased enforcement by campus police officers, i.e. posting speed limit signs, using electronic detection devices (radar), issuing citations for speeding, installing speed breakers, and so on. Mr. Smith has received only negative feedback. He has been reminded that his department is one of five others within the Physical Plant Division and whose primary responsibility should be the security of buildings and keeping trespassers off campus property. When Mr. Smith requested to take his problem a step higher, to the Vice-President for Business and Finance, he was strongly discouraged by his supervisor. Since there is no institution-wide policy for public safety function and, therefore, no clearly defined role and goals endorsed by the central administration, Mr. Smith can only respond to the continuing problem in frustration.

This problem illustrates the kinds of difficulties many campus public safety directors experience due, in part, to their position in the organizational hierarchy. Being placed several levels down from the top administrative staff often makes it difficult to approach institutional-wide problems and deliver a comprehensive public safety program. Of course, this will depend on a number of variables (i.e. size of the institution, organizational structure, personality of directors, authority and role of public safety). Historically, the campus public safety function was placed under the physical plant division. Its function was, in fact, only building and grounds security. However, with the expansion of its responsibilities and services over the past twenty-five years, this function is now much broader in scope. Since campus public safety is now concerned with students' safety, parking and traffic enforcement, fire safety, criminal investigations, and law enforcement, its position within the organization should be commensurate with its responsibilities and the influence it has on all segments of the campus community. The specific organizational position for all campus public safety departments cannot be easily identified under a blanket proposal, since, as with the institutions themselves, every organizational structure is uniquely designed in keeping with internal and external needs and constraints. However, some general conclusions can be drawn and recommendations made.

The results of a recent research effort conducted by the author as discussed in a preceding chapter supports the trend toward the campus public safety department reporting to a vice-president instead of the physical plant director.[1] Table II shows the titles of persons to whom campus safety report with a distribution of responses. These data are considered pertinent to indicate what positions the supervisors hold as well as add research on campus public safety.

TABLE II
FREQUENCY DISTRIBUTION AND PERCENTAGES OF TITLES
OF PERSONS TO WHOM CAMPUS SAFETY DIRECTORS REPORT

Titles of Persons to whom directors report	N	Percentage
Vice president	106	67.1
Dean of students	9	5.7
Director of physical plant	35	22.2
President	2	1.3
Assistant to the president	6	3.7
Total	158	100.0

There was a total of 158 responses from the direct supervisors of campus public safety directors. One hundred and six directors (67.1%) reported to a vice-president. While this does not specify the vice-president's title or area of responsibility, it does illustrate the level of the administrational organization to which the director reports. Nine directors (5.7%) reported to the dean of students. The second largest number of respondents in this table, thirty-five (22.2%), reported to the director of physical plant. Only two directors (1.3%) reported directly to the president. Six directors (3.7%) reported to the assistant to the president.[2]

While there are a number of organizational configurations, the campus public safety director should be placed at a level which will afford him the status with which to communicate directly with directors and deans and, at the same time, have reasonable access to all vice-presidents and the president when appropriate. There should be no more than one level or position between the campus public safety director and the president of the institution. If the law enforcement/public safety function must report through several bureaucratic layers, the reports and information tend to be filtered and, thus, the original meaning diluted. The ideal organizational model, particularly on a large multi-campus institution, would designate the campus public safety head as vice-president for public safety services. The University of South Carolina offers a good example of this (see Fig. 1).

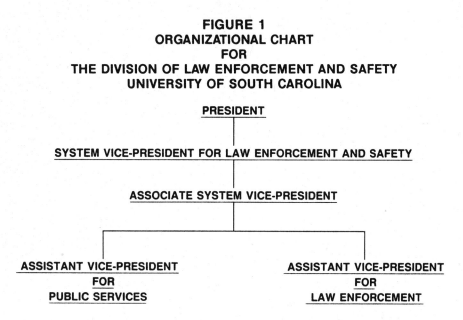

FIGURE 1
ORGANIZATIONAL CHART
FOR
THE DIVISION OF LAW ENFORCEMENT AND SAFETY
UNIVERSITY OF SOUTH CAROLINA

PRESIDENT

SYSTEM VICE-PRESIDENT FOR LAW ENFORCEMENT AND SAFETY

ASSOCIATE SYSTEM VICE-PRESIDENT

ASSISTANT VICE-PRESIDENT
FOR
PUBLIC SERVICES

ASSISTANT VICE-PRESIDENT
FOR
LAW ENFORCEMENT

The University of South Carolina, which uses a system-wide approach in organizing its public safety program, has eight branch campuses in addition to its main campus in Columbia. The system vice-president for law enforcement and safety, who reports directly to the president of the university, has general direction over law enforcement and safety needs on these campuses. He serves in an advisory and support capacity to the branch campuses. Auburn University, with an enrollment of approximately 21,000, provides a model for an institutional organizational structure depicting the position of the university police department. Auburn's organizational structure is illustrated in Figure 2. Here, the chief of police, along with four other department heads, reports to a vice president of the institution.

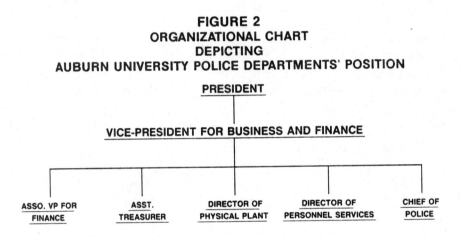

**FIGURE 2
ORGANIZATIONAL CHART
DEPICTING
AUBURN UNIVERSITY POLICE DEPARTMENTS' POSITION**

Figure 3 presents a typical organizational model for a small university with an enrollment of approximately 5,000 students. In this model, as with many actual institutions, the head of the campus police/security department reports to the director of the physical plant. This director then reports to a vice-president. There are many other organizational variations which can provide acceptable position and functional adequacy for the public safety department.

Organizational Concepts

It is important that students of criminal justice administration, campus public safety administrators, and top university administrative officials responsible for public safety services recognize and understand basic concepts of organizations. If those ensure the implementation of good sound concepts and practices, the organization will better fulfill its mission, goals, and objectives. Organizations represent man's attempt to achieve specified goals in an orderly and efficient manner. Organizations are shaped by the changing conditions around them and are

FIGURE 3
ORGANIZATIONAL CHART
DEPICTING
THE POSITION OF A CAMPUS POLICE DEPARTMENT
AT A SMALL INSTITUTION

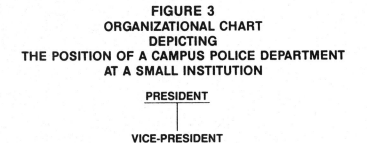

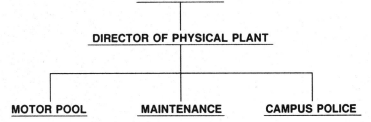

subject to a number of influences. Campus public safety administrators must understand this and be willing to adapt to these conditions and influences. Perhaps few other environments have changed so significantly as the campus community within the past twenty years.

The ultimate purpose of an organization is to establish conditions that will enhance the effectiveness of the organization in attaining its goals. An organizational structure is necessary when any group has a common task and/or goal. An unorganized group is only a mass of people. It can neither determine its purposes nor accomplish its ultimate objectives. Therefore, in order to survive, the group must be organized. The following concepts set forth the basic criteria for an effective organization.[3]

1. The effectiveness of an organization is enhanced by having a single executive head.
2. The effectiveness of an organization is enhanced by a clear definition of goals and purposes.
3. The effectiveness of an organization is enhanced when every person in the organization knows to whom and for what he is responsible.
4. The effectiveness of an organization is enhanced when superordinates delegate authority to subordinates.
5. The effectiveness of an organization is enhanced by the division of labor and task specialization.
6. The effectiveness of an organization is enhanced by the devel-

opment of standardized procedures for routine administrative operation.

7. The effectiveness of an organization is enhanced by assigning to each administrator/supervisor no greater a number of persons than he can directly supervise.

8. The effectiveness of an organization is enhanced by continuing policies and programs until results can be evaluated.

9. The effectiveness of an organization is enhanced when it makes provision for innovation and change.

10. The effectiveness of an organization is enhanced when the organization provides security for its members.

11. The effectiveness of an organization is enhanced by the personnel selected. This includes selecting the competent, training the inexperienced, eliminating the incompetent, and providing incentives for all members of the organization.

12. The effectiveness of an organization is enhanced when provision is made not only for evaluating the products of the organization but also the organization itself.

It is important that every department have a designated head or director who is trained in the area of security and/or law enforcement and who is directly responsible for the administration and operation of the campus public safety department. Too often a director of physical plant or business manager will serve as the only director and supervisor of the campus police/security program with no other ranking officer responsible for the operations. This is particularly true in some small institutions. This can result in serious problems when a major crisis arises and "on-the-scene" decisions must be made which may require special training and knowledge of the criminal justice system. This director, with no formal training or law enforcement experience, will have to make decisions which may impact students, officers, and the institution's liability.

THE CAMPUS PUBLIC SAFETY DEPARTMENT: ORGANIZATION

The organizational structure of most campus public safety departments resembles that of municipal police departments. Since police agencies are paramilitary organizations, campus police and security departments usually designate positions, titles, and rank with military terms (i.e. officer, sergeant, lieutenant, etc.). It is important that campus public safety departments be organized so as to enhance the effectiveness and efficiency of the operation. The size of the department, its function and other factors will determine the best organizational design.

While there are a number of factors to be considered in determining the most suitable organizational structure, generally, the campus public safety department should be centralized with bureaucratic authority vested in formalized positions which are hierarchically organized, with officers at each level reporting to persons at a higher level. All should ultimately report to the director or chief. It should also be kept in mind that there are many variations and possibilities in organizational structures for campus public safety departments. Perhaps one of the most important considerations should be an organizational design which provides for a clearly defined line of responsibility. Functional units should be arranged so as to effectively and efficiently meet the goals and objectives of the organization. Even in a small campus security department someone must be in charge; everyone must understand the organizational and functional responsibilities of the members of the organization. Every individual in the organization should expect clarification of the objectives, duties, authority, and relationships of his position. A well-defined chain of command with position rankings provides all members of the department with a clear understanding of who is responsible and who is in charge.

In order to gain a better perspective of the campus public safety organizational structure, three models are presented representing a large institution, a medium-sized institution, and a small institution. While these models are specifically designed to meet the needs of their particular institutions and may not be ideally suited for other universities, they do represent credible and effective organizational designs. Rutgers University, with an enrollment of approximately 50,000, provides an organizational structure for a campus police agency at a large institution. Figure 4 illustrates Rutgers's organizational chart. There are three major divisions on the main campus at New Brunswick: Service Division, Patrol Division, and Detective Division. A captain heads each division with supervisors under him in descending order or rank (i.e. lieutenant, sergeant, etc.). It should be noted that the Rutgers University Police Department is also subdivided into three campuses: Camden, New Brunswick, and Newark. Each campus is headed by an assistant police chief or captain.

The University of Arkansas, a public institution, located in Fayetteville,

**FIGURE 4
ORGANIZATION OF THE RUTGERS UNIVERSITY
POLICE DEPARTMENT
TABLE OF ORGANIZATION—RUPD**

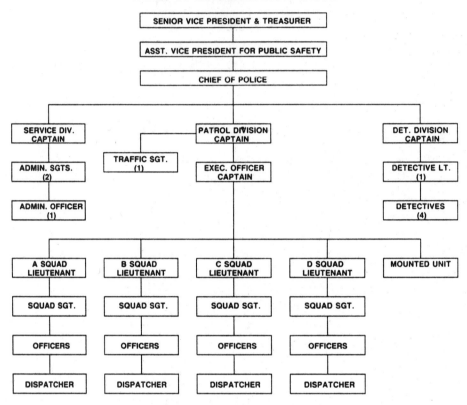

Arkansas, has an enrollment of approximately 13,000 students and is considered a mid-sized institution. Figure 5 depicts the University of Arkansas's organizational structure. Notice there are only two major divisions, each headed by a lieutenant. Basically, one lieutenant heads the law enforcement division which includes uniform patrol functions and investigation functions. The other lieutenant heads the support services function to include training and crime prevention. These division heads report directly to the director. This design is particularly suited to the single-campus institution with approximately 28 full-time sworn personnel.

The University of Montevallo, a small public institution in Alabama, has an enrollment of approximately 2,800. The campus police department is located within the physical plant division, both geographically

FIGURE 5
UNIVERSITY OF ARKANSAS—FAYETTEVILLE
UNIVERSITY POLICE
1986 ORGANIZATIONAL CHART

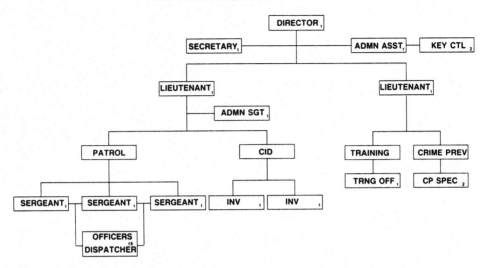

and organizationally. Figure 6 illustrates the organizational structure of this university's police department. Since there are only eight officers who provide a wide range of services to the campus community, there is no practical reason to divide the department into functional divisions. This structure functions adequately in a small campus setting.

FIGURE 6
UNIVERSITY OF MONTEVALLO
MONTEVALLO, ALABAMA

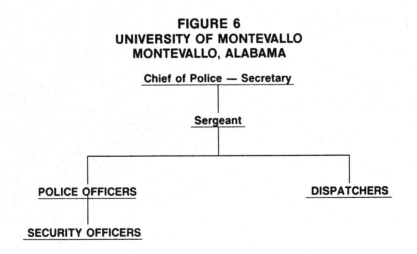

Responsibilities of Functional Units

The division of tasks within the campus public safety department is primarily by function. As discussed in a preceding section, functional units must be arranged so as to deliver the best possible services in the most efficient manner. By far, most campus police/security departments are small, employing fewer than twenty officers. Therefore, these functional units are usually under a single division with little specialization of function. The large departments are able to establish several major divisions, thus affording more specialization within each. Since specific treatment will be given to functional tasks and the delivery of services in a later discussion, broad characteristics and general areas of responsibilities will be discussed here.

While there is a variety of organizational designs, generally, most campus public safety departments' organizations can be structured into one or more of four major functions or categories: (1) administrative, (2) uniform patrol, (3) investigative, and (4) support services. Certainly, other major functional divisions exist on some campuses to include security, environmental and health safety, fire safety and protection, parking and transportation, etc. For example, the Michigan State University Department of Public Safety has three major organizational divisions: the police division, the staff division, and the environmental health and safety division. However, these four major categories are more widely accepted, usually encompassing other functions within their organizational jurisdiction. Again, the majority of campus police/security departments will be organized into only one division, the patrol division, and still perform the same wide range of functions as do larger departments with several divisions. A closer look at the description of each of these four major categories will reveal that most all other functions and areas of responsibility are included in one of these.

Administrative Division. This includes the director or chief, his secretary, an assistant director, coordinator of training, administrative assistant(s), and other specially designated positions. This unit is responsible for the police, administration, and operation of the department. The administrative staff is charged with maintaining and increasing organizational effectiveness and efficiency. Special units (i.e. internal affairs, public relations) may be included in this division.

Uniform Patrol Division. This includes command personnel, supervisors, and uniform patrol officers. It may also include secretarial/clerical personnel. This division often contains the building security and parking enforcement personnel. Its primary functions include law enforcement, security, traffic enforcement, vehicular patrol, and service tasks. It may also encompass criminal investigations, crime prevention, parking enforcement, building security, and escort service, particularly in smaller departments.

Investigative Division. This specialized division is usually found in larger campus public safety departments and includes a commanding officer, investigators or detectives, and secretarial/clerical assistants. The primary function of this division is that of criminal investigations.

Support Services Division. This includes a commander or director, secretarial/clerical personnel, radio communications operators, student employees, and other non-sworn employees. The primary functions include records administration, radio/telephone communications, parking decal issuance, vehicle and equipment maintenance, supply operations, key control, and fire safety. Other functions which may be assigned to this division are parking enforcement, training, and transportation services.

Position Classifications and Descriptions

Each functional division of the department, whether there be one or five, carries out its functions via personnel trained in specific areas to perform designated tasks. Some functional divisions may have few position classifications or categories, whereas others may have many. For example, an investigative division in a medium-sized department may have only three investigators with two position classifications: lieutenant and detective. On the other hand, the uniformed patrol division may have four or more position classifications (i.e. captain, lieutenant, sergeant, corporal, officer). The organizational hierarchy within each functional division is structured according to rank, with the highest usually being a deputy chief or captain and the lowest being officer, dispatcher, or trainee. Figure 7 illustrates Florida State University's Department of Public Safety's organizational terminology and brief functions/rank descriptions.

In order for each individual in his position to fulfill the assigned tasks within a particular functional division, it is important to provide detailed job descriptions. These also provide the basic organizational building from the lowest level to ensure the delivery of services, the achievement

FIGURE 7
FLORIDA STATE UNIVERSITY
DEPARTMENT OF PUBLIC SAFETY
General Order 85-3

DEPARTMENTAL FUNCTIONS/RANK DESCRIPTIONS

A. DIRECTOR—Department Head—Title: Mr. or Chief.

B. DEPUTY DIRECTOR—Assistant to the Director—Second in chain of Departmental authority and responsibility—Title: Captain.

C. CAPTAIN—an officer classified by the Department of Administration as a Law Enforcement Captain or any other officer so designated by the Director.

D. LIEUTENANT—an officer classified by the Department of Administration as a Law Enforcement Lieutenant or any other officer so designated by the Director.

E. SERGEANT—an officer classified by the Department of Administration as a Law Enforcement Sergeant or any other officer so designated by the Director.

F. CORPORAL—an officer classified by the Department of Administration as a Law Enforcement Corporal, or any other officer so designated by the Director.

G. OFFICER—a commissioned University Law Enforcement Officer—usually refers to a Law Enforcement Officer.

H. DISPATCHER—person assigned to communication duties—may be a police officer or duty officer—also called the Complaint Desk Officer (CDO).

I. INVESTIGATOR—an officer classified by the Department of Administration as a Law Enforcement Investigator or any other officer so designated by the Director, assigned to the Investigations Section. Title: Sergeant.

J. CHIEF INVESTIGATOR—an officer classified as a Law Enforcement Lieutenant or any other officer so designated by the Director. Title: Lieutenant.

K. TRAINING COORDINATOR—an officer, classified by the Department of Administration as a Law Enforcement Lieutenant or any other officer so designated by the Director. Title: Lieutenant.

L. SHIFT COMMANDER—the senior on-duty University Police Sergeant or Corporal.

of objectives, and the accomplishment of broader functional goals. They serve as criteria with which to measure the performance of employees. Figure 8 illustrates a job description for a Public Safety Officer I at the University of Arkansas at Fayetteville. While job descriptions vary in format, most generally include a general summary or description of the position, specific functions and responsibilities, job requirements, and qualifications.

FIGURE 8
UNIVERSITY OF ARKANSAS AT FAYETTEVILLE
PUBLIC SAFETY OFFICER I

JOB SUMMARY

A Public Safety Officer I is a trainee with less than one year police experience. Although this individual is a Certified Police Officer, he/she has not met all the training requirements established by this Department and the State of Arkansas. The Public Safety Officer I will not be armed with a revolver until basic training requirements are completed. The activities of the Officer include supervised and unsupervised patrol function, handling safety hazards, participating in training, assisting in special events, and performing other duties as assigned.

JOB DUTIES AND RESPONSIBILITIES

1. *Supervised Patrol:* The Public Safety Officer I will not engage in patrol activity unless supervised or until he/she has completed the basic training requests of this State and department. The Officer will utilize the patrol time in learning the campus, how to effectively patrol, how to perform security checks and recognize security violations, and other patrol functions as necessary. The Officer may assist in motorist assist/public service type functions.
2. *Handling Safety Hazards:* The Public Safety Officer I will assist trained officers in response to fires and/or bomb threats. The Officer will be constantly alert for safety hazards (e.g. defective lighting, electrical hazards) and immediately report these hazards for corrective action.
3. *Training:* The Public Safety Officer I must attend and successfully complete the Arkansas Law Enforcement Training Academy or show proof of acceptable training from another State. The Officer must successfully complete all phases of departmental recruit training.
4. *Special Events:* The Public Safety Officer I will work special events (e.g. concerts, basketball games, football games) while under supervision.
5. *Special Duties as Assigned.*

MINIMUM QUALIFICATIONS

1. Must be a high school graduate. No police experience necessary.
2. Must meet or exceed the minimum standards for law enforcement officers in Arkansas as per Act 452 of the 1975 Acts of Arkansas.
3. Must be public minded and demonstrate a non-rigid attitude with regards to human needs and problems.
4. Must be a team worker and capable of developing good rapport with the University community as well as area law enforcement officers.
5. Must successfully complete the departmental selection process:
    a. Interviews within the Department
    b. Selection committee interview
    c. Psychological examination
    d. Medical examination
    e. Background investigation
    f. Polygraph investigation
    g. Assessment testing

SUMMARY

In order for the campus public safety department to effectively provide services to the campus community, it should be afforded a position within the institution's organizational hierarchy which will facilitate administrative decision making and communications. Special provisions should be made to allow the campus public safety director accessibility to top administrative officials, to include the president, when circumstances warrant it.

The campus public safety director should organize his/her department in the most functionally efficient structure suited to the institution's unique environment and characteristics. It is essential that organizational goals, objectives, and functions be clearly defined and understood by all department employees. The department's philosophy and role should be identified and instilled in each member of the organization. An organizational hierarchy within the department must include a well-defined chain of command. Every member of the department should know what his/her responsibilities are via a written job description and understand his/her position within the chain of command.

Of course, an organization and its effectiveness is only as good as its leader. The director must be able to conceptualize basic organizational principles and translate them into practical, functional management. The director must be willing to adapt organizational goals and be flexible with the organizational structure when internal and/or external factors merit change. A sensitivity to the individual within the organization is essential in successfully administering any organization.

NOTES

1. David Nichols, "Perceptions of the Role of Campus Public Safety Departments by Public Safety Directors and Their Immediate Supervisors," (Doctoral Dissertation, The University of Alabama, 1985). Dissertation Abstracts International, 46, 1848A. (University Microfilms No. 85-19, 408), 1986.

2. Ibid., p. 55.

3. Edgar L. Morphet, Roe L. Johns, and Theodore L. Reller, *Educational Organization and Administration* (Englewoods Cliffs, New Jersey: Prentice-Hall, 1967), pp. 94–98.

Chapter 5

EFFECTIVE LEADERSHIP AND MANAGEMENT

THE KEY: EFFECTIVE LEADERSHIP

Effective leadership is a key ingredient in upgrading campus public safety administration. While great strides have been in all aspects in the field of law enforcement, the important role of leadership in police and security administration has been neglected. Against the backdrop of advanced, sophisticated police and public safety organizations set within an ever-changing society stands the police manager. He has the responsibility of effectively merging his organization's goals with those of society, whether it be a metropolitan area or a campus community. It is an unenviable, yet inescapable task that requires effective leadership abilities along with management skills. It is important to note that being a police manager does not guarantee that one is a police leader. With the position of manager comes the authority or right to command; with leadership comes the power to do so. Combining the two into a single person and position affects one's ability to effectively achieve results in a positive way. Whisenand and Fergusen state: "Fundamentally, leadership is a relationship between two or more people in which one attempts to influence the other(s) toward the attainment of a goal or goals."[1]

In the past, little emphasis was placed on the selection and quality of police managers. This was especially true in campus law enforcement and safety. The selection of an individual to head the campus public safety department should be of major importance to top university administrators. The right kind of leader can assist in setting goals and organizing and implementing programs. In the past, some college administrators gave little attention to public safety, which resulted in the director of the police/security department being chosen solely on criteria such as longevity within the department, being the oldest officer, and/or having extensive law enforcement experience (i.e. a retired state trooper, former municipal officer, retired military policeman). Frequently, there was no emphasis on advanced education, keen communication skills, or an acceptable philosophy of the role of public safety services within the academic community.

Today, however, the trend is toward selecting individuals who possess a bachelor's degree as a minimum, have proven experience in community relations, have successful experience in law enforcement (preferably in a campus setting), have the ability to communicate effectively with the various publics both on and off campus, and who possess human relations skills coupled with administrative abilities. An extensive, painstaking search and selection process is important when seeking competent candidates. A salary range should be attractive and commensurate with the credentials and qualities of a professional individual. Besides being able to relate to his personnel, this individual should be capable of communicating effectively with other administrative officials and students while developing a public safety program appropriate for that particular academic community.

In a study conducted with 404 responding campus public safety directors, Eastman (1982) found that 58.4 percent held a baccalaureate degree or higher. Over 110 directors were graduates of prominent national law enforcement institutes (i.e. FBI National Academy, Northwestern University Traffic Institute, and Southern Police Institute).[2] These data support the trend toward higher-caliber campus public safety leadership. One need only look at the classified section of the *Chronicle of Higher Education* to see that job requirements for directors of campus public safety usually include a bachelor's degree as a minimum.

Effective leadership is also important at all levels of the campus public safety organization, (i.e. chief, captain, lieutenant, sergeant). These police/security managers and supervisors should embrace the philosophy and goals of the department and be able to translate them into operational objectives and tasks. They should provide leadership for other employees and exemplify positive role models. A sergeant's influence on his/her shift employees can determine their attitude and support for major policy implementation or simple procedural changes. The development of leadership skills among all levels of management should be an essential part of every police/security executive's ongoing staff development program.

Generally, there are two types of leadership: status and operational. Status leadership comes from the position itself, sometimes referred to as positional or formal leadership. In a sense, this is not leadership in its purest form, since the individual derives his power or influence over others from the position and not from true leadership characteristics. Operational leadership refers to actual leadership. The actual leader does not depend on his status or position for his power to lead. The actual leader will inspire and enrich his followers, not dominate them. The actual leader may be an informal leader not holding a leadership position.

Leader effectiveness requires that the goals of the organization be definite. It is the responsibility of the campus public safety leader to identify the department's goals and ensure they are compatible with the mission of the institution. Leader effectiveness requires the ability to communicate the goals to the members of the organization. Every campus police/security officer must be afforded a clear understanding of the goals of the department and properly perceive his/her role in achieving these goals. Leader effectiveness requires the leader be potentially attractive to others. The members of the department must view and accept the director as being capable as well as popular.

Members of an organization will be attracted to and follow a leader who possesses certain personal characteristics or qualities which enhance effective leadership. Enthusiasm by the leader will be contagious throughout the organization. An enthusiastic director or chief will positively influence the attitudes and performance of supervisors and officers. Affection, a state of sympathetic warmth and conscious concern for the well-being of others is a key ingredient in gaining the respect and loyalty of employees. Integrity is an essential quality for the successful leader. Campus police and safety officers need to trust their chief and have confidence that he will not betray them or offend them. An effective leader must also possess technical mastery. While a director of a campus public safety department cannot be expected to be an expert in every phase of law enforcement, he should be perceived by officers to be thoroughly familiar with measures of sound performance, methodologies, techniques, and general knowledge of the profession.

Much can be said about qualities, characteristics, and standards of effective leadership. However, for simplicity's sake the following list, though not all inclusive, offers some basic, generally accepted concepts of leadership:

1. Leadership is the product of interactions, not status or position.
2. Leadership cannot be structured in advance. The uniqueness of

each combination of persons impinging upon the group will bring forth different leaders.

3. Whether a person is a leader in a group depends upon the group's perception of him.
4. The way a leader perceives his role determines his actions.
5. Most groups have more than one person occupying the leadership role.
6. Leadership fosters positive sentiments toward the group activity and persons in the group.
7. Leadership protects the critical group norms and provides security for the group.

In an address given to public safety directors in the Philadelphia area in 1985, Gary J. Posner, vice-president for administration at the University of Pennsylvania, suggested several qualities which he considers essential for the campus public safety leader. These are simple, practical qualities which he considers helpful in making the director a success as a professional leader within the academic community. He believes that the director should understand and be able to articulate the mission of the institution and approach students in an empathic manner. Mr. Posner also recommends that the director be cognizant of the political constituencies on campus and know which committee relationships need to be enhanced. He promotes the self-assessment concept and suggests that the director periodically step back and take a look at his image on campus. This affords a better perspective of his role and performance as perceived by others in the campus community. In terms of personal qualities, he recommends calmness, professional, human and a sense of humor. Mr. Posner states:

> I believe that the leadership role of the public safety director requires you to be assertive in your beliefs and aggressive in your desire to participate in the inner workings of the university. You are not an unneeded appendix, you are not a solution in search of a problem. Instead, you are critical to the education and teaching mission, and your opinions on areas other than safety and security are valuable and valued.[3]

Continued efforts by higher education institutions to select individuals who possess special leadership qualities and ongoing staff improvement programs aimed at developing leaders will enhance the image and effectiveness of public safety in the campus community. As this trend continues, a corresponding trend toward better campus public safety administrative techniques, better public safety personnel, and improved services will be evident. After some thirty years of accelerated development, campus public safety has already emerged as a respected, highly credible part of the law enforcement community. This has been accomplished to a great extent through effective and dedicated leadership.

MANAGEMENT CONSIDERATIONS

The campus public safety manager and leader today must be more than just an operational task-oriented supervisor giving orders to subordinates. The "head" or "chief guard" of yesterday needed only to exert authority over his officers and direct them toward the accomplishment of assigned tasks. He usually had little or no broad management responsibility for planning, organizing, or coordinating the programs as it related to the mission of the institution. This was usually the responsibility of his superior (i.e. the business manager, physical plant director, dean of students). However, the past thirty years have witnessed significant changes resulting in broader responsibilities and expectations for complex management skills for the campus police/security director. It is encumbent upon him to have a thorough understanding of organizational concepts and management principles and have the ability to translate this knowledge into practical, effective administrative approaches. He must be capable of establishing and maintaining an effective communication process. He must be skilled in the decision-making process, in conflict resolution, and in public relations.

Management can be divided into four major functions and subdivided into activities or subfunctions. A management function is a logical grouping of related kinds of managerial work and is made up of subfunctions which are closely aligned and have definite characteristics which are determined by the nature of the assignment to be performed. The management activities are the basic category of the management work product.[4] Figure 9 illustrates these functions with corresponding activities.

Perhaps one of the most common weaknesses in campus public safety administration and management, as well as police management in general, is the communication process. Because of the para-military bureaucratic organizational structure, many police managers are authoritarian in their style and, subsequently, communicate only orders and have little concern for clarity or feedback. Today's campus public safety director must understand the communication process and human nature and

FIGURE 9
MAJOR MANAGEMENT FUNCTIONS

Function	*Activities*
Planning	Forecasting, establishing objectives, programming, scheduling, budgeting, establishing procedures, developing policies
Organizing	Developing organization structure, delegating responsibilities, establishing relationships
Leading	Initiating, decision making, communicating, motivating, selecting people, developing personnel
Control	Establishing performance standards, performance measuring, performance evaluating, performance correcting

adjust his management style accordingly. Effective communication is to good management/leadership as what blood is to the body. Leadership will grow and mature with effective communication. Even though the campus police chief sends a message to all police personnel, he cannot assume that it will be understood. We communicate to facilitate understanding. Memos are not the most effective type of communication. Why? One-way communication with no opportunity for feedback is the main reason. Information dispensed in form of written decree is generally less well received than information dispensed in a face-to-face situation in which questions can be asked and answered. Of course, written communications in the form of directives and policy are appropriate, but care must be taken to ensure accuracy and completeness in the information.

A few helpful tips for improving the communication process include:

a. Send complete messages and information.
b. Repetition and consistency in communication efforts increase the chances of the message being heard.
c. Information being dispensed through several people or through various levels on an organization may be distorted in the process.
d. People tend to cooperate more fully if intended goals and outcomes have been accurately communicated.
e. The communication process at its best is free and open, with messages being transmitted vertically between leaders and followers, and horizontally between group members.

One thing is sure in campus public safety management: problems! Problems to include budgetary constraints, manpower allocation, crime, equipment needs, personnel grievances, and major policy implementations are just a few which police/security directors face almost daily. With problems come the responsibility to make decisions. Management decision making is a very important part of management. The campus public safety director must enhance his decision-making skill in order to more effectively solve problems. The public safety director must follow some organized thinking format and base his decisions upon factual data. This is not to de-emphasize the importance of subjective evaluation by the manager, but such subjective thinking must also be balanced by objective analysis. According to Griffiths (1957), six steps are taken in practically any discussion of the process of decision making:

1. Recognize, define, and limit the problem.
2. Analyze and evaluate the problem.
3. Establish criteria or standards by which a solution will be evaluated or judged as acceptable and adequate to the need.
4. Collect data.
5. Formulate and select the preferred solution(s).
6. Implement the preferred solution(s).[5]

The campus public safety manager who adopts this process as part of his management decision making will reduce frustration, time, and, in some case, expenses. These steps are generic to all management decision-making processes and will sophisticate the management skills of the campus public safety executive.

MANAGEMENT APPROACHES

Effective management approaches and techniques are required of campus police/security executives. Progressive and discerning administrators of campus police/security departments of all sizes should be looking for new management philosophies and approaches that will improve their ability to develop adaptive organizations that can plan for and respond to the demands of change. Generally speaking, top police management of all types has not kept pace with technological improvements at the periphery of the enterprise. Modern police agencies to include campus public safety departments find themselves called upon to provide complex and multi-faceted services, which include preventing crime, apprehending criminals, protecting citizens' constitutional rights, responding to exigent circumstances, facilitating traffic, resolving conflict, maintaining order, and providing assistance in various non-police situations. As if these tacks for the police manager were not enough, budgetary constraints and the pressure for efficiency and accountability add further to the complexity of the management role. It is inherent within this context of change that a new breed of managers emerge equipped to apply effective and innovative management approaches.

There are numerous successful approaches in police management today which demonstrates the emerging quality of police leadership. This is true in all types of law enforcement agencies to include campus police/security departments. Each agency must choose which management approach is best suited for its particular organization and circumstances. While some of the approaches outlined in this discussion have been predominately associated with state, county, and/or municipal police agencies, they have also been adopted by campus public safety departments. It should also be noted that often these management approaches are used but are not specifically identified by formal titles.

Management by objectives (MBO) has been adopted by some police agencies. MBO is concerned with the setting of performance objectives, tracking progress, and evaluating results. The practice of MBO usually involves a large number of people and extensive organizational development training within the department. The results could be a substantial reduction in the emphasis on obsolete ideas and programs, increased emphasis on self-management, and more attention to behavioral matters and values associated with contemporary organization theory. Management by objectives can be an effective means of breaking away from patterns that have proven to be ineffective and inefficient. The campus public safety director should carefully consider the impact of such an approach in terms of the compatibility with the institution's management process and his departments resources to handle the various activities required. A police-oriented MBO approach includes the following:

a. setting goals, objectives, and priorities in terms of results to be accomplished within a given time
b. development of plans for accomplishment of results.
c. allocation of resources
d. involvement of people in implementation of plans
e. monitoring progress
f. evaluation of results in terms of effectiveness and efficiency
g. implementation of improvements in objectives and results.[6]

While the above list is in simplified form, it offers the basic approach steps of the MBO process. Effective implementation will require effective leadership and involvement of all aspects of the organization. MBO is still not widely used or accepted among many police agencies.

Another approach to effective police management is policing by objectives (PBO). This is adapted from MBO which has had wide acceptance and usage in the private sector. Because the typical MBO system is not easily adapted to police departments or to the public sector in general, PBO has been tailored to fit the police agency. Unlike private, profit-motivated organizations, have little control over the demand for the kinds, timing, or frequency of their services. Police agencies cannot easily evaluate their effectiveness, because they produce services that are difficult to measure rather than tangible products.

PBO is different from the familiar management process in several ways. It is highly systematic and goal oriented, with the main purpose being to achieve results. Involvement is a key factor in PBO. It promulgates the participation of organizational members in every phase of the process. Most of the emphasis in PBO is placed on planning and assessment. If adequate emphasis is placed here, it will reduce the amount of supervision and monitoring of the organization's operation.[7]

The PBO philosophy is that police activities are only as good as the results they produce. PBO is a decentralized management process. All managers at all levels are involved in all stages of management-planning, administration, and assessment through a system of structural participation in the management process which makes greatest possible use of managerial talents at all levels.[8]

The author promotes a modified form of participatory management at all levels of the police organization. This includes the decision-making process of the department. Many municipal and campus police administrators are reluctant to allow their officers to have an effective part in influencing policies, procedures, programs, and changes with the department. Police administrators should recognize the significance of officer participation. The key to stimulating morale, promoting unity, and improving performance is involving officers in the management process. The effective utilization of officers' input, talents, and abilities will prove rewarding. While this approach may be flexible and requires iniative by the director or manager, a well-planned system must be developed to intentionally include all employees in various phases of the management process where appropriate. Effective leadership is a prerequisite for this approach.

Adaptive management is a style of management supported by Leonard and More.[9] They suggest that this approach is a balance between the humanistic and traditional approaches to organizational management. Adaptive management is an integrative management style based on an acceptance of bureaucratic organization, with an awareness of its good and bad features. Fundamental to this concept is the belief that traditional management does not have to be dehumanizing and detrimental to police or security employees. The importance of the individual must be acknowledged; management is the act of working with and through individuals and groups to attain organizational goals. The role of leadership must be pronounced to fuse life and purpose into the inanimate structure and organization and give it thrust toward the achievement of goals and objectives.

Since the environment of a police or security agency, whether traditional or a campus organization, frequently undergoes changes, some of the more structured approaches to management may not be as flexible as required. An approach which lends itself to change is the contigency approach. Managers who opt in line with the contigency approach are referred to as situational leaders. A contigency approach seeks to define the units within and between organizations, as well as the transactions among organizations and their environments. It also concentrates on organizations as being a complex series of processes that vary according to given situations. It justifies the need for temporary systems and plans. The contingency approach to departmental design has some strong points which should appeal to the police manager. This approach allows the manager/leader to determine which design, organization, or direction is best according to the current circumstances and situation. The contigency approach incorporates professional judgments about the situation facing an agency. The contingency approach also points out that various divisions within a single department may require different organizational designs to accomplish goals. This would be particularly applicable when organizing a parking enforcement division and an investigative division. Also each of these two divisions may require different management styles as circumstances change. The contingency theory supports the idea that there is no "one best way" to organize, but rather the selective process should be used as the situation demands.[10] As our campus communities, students, and problems change, managers must learn to adapt their styles and to use varied managerial tools in order to become more effective leaders.

ESTABLISHING POLICY

The provision of sound administrative policy should be a major concern to every campus public safety director. This is an often misunderstood area by many directors and chiefs and frequently neglected in terms of written policy provision and in adequacy of existing policies, regulations, and procedures. Policy is an important tool for setting the tone of the organization and in directing the actions of its members. Without clearly defined policies, members of the organization will be unsure of what is expected of them. In a day of increased accountability and high expectations of the campus public safety leaders, sound policy becomes more important than ever before. Written policy is needed for several reasons. It affords guidelines and direction for employees to follow. It serves as criterion by which employees are evaluated. It provides and maintains continuity and consistency of actions throughout the organization. It also supports and protects the director or chief when challenged by lawsuits from employees, criminal suspects, victims of crime, etc. In the absence of policy, neither the campus public safety director nor his employees have a basis for making decisions and, subsequently, defending their actions when challenged by complainants. In addition, the absence of policy often results in duplication of effort, inefficiency, waste of manpower, money, and materials, and a generally poor and inconsistent level of performance by the organization.[11]

It should be noted that not all policy may be in written form. Policy may be developed through practice and tradition. It may be established through communication by the director or supervisors. Policy may be adopted informally by following accepted standards. These accepted standards may have been established as policy or guidelines at state police training academies and, subsequently, adhered to by academy graduates in their respective departments even though these departments may have no written policy. Such standards include basic police conduct, arrest procedures, traffic enforcement, etc. While unwritten policy does exist, the importance of comprehensive written policy cannot be overemphasized. While unwritten policy tends to be ambiguous, written policy affords a formal record for consistency and equitable application for all employees.

Policy should be consistent with and be supportive of the mission, goals, and objectives of the department. Essentially, policy should be formulated to promulgate, delineate and implement these and serve to translate the department's philosophy into functional terms. Employees should understand policies, regulations, and procedure.

A policy is a broad statement of purpose or intent. Policies form the guidelines to measure progress toward goals and objectives. Policies embody the values and principles which underlly activities. Policy is usually reduced to more specific terms in the form of regulations, procedures, and directives. The following is an example of a written policy statement:

Public Relations

The Police Department, particularly its uniformed police officers, performs an important public relations function for the University. The initial impression of the University is oftentimes formed as a result of the impression created by the uniformed police officer. It is important that the officer projects an image favorable to the institution. It is the policy of this Department to strive to gain public approval and to win friendly University community coop-eration in its programs and procedures in order to facilitate the accomplishment of its objectives.

A regulation and/or rule is a specific statement of policy formulated to deal with specific functional areas and issues. They set forth concisely certain actions that are required or prohibited of employees. The following statement illustrates a departmental regulation:

Court Attendance and Demeanor

A member when subpoenaed into court to testify shall be punc-tual in attendance. He shall be dressed in full uniform or civilian clothes in good taste and businesslike appearance and shall not appear in business clothes without coat and tie. A member shall testify in a calm, distinct and audible voice. He shall not sup-press or overstate the slightest circumstance.

A procedure is a method of performing an operation or a manner of proceeding on a course of action. It differs from a policy, in that it directs action in a particular situation to perform a specific task within the guidelines of policy. Procedures are often classified as standard operat-ing procedures (SOP). The following describes a typical SOP:

Procedure

Any police officer making an arrest will do the following:

1. Attempt to minimize the danger to by-standers, suspect, and

yourself. (i.e., cuff suspect prior to placing in vehicle; remove subject from area, etc.)

2. If assistance is needed, contact other University Police Officers and/or City Police Officers.
3. If suspect is rowdy, unruly or in an intoxicated state it is advisable to transport directly to city jail. If subject is not giving you any problems, then transport to University Police Department and complete the following items of paperwork.

   a. warrant
   b. arrest report
   c. bond
   d. summons
   e. fingerprint cards—3 per person arrested
   f. photographed as required
   g. incident/offense report

A directive is an administrative/operational order to address a special situation, event, or operation. Usually, directives cover a specified period of time. It directs employees to follow certain guidelines or procedures. Directives are often in the form a memorandum or administrative special order. The following is an example of a directive:

> It is important that we maintain effective patrol and security checks throughout this holiday period. While the work load should be somewhat reduced, you are expected to stay out on campus and keep a check on all zones, check all buildings throughout your shift, and be responsive to any calls. Do not linger in the office.

There are four basic steps involved in policymaking: (1) formulation, (2) dissemination, (3) application, and (4) review and appraisal.[12]

Formulation. Policy formulation received the special attention of the President's Commission on Law Enforcement and Administration of Justice in 1967. The commission recommended a systematic process for formulating policy. The first step in this process was identifying the problem area or important issues. Assessing the current situation and determining needs is essential for sound policy formulation. The campus's public safety administrator must recognize the significance of this process and lend his full support. Too often policies are formulated by the director with little or no input from others and no assessment of the situation. Consequently, policies do not fit the circumstances and/or they do not gain widespread acceptance by employees.

The second step in the policy formulation process suggested by the commission is study and research of the issue or problem. This step includes researching current practices and trends in the field of campus public safety. A review of the literature will provide valuable information with which to measure the impact of the policy at hand.

The final step is consultation. Consultation both within and outside the campus public safety department will produce a better perspective with which to make policy decisions. Participation by command personnel should serve to elicit a commitment on their part to support the policies which are adopted.

Perhaps one of the major objectives of policy formulation is flexibility. It should be kept in mind that the department must be able to adjust its operating practices to the policy, and the individual officers and other employees must be able to adapt their activities to the varied circumstances that they confront. Therefore, when formulating policy it should be developed with some degree of flexibility in mind.

Dissemination. As stated earlier, policies should be written in order to minimize misunderstanding of the exact intent. Policy statements should be written in language that is clear and concise and, yet not so specific as to limit the reasonable exercise of discretion. Written policies should be distributed to all employees in a form that will be durable and easy to store. They should be prefaced with a statement(s) of explanation to inform employees of the general purpose and application of the policies. This will enhance the credibility of the director and promote cooperation by employees. Where feasible, it is recommended that the director or delegated command officers meet with employees to explain the policy and respond to any questions or comments. The director must be aware of the importance of proper disseminating policies to include clear communications and tact.

Application. As mentioned above, the application or implementation of policy will be easier for employees if the director has taken the time and effort to explain the purpose of the particular policy. Also, a thorough indoctrination and training process may be appropriate to ensure that employees understand the policy and know how to implement it. A reasonable amount of adjustment time, with a good deal of flexibility built in, should be allowed for implementation. Once sufficient time has been given, adherance to the policy must be ensured through effective supervision and direction of supervisory/command personnel. Uniform and consistent compliance is of utmost importance in making the policy effective.

Review and Appraisal. The final step in policymaking is that of review and appraisal. This step is essential to the effectiveness and relevancy of all policies. In essence, it is an ongoing assessment process to ensure that policies are keeping pace with organizational, environmental, and functional changes which naturally occur. Occasionally, technology makes some policies obsolete or in need of adjustment. Since change is inevitable, policies must be constantly reviewed and assessed to determine if they still serve the organization and support the goals and objectives set forth. This process should allow input from rank-and-file employees in order to get views from those in the field carrying out policies. This, in turn, will create a sense of ownership and commitment among employees. A number of employees from different ranks and functional areas should be given the opportunity to participate directly in the review and appraisal process. It is the responsibility of the campus public safety director to maintain this review and appraisal process and be willing to adjust old, traditional policies to better fit current circumstances.

In many departments, policies, procedures, directives and regulations are handed down in a "one-way-street" fashion, with no justification or purpose indicated. Because of lack of input and evaluation, some of these decisions lack practical application and may even be difficult to live with. A steady diet of these unexpected, unexplained "laws" often results in low morale and slack performance on the part of the officer, who may already feel like a peon in a caste system. Of course policies, procedures and directives are essential within an organization; changes and updates thereto must occur for the organization to be progressive and professional. Within this same context the value of officer participation should be recognized by the progressive administrator, rather than feared. It may be true that officers will usually follow one-way mandates, though often grudgingly. However, in order to create the camaraderie, high morale and positive performance that most administrators wish for, it would be wise to include the officers in making some of the rules.

The procedure for officer input need not be extensive or complicated but must simply allow two-way communication between the administration and the employees before the changes become "law." In procedural changes, as in the budget planning process, there are several methods that can be utilized. When it becomes obvious to the administrator that an existing procedure (e.g. patrol techniques, arrest procedures, vehicle maintenance) needs to be updated or replaced, it is a good time to let the officers put in their two cents' worth before implementing the new procedure.

One method would be to have the shift supervisor or chief announce to the officers that a change is being considered in a particular procedure and explain that before such a change is made they will be given the opportunity to voice their opinion regarding the change and/or offer a proposed procedure. The next step should include a meeting (if a small department) or several small group meetings for the purpose of discussing the procedure change. Again, this need not be an elaborate process; regularly scheduled meetings may be appropriate for this purpose. Whenever the meeting is held, an atmosphere of mutual respect and professionalism must be maintained, coupled with open and honest two-way communication. Remember, the purpose is to allow participation through suggestions, questions and discussion, not to make final decisions. The results of the meeting should be passed on to the administrator, who must decide the best plan for change based on his own perceptions and the input received from the officers.

Still another method for officer participation in policy and procedure formulation is the utilization of a standing committee selected from among officers and supervisors. Not only could this committee offer input regarding new proposals made by the administration, it could also periodically review existing policies, procedures and regulations and propose changes to the administration for consideration. Representative participation gives the other officers a feeling of involvement, since their ideas and suggestions can be relayed through their peers on the committee.

The development and provision of policy is a most onerous, but most necessary task. Many campus public safety directors have not recognized the significance of this task. It is time that these leaders/managers become aware of the importance of sound, comprehensive policies and be willing to find and utilize a systematic process for policymaking. It will benefit his leadership role, the organization's goals and objectives, and the functional efforts of all employees. It should be made part of the overall departmental planning process and placed on a continuum of assessment and improvement. No longer will "we've always done it that way" be acceptable or sufficient. In a day of unionization, liability suits, and performance accountability, it behooves the campus public safety administrator to ensure that his department's policies are complete, relevant, and flexible.

PLANNING AND GOAL SETTING

An important part of effective management is planning. Systematic planning is essential to a campus public safety department, whether it is in a public, private, large, small, urban, or rural setting. Planning is necessary to set realistic goals for the department, to develop goals and objectives to determine appropriate operational strategies to ensure goal attainment, to allocate available resources in the most effective and efficient manner, and to evaluate the impact of public safety operations and programs.

The National Advisory Commission on Criminal Justice Standards and Goals in its report on the police stated:

> A police agency that fails to plan ahead is forced to operate from day to day, adjusting to new demands as new demands arise, but never undertaking long range projects to upgrade police services. The agency may appear effective, but it could be much more effective if it charted its course. Such an agency delivers less than maximum police services and shortchanges its community.[11]

This philosophy holds true in the operation of a campus public safety department. Often, directors or chiefs of campus police/security departments limit their planning to short-range activities and fail to utilize the planning process for the entire public safety program. Planning must not be fragmented and uncoordinated. It should be an intergral component of every aspect of campus public safety management. Many campus police/security departments have adopted innovative techniques, computerized investigative processes, higher standards for officers, and better public relations programs. Modern equipment, additional officers, new and improved facilities, and bigger budgets have certainly afforded campus public safety administrators tools with which to protect and serve their constituents. However, while many departments have prospered in terms of these "add-ons" and even enhanced the quality of their performance, far too many fail to effectively utilize these benefits in reaching their full potential.

New approaches and improvements are often obtained and implemented without a clear and realistic plan based on what is, what is needed, and what the goals for the organization are. Often, increased budgets and expanded programs are simply unintentionally misapplied, because the real needs and goals of the department have not been properly identified. Such crisis management ignores or fails to recognize existing and future needs as they relate to goal setting and effective planning. Consequently, decisions on how to spend funds, what equipment to purchase, what programs to implement, what personnel changes to make and how to enhance operations are often made "from the hip" and may result in inefficiency and ineffectiveness.

A comprehensive, yet simple needs-assessment and goal-setting approach to police management will yield rich rewards to the police administrator. The police chief, administrator or director who is willing to involve all personnel of his department in an open process to evaluate current programs and operations and assess the effectiveness thereof will discover not only the status with regard to what is but will also realize positive effects on employees as they are allowed participation in this process. He will gain wide support among his employees, who will feel a part of his decision instead of simply victims. What is perhaps more significant is the sense of camaraderie and belonging that can be created among personnel when they observe effective changes, improvements and goals reached resulting from their input and ideas.

Ultimately, planning is the responsibility of the chief or director of the campus public safety department. Depending on the size of the organization, the planning process should be delegated to subordinates. In a small campus department the chief may spend more of his management time actually leading, directing, and controlling the planning process. In a medium-sized institution, one of the safety officers may be assigned as a planning coordinator along with his other responsibilities. In larger departments, the chief may delegate the entire process to a designated full-time planner whose responsibility is to carry out the planning process for every phase of the department to include constant needs assessments and evaluation of the various plans. The involvement of all members of the organization should be a foremost consideration for the head planner.

Many chiefs and directors are intimidated by formal planning process or feel that the benefits are not worth the effort. Planning can be relatively simple and can be accomplished without a great deal of cost or manpower. Basically, there are seven steps in a planning process:

1. **Prepare mission statement.** The leader, with input from his staff, will identify the need for planning. There must be a problem or goal in order to initiate a planning process for improvement.
2. **Involve members of the organization.** Begin by encouraging participa-

tion from all members in at least some phase of the process. Input from every one is important. Designate leaders from within the department and organize into functional units.

3. **Conduct a needs assessment.** This is an important step and should determine "what is" with regard to the need or problem.
4. **Prepare assumptions and forecasts.** All possible changes, future circumstances, and influences must be taken into consideration as they relate to the problem or need. This should be developed both on a short- and long-range basis.
5. **Select short- and long-range goals.** This should be fairly general and be based on the needs-assessment findings coupled with the assumptions and forecasts.
6. **Identify strategies for solving the problem or accomplishing the goals.** Several alternate strategies or plans should be identified. These should be in the form of specific objectives and activities.
7. **Initiate operational planning.** A decision must be made from among the strategies and then drawn up for implementation.

A Model: Needs Assessment and Goal Setting

A needs-assessment and goal-setting project was undertaken by the Jacksonville State University Police Department in Jacksonville, Alabama. It was recognized that, while progress had been made, there were areas of neglect, lack of direction, and unclear goals for future planning improvements.

The decision to conduct an assessment and goal setting at the Jacksonville State University Police Department was made because of a lack of direction in designing programs, purchasing equipment, training employees, and developing operational procedures. It was realized that decisions made isolated from any long-range plan often resulted in duplication and inefficient utilization of money and manpower. This was discussed with the entire staff in terms of the need and plans to set in motion a department effort to meet that need. Employee involvement and participation was stressed. Subsequently, the chief of University Police selected a committee made up of police officers, student patrol officers, student office workers and radio dispatchers. A chairperson was selected: a rank-and-file patrolman. The chief presented the problem to the committee and charged the committee with its task to develop an information-gathering instrument, determine areas of need, and recommend both short- and long-range goals and objectives. A flexible time-table was suggested to the committee, which allowed one year to complete the study and subsequent recommendations. The committee took it from there and proceeded with its assignment in a series of meetings over an eight-month period. A self-study plan was developed as illustrated in Figure 10.

FIGURE 10
UNIVERSITY POLICE DEPARTMENT
JACKSONVILLE STATE UNIVERSITY
SELF–STUDY PLAN

1. Determine scope and mission of self-study.

2. Define and confirm goals and objectives of the department.

3. Organize the areas and functions to be evaluated—develop a plan of action.

4. Collect and analyze data, i.e. statistics, records, reports, charges, budget, personnel, etc.

5. Develop/design a survey questionnaire to aid in evaluation of programs by employees.

6. Distribute survey instrument and collect.

7. Set up and conduct informal meetings with employees to determine needs and problem areas.

8. Evaluate the results of survey and informal discussion with employees.

9. Devise a survey instrument for the public (students, faculty, staff) to evaluate department's effectiveness.

10. Distribute public survey and collect.

11. Evaluate results of this survey and log.

12. Compile all data and results of evaluations, analyze, and make a findings report.

13. Make recommendations report to be submitted to chief and other university administrators.

The committee set its own schedule of deadlines for each phase of the study. A survey instrument was developed to elicit responses from employees as to their perceptions and suggestions with regard to what is and what is not needed. This survey was divided into four major areas: administrative, operations, personnel, and public relations. These survey forms were distributed to all employees. When the completed forms were returned, the committee calculated the responses and compiled the date in a final report that indicated the perceptions and wishes of the employees.

Using this information, the committee drew conclusions and translated these into short- and long-range goals and objectives. This draft report was then submitted to the chief for his review and subsequent questions and/or comments. After another month of careful review of the study, the chief met with the committee chairperson to discuss the findings and recommendations. A copy of the report was made available for all employees to read. Department meetings were then announced for the purpose of presenting the findings to employees. At these meetings, the chief, with the help of committee members, presented the final recommended goals and objectives in terms of their feasibility, time schedule and priority. A good deal of response came from all of those present, which helped further develop and adjust goals and objectives into a firm plan of action. In fact, many of the short-range objectives were accomplished immediately (i.e. change in procedures, equipment needs, administrative approaches, etc.). Some long-range goals and objectives were reached at the completion of the study, and others were forthcoming within the next year.

EVALUATING THE PROJECT

As with any effort, an effective evaluation is important to determine its validity and its worth for future efforts. An evaluation form was developed and distributed to all employees of the JSU Police Department for the purpose of evaluating the assessment and goal-setting process. Some items included on the evaluation form were: the process was worth the effort—yes or no; the time frame was—too short, about right, too long. I think the process was conducted well, and I have the following positive and/or negative comments about the assessment process. The employees seemed eager to respond to this. The overall indication was very positive. Employees expressed their good feelings and support for the effort. Results indicated a high degree of confidence in the credibility of the effort as well as the projected outcomes.

This program proved beneficial both for the University Police Department and for the individual employees. The department now has a plan of action with clearly stated goals and objectives that were arrived at by the employees and have their support. This plan also assists the chief and his superiors in budget planning and decision making. It affords the chief a plan of action supported by his subordinates with which to organize, operate and direct the total public safety program for the campus.

Employees have a better understanding of the administration and operation of the department and feel a sense of direction with regard to decisions relating to all facets of the department. They also have a sense of involvement and feel part of the decision-making process. They are confident that their ideas and input do make a difference. They feel like they have a vested interest in their job. This enhances morale and efficiency among employees.

Such an assessment and goal-setting effort can be accomplished at a very minimal cost and can be done effectively by any size department. A commitment to the process by the administration, employee involvement, and an open and honest approach are essential ingredients for a successful outcome. It will foster employee job satisfaction and strengthen the department administration's credibility and its ability to provide leadership.

SUMMARY

It has been said that the degree of effectiveness achieved and the kind of image projected by an organization reflects the leadership and management ability of that organization's chief administrator. Campus public safety can no longer endure inept chiefs and directors who have no sense of public safety's role within higher education nor possess the professional and personal capabilities required to administer a unique service-oriented organization within the academic community. Chief administrators of campus public safety departments must be expected to be accountable to the institution's administration, their department's staff, faculty and staff, and, most importantly, the students for which campus public safety exists. The campus public safety director must have a strong commitment to high standards for his/her personnel, to increasing the quality of service, and enhancing the image of his/her department. With the right kind of leadership and management approach, campus public safety will continue to achieve respect within the campus community as well as in the law enforcement/security community.

NOTES

1. P. M. Whisenand and F. R. Fergusen, *The Managing of Police Organizations* (Englewood Cliffs, New Jersey: Prentice-Hall, 1973), p. 17.

2. George Eastman, "Campus Law Enforcement Administration: An Analysis of the Role of Higher Educational Administration." *Campus Law Enforcement Journal,* 12 (May–June 1982):20–31.

3. Gary J. Posner, "Leadership Role of Public Safety Directors." *Campus Law Enforcement Journal,* 15, Nov./Dec. 1985, pp. 21–22.

4. Louis A. Allen, *Principles of Professional Management.* (Palo Alto, California: Louis A. Allen Associates, 1969), p. 2.

5. D. E. Griffiths, *Administrative Behavior in Education.* (New York: Harper and Row Publishers, 1957), pp. 132–133.

6. Whisenand and Fergusen, *The Managing of Police,* p. 174.

7. Victor A. Lubans and J.M. Edgar, *Policing by Objectives.* (Hartford, Connecticut: Social Development Corporation, 1978), p. 19.

8. Ibid, p. 17

9. Vivian A. Leonard and Harry W. More, *Police Organization and Management.* (Mineoia, New York: The Foundation Press, 1978), p. 321.

10. Whisenand and Fergusen, *The Managing of Police,* pp. 239–251.

11. Charles D. Hale, Fundamentals of Police Administration, (Boston: Holbrook Press, Inc., 1977) p. 90.

12. Justin G. Longenecker, *Principles of Management and Organizational Behavior* (Columbus, Ohio: Charles E. Merrill Co. Inc., 1969), p. 104.

13. National Advisory Commission on Criminal Justice Standards and Goals, Report on Police, 1973 (Washington, D.C.: U.S. Government Printing Office, 1973).

Chapter 6

BUDGET PLANNING AND RECORDS MANAGEMENT

THE BUDGET

Budgeting is a critical consideration for the campus public safety director. The budget process is an ongoing, year-round planning process. The importance of careful planning, preparation, and implementation of the budget should be recognized by the chief or director. However, many campus public safety administrators have not given sufficient attention and effort to the budget process. It should be noted that some small campus police/security departments do not have their own budgets but may be part of another division's budget (i.e. physical plant, business office, student affairs). Consequently, some chiefs and directors do not have budget planning and management responsibilities. Others have limited input and responsibilities with their direct supervisor making most of the budget-related decisions. This is unfortunate, since the police/security chief should have more input and control over the budget which is directly tied to the program for which he is responsible.

A budget is a quantitative expression of a plan of action and a means of coordination and control. Since most campus public safety programs are not revenue producing, their budgets do not reflect income. They do indicate a beginning balance or proposed expenditures to be expended over a twelve-month period, called a fiscal year. A fiscal year may not coincide with a calendar year but cover a period such as July 1 through June 30 or October 1 through September 30. While budget formats vary from one institution to another, most universities use the line-item type. Under this format, proposed expenditures are divided into specific categories or object codes (e.g. salaries, office supplies, postage). (Table III)

One of the most frequent misconceptions among many department heads is that the institutional budget process occurs over a three- or four-month period. This is due to the fact that in most cases these directors involve themselves with budget planning and preparation for only this length of time. They are called upon to submit their budget

90

TABLE III
BUDGET REQUEST (FORM 10)
FOR THE FISCAL YEAR OCTOBER 1, 1985 THROUGH SEPTEMBER 30, 1986

DEPARTMENT ___*SECURITY & TRAFFIC OFFICE*___   BUDGET UNIT NO. ___*1-000-50-1130*___

REQUEST   ALLOCATION

OBJ Code	Description of Line Items	Actual Expenditures 1984–85	Requested 1985–86	Adjusted* Request 1985–86	Approved Budget 1985–86	Projected 1986–87
		(1)	(2)	(3)	(4)	(5)
110	SALARIES	190351.00	215400.00	215400.00	215400.00	235500.00
150	WORK STUDY–STUDENT	1396.00	1400.00	1400.00	1400.00	1500.00
151	UNIV AID SPECIAL	90048.00	84000.00	84000.00	84000.00	84000.00
240	LIFE, DISABILITY & H	24192.00	25700.00	25700.00	25700.00	27000.00
255	MATCH PR EXPENSE TI	1668.00	2000.00	2000.00	2000.00	2200.00
	TOTAL PERSONNEL	307655.00	328500.00	328500.00	328500.00	349700.00
330	OFFICE SUPPLIES	500.00	650.00	650.00	650.00	750.00
390	EXPENDABLE SUPPLIES	1900.00	3200.00	3200.00	3200.00	3600.00
410	TELEPHONE	1500.00	1500.00	1500.00	1500.00	1700.00
0	POSTAGE	120.00	120.00	120.00	120.00	140.00
435	MEMBERSHIP DUES	120.00	120.00	120.00	120.00	150.00
440	PRINTING DUP & BIND	3400.00	3800.00	3800.00	3800.00	4400.00
460	TRAVEL	900.00	1200.00	1200.00	1200.00	1400.00
530	MAINT–MACHINERY & E	1400.00	2600.00	2600.00	2600.00	2900.00
535	MAINT–GAS OIL & AUT	14000.00	14000.00	14000.00	14000.00	16000.00
546	EQUIPMENT MAINT CON	2400.00	2800.00	2800.00	2800.00	3200.00
668	STATE BOARD ADJUSTM	.00	–	–		–
	TOTAL OTHER COSTS	26240.00	29990.00	29990.00	29990.00	34240.00
820	EQUIPMENT	.00	5000.00	.00	.00	8000.00
	TOTAL	333895.00	363490.00	358490.00	358490.00	391940.00

requests sometime in the spring, attend budget meetings in early summer,
and are finished with their part by mid-summer (this assumes that the

fiscal year begins on October 1). Therefore, their perceptions of the institutional budget process is somewhat limited. It is important that campus public safety directors understand the scope of their particular institution's budget process and their department's place within that process.

The budget process will vary from institution to institution depanding on the size and type of institution. The type of institution, whether public or private, will determine to a large extent the format and length of the budget process. Generally, the private institution's budget process is initiated and implemented internally within a relatively short period of time. Since the final approving authority will be the institutions board of trustees, the entire process may take only about three months,[1] whereas the public institution's process will require several external steps to include state coordinating boards or commissions, the state executive branch or finance office, and the state legislature for final approval and funding. The total time for a full budget cycle, from beginning to end, may take from 18 to 24 months. This rather complicated process is necessary due to the fact that the public institution is dealing with three budgets at one time. For example, the budget on which work begins in January 1985 is for the fiscal year beginning October 1, 1986, a period of 22 months. Three budgets are under consideration: (1) the one currently in operation; (2) the one for the next fiscal year which is at an advanced stage in the process; and (3) the one on which work is just beginning.[2]

The preparation of the budget is perhaps the most neglected and misunderstood process within the campus public safety department. It is viewed as a once-a-year chore and often hurriedly put together to meet a deadline. Usually, little thought and planning is involved in the budget preparation. Few campus police/security chiefs or directors really understand the relationship of the budget to the operation. Certainly, the institution's approach to budgeting often hinders the creativity and flexibility of the departmental budget planning and preparation; yet, it behooves every chief or director to maintain an ongoing assessment of his operation, to include detailed record keeping of all activities, expenditures, and manpower allocation. These, then, should be translated into justification for future needs and requested expenditures.

Hanna and Gentel suggest that the following information be included in the final budget request:

1. A statement of what the department is trying to accomplish, the scope of the task, and how well it is being accomplished.
2. Review present activities in detail, recommend discontinuance of those which are obsolete or unnecessary, and propose changes which will reduce expense.
3. Budget salary increases in accordance with the present compensation plan.
4. Budget non-personal expense and commodities at current prices except for specific items as indicated in the memo from the purchasing agent.
5. Consider long-term economy of operations and improvement of performance efficiency in planning expenditure requests.
6. Submit copies of the department's performance, justification data, and expenditure estimates not later than the date specified.[3]

There are several approaches to budget preparation. Drewry identifies three general approaches: (1) the incremental approach, (2) the program approach, and (3) the zero-base approach.[4] Not one of these is likely to be used in its pure form, nor can any single one be identified as the best approach. The approach adopted by a college or university will determine the way the campus public safety department must plan and prepare its annual budget.

The incremental approach is also known as the "add-on" approach. Its major characteristic is that it simply increments or adds to the previous year's budget a percentage or dollar amount. This approach to budgeting has several advantages. It is simple and easy to explain. If the institution has a 10 percent increase in funds, most divisions within the institution can usually expect a 10 percent increase in their budgets. Little time and effort are required in program planning and budget preparation. Only special needs (e.g. additional personnel, major equipment) need to be explained and justified. The incremental approach lessens the need for evaluating program effectiveness and efficiency. Policy and personnel decisions are not required each year in order to justify requested expenditures. Its major weakness is that it does not necessarily reflect the real needs of the department. For example, while the institution increments 5 percent to all divisions' budgets, the campus police/security may find this inadequate to support increased costs associated with equipment maintenance, replacement uniforms, and overtime hours due to increased manpower demands. In some cases adjustments can be made to compensate for such circumstances.

The program approach centers on the resources required to conduct programs. The best known program approach is the Planning, Programming, Budgeting Systems (PPBS). This system does not utilize the line-item format for budget preparation which is most common to the incremental approach. This approach originated in the private-profit sector of the economy. PPBS is concerned with translating the organization's goals, objectives, and programs into quantitative units of a budget. William J. Bopp (1983) believes it can be adapted to the public police organization and suggests that PPBS can do the following for a police organization:

1. A Program Planning Budgeting System will compare and evaluate the various police department's activities in determining how they are meeting their objectives.
2. Program budgeting incorporates a financial projection over an adequate time period (3 to 5 years), resulting in data for rational decision making.
3. Scrutinization of various objectives, programs, and budgetary allotments will continually be evaluated due to the in-depth analysis necessary with a program budgeting system.[5]

Bopp (1983) further promotes better planning which will be needed with PPBS. He states, "Judgment of planning quality must involve how the product copes with proposed programs in relation to available resources."[6] This is just as true in the campus setting as it is in the municipal or county law enforcement agency. The PPBS is responsive to the needs of the organization and demands placed on it by the community it serves. It should also be more flexible and adapt to changes easier than the incremental approach.

Zero-based budgeting may be considered a special form of program budgeting with a radical assumption underlying it. That assumption is that each new budget year base starts at zero, that is, there is no previous budget to which it has any relationship. While this would probably be acceptable with a new department, it lacks credibility if it is applied to an ongoing department or program. Actually, zero-based budgeting originated in the private business sector as did PPBS and is not considered practical for public institutions. It is cumbersome and time consuming, requiring detailed paperwork. Perhaps the major positive feature is that it makes no assumptions about personnel or programs and requires a thorough assessment and decision-making process each year to determine if the current number of staff, the number and types of programs, and resources are needed for the new fiscal year to accomplish its goals and objectives.

Whatever approach is used, it is incumbent on the campus public safety director to focus adequate attention and direct significant effort toward budget planning and preparation. Accountability is a key aspect of fiscal management which must be demonstrated by the police/security administration. This includes maintaining accurate statistics and records, directing an ongoing planning and assessment process, and demonstrating integrity and adeptness in budget justification and presentation. He should have an understanding of his institution's budget preparation process and the significance of adequate preparation on behalf of his department.

The assiduous chief or director will involve all members of his department in the budgeting planning process. As with planning, assessment and goal setting, officer participation will provide meaningful input for determining programs, equipment, and other needs which should be reflected in the annual budget. The chief or director should surround himself with competent individuals to assist him in preparing the budget for submission.

RECORDS MANAGEMENT

An accurate and efficient records system is essential to every campus public safety operation. While it seems almost inconceivable, many police/security departments at small institutions have no formal records system! In such cases, reports, when written, may be submitted to an administrative official (e.g. dean of students, director of physical plant). But records may not be kept in the police/security office at all. Often, this may be a result of the attitudes of some college officials who either consider the police/security operation insignificant or who wish to suppress the reality of crime on campus.

A variety of records systems exist at colleges and universities. It is not the purpose or design of this discussion to present all of these nor to elaborate on specific forms and procedures. However, some basic features of sound records management are presented in an effort to provide the campus public safety administrator with a framework for assessing the current operation and establishing an improved records system. It should be noted that records systems in industry, educational institutions, and even in law enforcement agencies of all sizes have recently undergone a transformation from "paperwork" to computer-based programs. Yet, many departments may be restricted to the traditional records system for the foreseeable future. Whatever type of system is used, it should be tailored to the individual departmental needs. Again, the planning process should be utilized in determining which system is best and ensure its continuous updating.

Generally, records management for the campus public safety department can be divided into three broad categories: police records, safety and security records, and administrative records. There may be other designations, but generally most types of records can be placed under one of these.

POLICE RECORDS

The police records system includes report writing, filing, and records control. Police records within this context also include criminal-related incidents and records within a campus security department even though the department has no sworn police authority. While the terminology is different, the principles are generic. Police records are needed for the following purposes:

1. to determine the nature and extent of crime and traffic problems;
2. to determine the need for additional personnel and financial resources;
3. to properly allocate available resources proportionate to actual service requirements;
4. to evaluate past performance;
5. to plan future manpower requirements, goals, objectives, and operational strategies;
6. to document police activities.[7]

A police records system should provide complete and accurate information on all police activities. The system should be kept as simple as possible yet flexible enough to expand as the need arises. The records should be accessible on a 24-hour basis for those who may require information. There should be definite guidelines and procedures fixing responsibility for records dissemination, confidentiality, and control. A clearly defined policy and procedural guide should be established regarding the release of records to other campus officials. This enhances communication between the campus police/security department and other departments with which good relations are essential (i.e. student affairs, housing office, physical plant). Adequate report forms should be designed and made available. Where possible, consolidation of forms can reduce the number of forms and simplify the system.

Most police records are initiated by police/security officers in the field completing an incident/offense report form. Other incident/offense reports may be completed by a desk supervisor or radio communications dispatcher. The incident/offense report form should include the time of the incident or offense, date, location, victim, suspect, description of property, type of incident or offense, and a narrative of the occurrence. The incident/offense report can provide the basis for the collection of detailed information on police activities with either manual or automated systems. It is important that such reports be accurate and complete. Proficiency in report writing should be stressed.

An accurate and complete records filing system must be maintained. While there are many variations of a records filing system, there are some basic concepts which should be followed. A sound police records filing system should include:

1. a centralized filing system to minimize duplication and maximize efficiency
2. qualified personnel to direct and operate the system
3. accessibility by the line operation of the department
4. simple procedures for retrieving information
5. safeguards for ensuring the security records

The author recommends two basic types of indexing case files: a master name index and a incident-type index. Certainly, there are other variations which may better serve some departments. The larger the department, the more complex the system will need to be. The master name index file provides the police agency with a central reference to all other police records maintained by the department and is the core of the police records system. The master name index file is simply an alphabetical listing of all persons with whom the police/security department comes into contact. This includes victims, witnesses, complainants, suspects, and persons arrested. This system can be utilized in a computerized system to be called up by name or simply implemented using 3-×-5 index cards.

The incident-type file generally refers to referencing all incidents according to the type of incident (i.e. murder, rape, theft, traffic accident). There are a number of variations to this system. Usually, a numerical reference system is designed to adjust to the volume of cases, provide case numbers, and increase the security of the files.

There are other types of files which may be needed for a police records system. They include *modus operandi* files, stolen property files, warrant files, evidence control files, photograph files, and juvenile offenders' files. The campus public safety director must ensure that these files are simple and accessible. A cross-reference system may be utilized to make the filing system more efficient. For example, if an officer is looking for a suspect but does not know his name, he may look at the incident-type files under the offense the suspect committed, or in the *modus operandi* files if he has knowledge of the suspect method of operation.

SAFETY AND SECURITY RECORDS

Safety and security records are particularly unique to the campus public safety department. These records relate to such functions as fire safety, health and environmental safety, building security parking, and other general security or non-police functions. Not all police/security departments have all of these responsibilities. The trend, however, is toward the comprehensive public safety program which includes most of these functions.

Fire safety records include accurate files of all fire safety expections, fire extinguisher expections, and reports of fires and/or fire alarms. If the department has an adequate number of personnel, one individual would be designated as the functional head of fire safety, with records management under his direction. He should organize fire safety records with the basic concepts in mind similar to those outlined for a police records system to include accuracy and completion of report writing, the filing system, and control of records.

Health and environmental safety records may include construction safety, physical plant safety standards, safety considerations regarding hazardous material and chemicals, and emergency medical services. This area may include the monitoring of Occupational Safety and Health

Administration standards. A health/safety specialist should be designated as director or coordinator over this function and should ensure the integrity of an accurate records system. These records should include inspection reports, violation citations, location records on a hazardous material and dangerous chemicals, and emergency medical incident reports. General rules for accessibility, confidentiality, and simplicity should be followed when establishing and assessing the records system for this area.

Building security is a major area of concern for most public safety departments whether on a small junior college, a private college, or a major urban university. A sound records system is essential for maintaining information regarding security programs, problem areas in particular buildings, security equipment effectiveness, and the performance of security personnel. Reports by security officers, building monitors, and managers of buildings should be filed according to the type of occurrence or circumstances (i.e. inspective security hardware, unauthorized entrance incident, burglar alarm report). Accurate reports and records provide information for planning and decision making as well as substantiate security efforts by security officers.

An effective parking system must be supported by a good records system to include issuance of parking decals, enforcement records, and data regarding problem parking areas and violation records. The parking records system should be under the general direction of a parking director where feasible. This system includes the initial application for a parking decal which is completed by the student or faculty member. This must be accurate and filed either manually, on computer, or both. Files may be indexed by name alphabetically or by decal or tag number. Parking citations must be processed, filed, and sent to the business office for billing purposes. Parking violation records must also be filed. Other data relevant to parking patterns, special parking problem zones, and parking for special events should be kept in the parking records system. This records system usually handles the largest volume of records and requires adequate supervision and clerical workers. Computerization for this system is highly recommended due to the volume and nature of the information. A computer also makes information retrieval more efficient.

ADMINISTRATIVE RECORDS

An effective and efficient administrative records system is essential for any size or type of campus public safety operation. This staff operation provides support for the operational functions of the department. These records should be separate from other centralized police and safety and security records. In contrast to the other records systems, the administrative records should not always be accessible to all employees. The director or chief should administer this area with scrutiny and close supervision. The administrative records system encompasses budget and financial records, personnel records, policy and procedures, and general administrative data and communications. Each of these areas should have its own separate system within the overall framework of the administrative records system, yet sometimes with overlapping applicability. In the larger department, each area may have a staff supervisor to direct and control the records system. However, in medium-sized departments with 25 to 50 officers, one supervisor such as a captain or lieutenant may oversee all of these areas. In small departments with 25 officers or less, the director or chief may directly supervise all administrative records with only secretarial and clerical assistance.

Budget and financial records must be afforded special consideration and handled with circumspection. The budget provides the wherewithal to operate programs, compensate personnel, and purchase equipment and supplies. Wise budget management demands accurate direction, control, and operation of all budget matters on a day-to-day basis. Competent clerical staff is essential to ensure such accuracy and efficiency. Whether the budget is on computer or a paper printout, it must be kept undated and scrutinized for accuracy. Each expenditure and line-item balance should be indicated on a current basis. Requisitions, purchase orders, and invoices must be filed in such a manner as to make retrieval reliable. Some departments accept cash for decal purchases and special events. Strict security and accurate record keeping must be maintained with such monies. Often, some departments maintain "slush funds" for departmental social activities, flower funds, and charities. All transactions should meet with acceptable audit control standards.

Budget and financial records should be open for inspection, and such information should be shared with employees. This enhances a feeling of being involved on their behalf. It also precludes suspicion and accusations of secrecy and deception by those responsible. However, the actual responsibility and control of budget and financial records should be limited to only a few individuals who have access to these records and, subsequently, are liable for misapplication of funds. This should be a primary concern for the campus public safety administrator.

Personnel records affect everyone, and everyone will let the director or chief know when these records are not accurate! This area of the administrative records system overlaps with the budget records, since approximately 80 percent of the budget is committed to personnel. Personnel records are sometimes referred to as personnel information system, performance appraisals, time cards, compensation records, and employee work and personal data. As with the budget records, personnel records must be secured and be accessible by only a few designated people; where feasible, one person should be designated as the department personnel coordinator or director. He should be responsible for protecting the integrity of the system. As a general rule, access should be limited to strictly official use by authorized personnel or to the subject employee for specific purposes, such as:

1. Employee concerned (review)
2. Error correction by employee concerned
3. Identification of employees with special skills
4. Career development-advancement and promotion
5. Statistical analysis of personnel resources
6. Official agencies[8]

Personnel records are particularly important to the campus public safety administrator when employees are unionized and an adversarial relationship exists between management and staff employees. Reliability and completeness become extremely significant.

Department policies and procedures may be considered a part of the administrative records system. While such records are usually bound in one or a few volumes, no extensive filing system is required. However, these records are of paramount significance, since they provide the basis for the personnel functions, activities, and rules of conduct. These records should be kept updated and disseminated to all employees as changes are made. An ongoing assessment and adjustment process requires continuous attention and effort by the campus public safety administrator. Policy and procedures development and implementation will be treated in greater detail in a succeeding chapter.

There are other general administrative information and records which must be maintained. Accurate inventory records of all equipment and supplies is one area which demands close supervision and control. Records for special services (e.g. crime prevention programs, escort services, in-service training) should be maintained for assessment and planning purposes as well as for statistical benefits. All meaningful correspondence, both in-house and external, should be copied and filed. The author has experienced the need to refer to memos written two or three years back. It can be very helpful to maintain such records for a reasonable period of time. These records may be categorized and indexed in several ways depending on the style of the administrator and needs of the department. Minutes of all department meetings should be filed in a systematic method to make their retrieval convenient.

The wise administrator will be sure to maintain a viable administrative records system in order to accurately support the operations of the campus public safety department. The number of record systems and types of filing and indexing will vary, but the completeness of record keeping must be assured.

The trend in records management for police and public safety agencies is toward computerization. College and university public safety departments across the country are converting their traditional records systems to computer systems. This has streamlined the operations and made the records system more efficient and accurate. There are many example and testimonials to support the success of this trend. The Harvard University Police Department is one each success story and proof that computerization works. At Harvard, a needs analysis was conducted preceeding the decision to obtain a comprehensive computerized records system. This needs analysis included the following:

1. Computerization of all internal files, enhancing both file security and records management.
2. Decrease communications dispatcher work load by eliminating several manual tasks.
3. Development of clear, concise, and accurate reports.
4. The capability of directly accessing information for administrative, investigative, and other uses.
5. Crime analysis.
6. Resource allocations.
7. Elimination of manual file search for reports, information, court appearances, etc.

8. The development of a system would be cost effective and offer a payback of less than three years.[9]

A system was selected and implemented within five months after the decision was made. It fulfills their needs and provides for future growth. The system contains 12 different modules which receives information from the operator's data or by programmed input from information in other parts of the system. Each module contains a principal file. Some of the modules in the system include: calls for service, offenses, wants-warrants, arrests, complainants' names, and UCR/crime reporting.

While this is an abbreviated description of the system, it serves to demonstrate the utility of a computerized records management system. Recent technological advances have made the mini and microcomputers more affordable and cost effective. These new small computers do not require highly skilled operators as in the early years of computers. They can be easily adapted to small and large departments. As Harvard did, it would be wise to conduct a thorough and comprehensive needs analysis to determine which system best suits the department's unique circumstances.

Whether a computerized records system is used or the traditional records system is in place, it is the responsibility of the campus public safety administrator to establish and maintain a sound records management system. The benefits that a good system has are many. Perhaps foremost in the minds of many chiefs and directors is the liability-risk protection, commonly known as "covering your bases." Good records have saved many administrators from tremendous financial loss when they were sued by employees, victims, and suspects. Co-employee suits have increased in recent years. For example, at a small private college in Alabama, the chief of security and two of his supervisors were recently the defendants in a $5 million coemployee civil suit charging a lack of policy and procedures.

Accurate records are also beneficial in court appearances which require facts, times, and support information regarding incidents, accidents, and arrests.

Good record keeping will also be beneficial to the campus public safety administrator with respect to employee performance. Personnel evaluations and disciplinary actions should always be documented. Accurate records will prove helpful when the chief or director is the recipient of an employee grievance.

A final benefit is the utilization of accurate information from records for statistical purposes. Accurate and complete statistics of activities, programs, responses to call, and man-hours worked can provide justification for future budget request as well as be instrumental in planning and the decision-making process. Statistics can indicate areas of need and be used to forecast programs and approaches to problems.

A good records management system is a friend to the campus public safety administrator. It should be designed, developed, and continuously improved to enhance the overall public safety operation.

SUMMARY

Budget planning and records management are important areas of administration with which the campus public safety director must be concerned and put forth special efforts to ensure their establishment accuracy, completeness, and effectiveness. These areas are the basis for support of all other services. Without a budget, programs, services, and personnel allocation would be difficult to forecast. Without an effective records system it would be impossible to retrieve much needed information, measure the quantity of functional activities, and determine the effectiveness of public safety efforts. Experienced campus public safety directors know well the advantages and value of keeping records. Not only will accurate records reduce liability risks, they will also provide the basis for justification for needs requests. Since every campus public safety director is held accountable to some degree for the operations of his/her department, it is encumbent on him/her to be a "good steward" and assess the effectiveness of the current budget and records systems to determine if better methods are feasible.

NOTES

1. Galen N. Drewry, "The Next Lean Years" (Tuscaloosa, Alabama: Unpublished Manuscript, 1983), pp. 98–99.

2. Ibid., p. 105.

3. Donald G. Hanna and William D. Gentel, *A Guide to Primary Police Concepts* (Springfield, Illinois: Charles C Thomas, 1971), p. 175.

4. Drewry, "Lean Years," p. 76.

5. William J. Bopp, *Police Personnel Administration* (Boston: Holbrook Press, 1983), p. 65.

6. Ibid., p. 68.

7. Charles D. Hale, *Fundamentals of Police Administration* (Boston: Holbrook Press, 1977), p. 289.

8. Paul B. Weston and Preston R. Fraley, *Police Personnel Management* (Englewood Cliffs, New Jersey: Prentice-Hall Inc., 1980), p. 108.

9. Henry J. Delicata, "Harvard Develops System To Manage Police Reports," *Campus Law Enforcement Journal* 14, (May–June 1984), p. 28.

Chapter 7

PERSONNEL MANAGEMENT

The most important component of campus public safety administration is personnel management. Personnel management must be performed in every campus police/security organization, regardless of type, size, or administrative arrangements for its operation. To a large extent personnel policies, regulations, and procedures affecting campus public safety employees are formulated and disseminated on a institution-wide basis by a central personnel department. These usually include position classifications, compensation, working hours, benefits, holidays, leave conditions, appointments and terminations, and grievance procedures. In addition to these, public safety departments should develop and disseminate their own set of standards which are more extensive and applicable to specific job performance activities. They may duplicate the institutional standards but should never contradict them. While the institutional personnel system provides a framework of standards and guidelines for the campus's public safety administrator, it is his responsibility to develop a personnel management plan, formulate departmental personnel standards, and effectively manage the personnel function toward the attainment of the organizational goals. The primary mission of the personnel function in any organization is to attract, develop, and maintain an effective group of personnel who will contribute willingly to the department's goals and objectives. While the focus of this discussion is on uniformed officers, good personnel management will include all classifications of employees within the campus public safety organization.

PERSONNEL PLANNING AND MANPOWER ALLOCATION

Common statements made by many campus police/security directors are "I need more manpower" or "I could do a better job if the administration would provide me with additional personnel." Certainly, this could be true. Yet, in many cases such statements are not based on reliable facts and lack valid justification. Most directors exert little effort toward assessing and planning personnel needs. This lack of effort often results in so-called efficiency experts being called in by top university officials to determine manpower needs and scope of responsibilities. It is time for public safety administrators to dispense with whimpering and complaining about their personnel needs and become accountable in the support of these needs.

It is of paramount importance for the successful campus public safety director to recognize the importance of developing a personnel plan based on a comprehensive assessment of "what is" coupled with supported documentation to include information and statistics about the total operation of the department. An annual report can serve to compile and present this kind of information. Such a report is utilized by the Yale University Police Department, the University of Arkansas Department of Police Safety, and other progressive campus public safety agencies. In his introductory statement prefacing the University of Arkansas's Department of Public Safety Annual Report, Mr. Larry Slamons states: "This report is intended to be a succinct overview of how DPS is structured, the type of activities in which it becomes involved, and a statistical accounting of what occurred throughout the year."[1]

While the kind of information contained in an annual report is essential in justifying personnel needs, this is only a part of personnel planning. A thorough program and manpower assessment must be conducted to determine areas of need which are not directly addressed in an annual report. A similar planning process as outlined in a previous discussion is applicable to personnel planning. It is essential to link personnel needs to program goals and objectives. The overall program or operation should be viewed in terms of current goals and objectives to identify areas of need and, in some cases, areas which need revamping or abolishing. Programs should be evaluated to determine their effectiveness and the proper amount and kind of manpower needed to accomplish program objectives. The personnel function should also be assessed to identify existing needs in all areas (i.e. recruiting, selection, development, appraisal, manpower allocation, etc.). All internal and external influences on the organization's program should be viewed in terms of future changes. This is called forecasting. A short range forecast (e.g. two years), and a long-range forecast (e.g. five years) should be included in the personnel planning process. Such influences or circumstances to forecast include: student enrollment, geographic/jurisdictional expansion, surrounding community features, the crime rate, economics/fiscal trends, new programs and areas of responsibility, and personnel changes (i.e. turnover, organizational structure, salaries, unions, etc.).

Special consideration must be given to manpower allocation. This is an often overlooked aspect of personnel management. While no in-depth discussion is attempted here, the assiduous campus police/security administrator will evaluate the current allocation of personnel to various functions and time periods. By doing so, he can determine if man-hours are being wasted and efforts duplicated. Manpower allocation will be determined by analyzing programs, functions, activities, and personnel needs. For example, it may be determined that a campus police department has enough uniformed patrol officers but too few assigned to the day shift which has the largest volume of vehicular and pedistrian traffic, complaint calls, and routine activities. Efficiency in allocating personnel to better meet the goals and objectives of the department will provide a true picture of personnel needs. A continuous evaluation of programs and employee performance will ensure maximum productivity. Manpower allocation analysis is an important process within the overall personnel planning process. A willingness to take a close look at this area will lend credence to the genuine efforts of the campus public safety administrator.

Upon completion of these processes, the director should pull together all data collected for analysis and prepare a comprehensive personnel plan to include short- and long-range goals and objectives. There should relate directly to existing data (i.e. the annual report statistics), the program and personnel assessments, and forecast data. All of these data afford justification and support for recommendations. Problems and needs should be identified and clearly stated along with recommendations and appropriate strategies to accomplish the goals and objectives. Such a comprehensive personnel plan will provide the campus public safety director with a clear perspective on the real personnel needs of his organization and enhance his credibility and accountability with top university administrative officials. By being his own efficiency expert, he will preclude the need for external examination. Then, when he says, "I need more officers and more money for training," he will have information to support his request and a plan to present. His superiors will recognize that he has done his "homework" and it will be difficult to ignore his request.

PERSONNEL PROCUREMENT

Success in attracting and employing suitable individuals as campus public safety officers and support personnel will greatly enhance the effectiveness and image of the public safety department. Historically, campus police and security officers were recruited and selected from the ranks of former, and usually retired, municipal, county, and state law enforcement officers. Little attention and effort was placed on the recruitment and selection of the most qualified and most suitable individual for the position within the campus environment. Today, progressive public safety officials and criminal justice professionals recognize the significance of procuring highly qualified and suitable individuals to fulfill the sometimes difficult role of campus police/security officer. While the days of hiring the retired cop are generally gone, many campus public safety departments still neglect this important function of personnel management. These agencies have no formal program or process for recruiting and selecting quality applicants and often operate on a personal and political basis. Others have developed comprehensive, sophisticated approaches to recruiting and selecting public safety personnel. The campus public safety administrator must recognize that the employment of good people is the key to the success of the operation and will greatly reduce problems for him as the leader/manager of the organization.

RECRUITMENT

Many municipal law enforcement agencies have established extensive recruitment efforts to attract the best individuals possible for employment consideration. Some large municipal police departments are blessed with their own personnel divisions devoted to recruiting, selection, training, and other personnel functions. They develop a large pool of applicants from which to select the most suitable individuals. For the most part, campus police/security agencies have neglected this important aspect of the personnel function. In most cases, campus public safety administrators have no formal recruiting plan or procedures with which to attract highly qualified individuals particularly suited for the academic community. Usually, they must rely on their institution's central personnel department. Campus public safety departments often look no further than their surrounding community and choose from among local "known quantities." These may be members of local municipal and/or county police departments, friends of campus police/security officers, and retired police officers or military retirees looking for security in a second career. This practice limits the potential pool of qualified applicants which could be established with some effort.

Most institutions of higher education, both public and private, adhere to the affirmative-action concept. Institutional personnel departments coordinate and implement these Equal Opportunity guidelines and direct a variety of recruiting efforts. However, it is the responsibility of the campus public safety administrator to ensure adequate information is made available to central personnel officials. His input should include clearly defined position qualifications necessary for potential candidates. He should suggest specific mediums for advertisements to recruit applicants. He should also express any special personnel needs such as minorities, women, or specifically experienced/skilled individuals. A good relationship and understanding should exist between the public safety director and the director of personnel services in order to better accomplish personnel needs.

There are some basis considerations which the campus public safety administrator should take into account in his recruiting efforts. It is important to ensure equity and openness in the recruiting process; regardless of "known quantities" on hand, every effort should be made to recruit as many good applicants as possible and allow ample time for recruiting efforts. On many occasions the author has made early judgment regarding certain individuals interested in employment, only to discover later that these individuals were not as attractive for employment relative to other applicants.

A variety of advertisement mediums should be utilized. Classified ads in the local newspaper will reach individuals, particularly the unemployed. Radio spots are excellent means of publicizing vacant positions. Some campus public safety departments send job announcements to other campus police/security agencies for posting on bulletin boards. Regional and state campus and municipal law enforcement association newsletters also provide means for publicizing position vacancies. There are other methods for recruiting individuals for campus public safety positions. Whatever the method used, it is important to make the announcement or advertisement attractive and complete as possible. Such efforts should be designed not only to fill current vacancies but to establish a pool of applicants for future position openings.

Another important recruiting consideration for the campus public

safety director is the recruitment of minorities. In many campus police/
security departments little or no minority representation exists, despite
significant numbers of minority students, faculty, and staff in the
university's population. While this problem is not unique to campus law
enforcement agencies, it does not relieve the responsibility to shore up
this aspect of personnel management. The President's Commission on
Law Enforcement and Administration of Justice expressed concern for
sufficient minority recruitment and urged police agencies to afford reasonable efforts to recruit minority applicants:

> In order to gain the general confidence and acceptance of the
> community, personnel within the police department should be repre-
> sentative of the community as a whole. . . . Minority officers can pro-
> vide a department an understanding of minority groups, their languages,
> and subcultures, that it often does not have today. . . . [2]

Minority recruitment appears to be a pressing problem for many
campus public safety directors, whether real or contrived. In most cases,
where this problem exists, there is simply a lack of genuine commitment
and purposeful effort on the part of public safety administrators. There
are far too many examples of campus police/security agencies with
sufficient minority representation to refute the excuse that qualified
minorities are not available for employment. The problem is the lack of
effort to recruit minorities.

There are several ways to target qualified minorities. Perhaps the best
and most often overlooked approach is minority recruitment within the
institution. Today, most universities have a percentage of minority students,
many of whom might be interested in a career in law enforcement/public
safety given the proper information about job opportunities, benefits,
and working conditions. Many institutions have criminal justice programs and have a number of minority students enrolled. Another way to
attract minorities is through communication with local minority leaders
who can inform qualified minorities of job possibilities within the campus public safety department. Job announcements may be sent to other
university equal opportunity employment officers encouraging minorities to apply for vacant positions. Special emphasis should be included
in advertisements. Features such as pictures of minority police/security
officers may be attractive and encourage minorities to apply. There are
other ways to target and attract minorities for campus public safety
positions, such as personal contacts with other law enforcement administrators for referrals and spots on radio stations targeted at minorities.

Recruitment efforts for women should not be slighted in a discussion of recruitment. This is particularly applicable for the campus police/security department, since, in most cases, the majority of students are females; yet, many departments have not one single female officer! In general, women have increasingly become accepted, either voluntarily or by mandate, into the field of law enforcement. Restrictions such as physical requirements have been dropped, thus affording women equal access. The Civil Rights Act of 1964 (Title VII) requires that all jobs be open to both men and women on an equal basis.[3] Many large metropolitan police departments have taken the initiative to encourage women to apply for police officer positions. Campus police/security agencies should follow suit and actively recruit women for their ranks.

Recruitment is an essential component of the procurement process and will greatly enhance personnel selection efforts. Campus public safety administrators must demonstrate their commitment to effective recruitment efforts. They must be aggressive in their efforts to identify and attract qualified individuals with special emphasis on minorities and women. Once a large pool of qualified applicants is established, continuous recruitment efforts should be made to keep a fresh supply on hand from which to select the best qualified and most suitable individuals.

SPECIAL CONSIDERATIONS FOR SELECTING CAMPUS POLICE OFFICERS

The officer selection process is an important component of the personnel function in law enforcement administration. It is encumbent on every police administrator to give due consideration and subsequent efforts to selecting the most qualified and suitable individuals to fill police officer positions within his department. The selection process is generally generic in terms of basic principles, whether choosing teachers, mechanics, factory workers, or police officers. However, every profession and/or occupation has special requirements, standards, and characteristics for its employees. Campus public safety/law enforcement is no exception. The uniqueness of police and law enforcement in the academic community merits some special consideration, particularly in the officer selection process. While the basic requirements for municipal and campus police officers may be similar, there may exist some very real differences in desired characteristics which the campus police administrator should consider.

The selection of officers may be one of the most critical factors in determining the overall effectiveness of a police department. It is the officer on the street who interacts with the public and becomes the police department in the eyes of the citizens. If the officer makes a positive public impression, the department can expect public support. However, if the impression is not positive, the result can be criticism and reduced community backing. Similarly, the bottom line for all other aspects of departmental operations depends on the quality of the individuals wearing the uniform. Therefore, officer selection becomes a key factor in determining overall departmental effectiveness.[4]

When determining the "special" aspects for consideration in the selection of campus police officers, it is essential to identify the "special" conditions and characteristics of the job environment. Thereto, a basis is established for matching campus police officer candidates to the "special" setting and responsibilities so that a measure of compatibility can be achieved. The following are some major characteristics of the campus environment and conditions with which a campus police officer must deal:

1. The clientele of the campus community is different from its municipal counterpart. The campus community is comprised primarily of young, highly educational individuals all involved, either directly or supportively, in the business of higher education. This group of people is composed largely of middle- to upper-middle-class scholars and students—a rather select clientele compared to the general populace of a municipality.

2. Campus policing takes a different and unique philosophical orientation to law enforcement. It is one of emphasis on prevention and service, not strict law enforcement and arrest.

3. The physical environment of the campus community is different from most other communities. While the concept of the "closed campus" has been replaced with the open access campus community, it is still one of relatively distinct, close boundaries with unique characteristics. Usually, on residential campuses in particular, students freely walk about campus at all times of day and night. Parking and vehicular traffic is normally congested.

4. Most crime on campus fits into the property theft and public order categories, with few violent and other serious crimes.

5. The social life is unique. Group social activities tend to occur more

frequently than in the more traditional community. These activities include rock concerts, major athletic events, fraternity/sorority parties, etc. The use of alcoholic beverages is usually the rule rather than the exception and often produces violations and misconduct.

6. There usually exists an internal discipline process for student misconduct and is often used as an alternative to arrest by the campus police and college administrators.

7. The typical campus police officer has, in addition to traditional law enforcement responsibilities, varied functions, such as parking enforcement, building security, escorting females, fire safety inspections, and other service/security-related activities.

Bordner and Peterson's (1983) study revealed that the role, functions, work characteristics, and general nature of campus police officers differs markedly from their municipal counterparts.[5] Because of these differences and the uniqueness of the environment as cited above, it is encumbent on university administrators to identify the characteristics of campus police officers necessary for compatibility purposes. These special considerations will enhance the selection process.

Several studies have been conducted to determine which characteristics were most appropriate for campus police officers to possess. Meadows (1982) conducted a thorough research project to determine the role orientation of campus police officers. His study included the entire population of campus safety officers in the California state college and university system. His findings are pertinent in identifying the perceptions of campus police officers and the characteristics most appropriate in fulfilling the service role of the university. This has a definite impact on determinations for officer selection. Among his findings were the following:

1. Public safety officers (campus police) perceive their role as being one of service rather than one of law enforcement.

2. Supervisory officers are more service oriented than non-supervisory officers.

3. Officers who possess a baccalaureate degree or higher are more service oriented than those officers with less education.

4. Public safety officers perceive their role as being different than municipal police officers.

5. The main variable influencing a service role was higher education.[6]

He further recommended that when recruiting and selecting campus police officers, "special" consideration should be given to those persons with significant academic and/or professional experiences conducive to serving an academic community.[7]

Telb (1980), in a related study in Ohio, offered the following recommendations regarding special considerations when selecting campus police officers:

1. Eliminate those applicants who strongly favor law enforcement over security.
2. Applicants who have prior experience with a public police agency (i.e. municipality) should not be favorably considered for a position as a campus police/security officer.
3. The minimum educational level for new campus police officers should be at least two years of college.[8]

Powell (1981) supports a combination of higher education and work-related experience. He contends that previous police experience enhances the individual's ability to relate to the campus community.[9] Good physical condition is another condition Powell believes to be important. Nielson (1971) recommends specific minimum physical requirements for all campus police officers, with preference given to the "large man."[10] He also supports hiring younger officers who are not set in their ways and may also relate better to the student population. Of course, it is essential that candidates have no felony or sufficient misdemeanor record.

Selecting and employing well-educated, intelligent individuals with the potential to be trained professionally and the ability to adapt to the campus environment is the key to establishing an effective campus law enforcement/security department. These professional "protectors" can better communicate with faculty, staff, students, and visitors while providing quality performance to meet the various needs that may arise in the campus community.

It is within the actual selection/screening process that these characteristics must be considered and applied in order to determine which applicants will be hired. It is important to point out some of the basic approaches and techniques of more traditional police agencies, such as intelligence testings, criminal background checks, physical fitness requirements, etc. However, it is the purpose of this discussion to focus on more special selection considerations and approaches relevant to choosing campus police officers. Admittedly, it is difficult to identify the personal characteristics of a particular applicant which prove whether or not he/she is suitable to be a campus police officer.

Telb (1980) recommends specially designed written and oral examinations as well as a psychological review designed and used to eliminate those applicants who strongly favor law enforcement over security.[11] Perhaps one obvious technique available for use in identifying special desired characteristics is the exhaustive interview based on a detailed application form. This will indicate a number of both desirable and undesirable characteristics such as employment background, education, training, and attitudes and perceptions regarding the role of campus law enforcement. Another approach which may be particularly helpful in the campus setting is the use of an advisory committee made up of faculty members, administrators, students, and others. This group can be helpful in setting up criteria and guidelines for positions and, perhaps, be directly involved in the applicant screening process. A well-defined job description to include specific qualifications and personal characteristics will be helpful as a basis for evaluating and measuring the suitability of the applicant as a campus police officer. This might best be developed on a campus-by-campus basis, since some campus departmental philosophies differ from others. A case in point is the job description for Rutgers's university police for their entry-level position of police intern (See Fig. 11). This position serves the department during the training and evaluation phase prior to appointment a police officer.

For the purposes of administering and interpreting psychological tests, the university's testing and counseling center can be of aid. These resources coupled with statisticians can also develop specially designed instruments to evaluate the applicants' role orientation, attitudes, and personality as applicable to law enforcement/security in the campus setting.

There is no panacea to the problem of selecting campus police officers. However, there are some realistic procedures that can be employed with some degree of success. Perhaps the most important concern is recognizing the complexion and uniqueness of campus police work and determining generally what kind of individual is most suitable thereto. Relying on research findings and utilizing the best applicant selection techniques available will increase the chances for selecting the best individual. While this discussion focused on the selection process, it should be noted that an effective and well-planned recruitment process discussed within the preceding section can generate a pool of applicants with the charac-

FIGURE 11
RUTGERS UNIVERSITY POLICE DEPARTMENT

Requirements for the Position of Police Intern

The Police Intern is the entry-level position leading to the position of University Police Officer.

The Intern program is an intense training and evaluation program. it is designed for the individual Intern and allows the Intern to progress at his or her own speed. The program is designed to be completed in 12 months or less. During the program the Officer will attend a recognized Police Academy approved by the New Jersey State Police Training Commission. A background investigation will be conducted by the New Jersey State Police who must certify the Intern is qualified under Title 18 NJS for appointment as a University Police Officer.

The Intern is assigned to a training Officer in a Patrol Squad for on-the-job training. The training Officer insures that the Intern is exposed to a wide variety of Police situations and develops confidence in the ability to properly handle all situations. The Intern training Officer, Squad Sergeant and Division Captain participate in the evaluation process, which is conducted bi-weekly.

The guidelines for promotion of Police Interns to Police Officers are covered in Policy U–PDB–88 dated August 18, 1981.

The requirements for appointment as a Police Intern are as outlined below:

1. Applicants must be high school graduates or hold state-approved equivalency certificate.

2. Applicant must possess a valid automobile driver's license issued by the New Jersey Division of Motor Vehicles.

3. Applicants shall not be less than 18 or more than 40 years of age.

4. Visual 20/100 in each eye without artificial correction, corrected to 20/20 and normal color perception.

5. Teeth in good condition with satisfactory restoration.

6. Applicants will be required to pass a thorough medical examination.

7. Applicants will be required to pass a physical fitness examination.

8. Applicants will be required to pass a psychological examination.

9. Applicants will be required to pass a departmental oral review board.

10. Applicants must have good driving record and be free from conviction for criminal offenses.

11. Applicants shall be at least 5' 6" with weight proportioned to height.

12. A thorough background investigation shall be conducted on each applicant to determine that the applicant is of good character.

13. Finalists are selected by interview with key Command Police personnel.

teristics suitable to the campus environment. This will enhance the effectiveness of the selection process.

STAFF DEVELOPMENT: ORIENTATION, BASIC TRAINING, AND PROBATION

Following the selection of individuals as members of the campus public safety department, it is important to adequately prepare them for permanent service within the department. This is applicable to all new employees but especially important for the uniformed officers. In years past and in some instances today, small campus police departments simply hired a "good Joe," put a uniform and gun on him, and placed him on a regular shift within a week of employment with little or no formal orientation and training. Fortunately, this practice is on the wane and has been replaced with comprehensive plans for orienting and training new employees.

Orientation

The orientation process should begin immediately upon selection for employment. The length of time for this process may vary, depending upon the policy and procedure of the department regarding basic training and the probationary period. The orientation process should extend throughout the probationary period.

Orientation includes acquainting the new employee with the department's personnel, policies and procedures, facility, and mission. It also includes familiarization of the physical environment of the campus community, the institution's organizational structure, and key officials on campus. The new officer should also be introduced to local municipal public safety officials with whom he will be expected to communicate.

There are various methods of orienting new officers. Basically, there are two categories or phases of orientation: (1) classroom instruction and (2) field instruction. The classroom instruction phase of orientation should cover a period of at least two weeks and may be conducted simultaneously with field instruction. The classroom instruction should include an overview of departmental policies, regulations, and procedures. The officer should be issued a copy of the department's policies, regulations, and procedures manual and instructed to read it. An introduction to campus public safety work and its philosophy and role within the institution of higher education should be conducted. There are films available for this type of presentation. A general introduction to criminal law and basic police procedures should be included in the classroom instruction. Some principles and concepts of physical security should also be presented and, if the officers are not sworn peace officers, basic security procedures should be included.

Field instruction should afford the new officer with practical, on-the-job experience coupled with instruction and guidance by an experienced officer or supervisor. The field instruction phase of the orientation process should continue until the formal or basic training begins. The new officer should be exposed to a variety of duties and circumstances. He should be encouraged to ask questions and apply field experiences to classroom instruction. The officer should always be assigned to another officer or supervisor and never be placed in a situation requiring decision making beyond his preparation.

Basic Training

Basic or formal training for campus police and security officers is essential. As pointed out in a previous discussion, most states police minimum standards training legislation includes sworn campus police officers. In other states, such as Tennessee, campus officers may receive this basic police training through the authorization of the local municipal police department in whose jurisdiction they are located. Many private institutions have no such mandate or opportunity to acquire this police training for their police or security officers. Yet, they must ensure their officers some extensive formal training in order to equip them with the knowledge and skills to perform their duties and protect the institution from litigation which could result from action or lack of action of untrained officers.

The length and type of basic training varies from state to state and department to department. Normally, basic police academy training sessions last from six weeks to sixteen weeks. Some states have one state training academy. Others have regional academies located in several locations throughout the state. Some large police departments have their own approved basic training academy which may exceed their station-required minimum number of hours and courses. Alabama has all three: (1) a state police academy, (2) five state approved, and (3) municipal police academies. Alabama's minimum number of hours required for minimum standards police certification is currently 280 hours. However, the state academy and several municipal police academies exceed this requirement up to twice that number of hours. All public campus police agencies in Alabama send their officers to one of the regional academies which require the minimum of 280 hours or seven weeks of basic police training.

Generally, most police academies across the country teach the same basic curriculum and train with similar methods. Basically, every basic police training program must:[14]

1. Satisfy state standards for police training
2. Meet the stated needs of participating police agencies
3. Be job related
4. Communicate expectations.[12]

The National Sheriff's Association's *Manual on Training for Sheriffs* and The International Association of Chiefs of Police's *Police, Reference Notebook* generally agree on the following areas of study for basic police training:

1. Introduction (orientation to ethics, conduct, performance standard, etc.)
2. Criminal justice
3. Basic law (i.e. criminal law, local codes, etc.)
4. Police procedures
5. Traffic control
6. Investigation
7. Juveniles
8. Proficiency areas (firearms, defensive tactics, first aid, etc.)
9. Community relations
10. Department policy and procedures.[13,14]

While all of the above areas have some application to campus police departments, it should be noted that much of the training is geared toward circumstances which more commonly exist in municipal and county law enforcement work than in the campus police/security setting. Therefore, it would be wise to continue orientation and in-service training emphasizing the role and scope of the campus public safety department within the campus community. It is encumbent on the campus public safety director to ensure that his personnel receive this basic training if at all possible and adapt it to the campus setting. If the officers do not qualify for attendance at police academies, the campus police chief should seek alternative methods and sources for acquiring acceptable compensatory training for his officers. Many large municipal or county law enforcement agencies will provide certified instructors at no cost to instruct workshops and special training seminars for these campus agencies. For example, most medium- to large-sized police agencies have officers certified as firearms instructors, defensive tactics instructors, and experienced investigators who are available to assist upon request.

All sworn campus police officers should receive their basic training as soon as possible. Whereas many large metropolitan police agencies send their officers to the police academy almost immediately after selection, most campus departments usually delay this for several months and provide orientation and on-the-job training during much of the probationary period. This is due, in part, to manpower and budget constraints. Also, some campus police agencies prefer to send new officers to the police academy during the "off season" in the summer months. Another advantage of delaying this training is that it gives the department an opportunity to evaluate the personal characteristics and general work habits of the new employee during the probationary period to determine if he is suitable for the significant investment of time and money which is involved in police academy training.

Probation

Most probation periods range from six months to a year. This phase of the employment process gives both the new employee the opportunity to evaluate and determine the employee's suitability and adaptability to campus public safety. Not everyone who wants to be a police officer and is selected is really suitable for the type of work required. It also affords the chief and his supervisors the time to work closely with the new employee and begin the career development process. A one-year probationary period affords the new officer the opportunity to attend the basic or formal training to determine if he is capable of passing all of the required training. In turn, if the new officer fails to complete this training, it allows the employer to release him under probationary rules. This is an equitable arrangement.

Probation is a safety value for the campus public safety administrator to ensure his selection decision was a good one. He must be confident that this individual is the caliber and quality worthy of future investment, training, and development. He should expect and demand quality performance and a positive attitude by the new employee. He should not assume anything but direct, close supervision and scrutiny of the recruit. If this is done and the employee survives the probationary period, a better, more conscientious employee will emerge to serve the department with distinction.

Staff Development

Every campus public safety administrator should implement and maintain an employee development program designed to further the on-the-job growth of employees. While most large police departments operate separate training divisions and formal training programs for personnel development, they represent only a small percentage of the number of all police departments in this country. The overwhelming majority of campus public safety departments are considered small. There are approximately 18,000 law enforcement agencies in the United States. Of this number, 50 percent have less than 10 officers and 80 percent have less than 25 officers.[15] This indicates where the emphasis on training is needed—in small departments. Yet, small departments may often find it difficult to fulfill the responsibilities of an effective staff development program.

Numerous constraints face the campus police chief of the small department, one of which is the number of sworn personnel in the department. If the entire organization consists of 10 members, then sending 2 officers for advanced training would create a manpower shortage. Another area of concern is the funds available to support staff development activities. Also, while an in-house development program may be an alternative, some administrators do not have qualified instructors or a plan for such a program. Yet, there exists a definite need for viable staff development programs in campus police and security agencies.

Today, all states except Hawaii require minimum standards training for entry-level police officers.[16]

Under the Alabama Minimum Standards and Training Act of 1972, all police officers or peace officers in the state are required to receive a minimum number of training hours—currently 280 hours. This includes all public college and university police officers. Most states now have legislation which requires minimum standards training for campus police officers. These efforts have served to upgrade the quality and performance of police officers. However, it is becoming increasingly evident that the individual police employee must be afforded continuous development opportunities to be effective and enhance job performance. The influx of intelligent, inquisitive, and social-conscious young officers serves to emphasize the need for education and training. In many instances, these officers have been exposed to the college environment and desire to continue their education after entering law enforcement. The advent of college-trained/educated officers serves to emphasize the need for training.[17] Minimum standards aren't enough.

Society's increased awareness of crime, its subsequent demand for better services, and its misconceptions about the police require that the quality of personnel be improved. It is imperative that police officers receive adequate training to keep pace with our fast-changing technological society. As times change, so do problems and their complexity. In order to ensure the preparedness and effectiveness of small campus public safety agencies, their personnel must be involved in continuous professional development beyond minimum standards training.

The chief administrator has the main responsibility for staff development, which is closely linked to the expectations of the general public. If the general public expects a certain level of performance, then public safety personnel must be equipped to fulfill this expectation. In meeting these responsibilities, the chief administrator should have certain objectives in mind. The training function should be viewed as a process whereby the organization can aid its members in becoming more effective in their present or future positions. Training not only improves and increases the skills and knowledge of individual officers but also improves the efficiency and proficiency of the organization as a whole.

Many campus police and security chiefs are faced with training personnel while staying within their budgets. Too often, administrators send officers to school arbitrarily without any plan or purpose in mind. Consequently, they often run low or out of funds before training the expected number of personnel is completed.

Planning is essential to the operation of any organization, and when feasible, the chief administrator should appoint a training officer to lead in the planning and implementation.

The Florida State University Department of Public Safety has such a position, which is called a *training coordinator.* This Training Coordinator is responsible for:

1. The maintenance of complete and accurate training files for all department members.

2. The total coordination of in-service and on-the-job training programs.
3. Acting as departmental personnel and inspection officers.[18]

A training program must be included in planning decisions as well as budget proposals. One relatively novel approach is policing by objectives (PBO), which involves every aspect of the police organization. An interal part of the PBO approach is a comprehensive staff development/training program incorporating input from all members of the organization. Subsequently, the end result should meet the needs of the organization as expressed by its members.[19]

In-service training is only a part of a comprehensive staff development program; yet, it is a very significant component. There are various traditional approaches to in-service training and education, most of which can be used by the campus police department. It is important to include all personnel in some training activities (i.e. dispatchers, investigators, clerical staff, and patrol officers). Regularly scheduled training sessions using film, tapes, guest speakers, and/or training officers are well-accepted methods and are particularly adaptable to the small department. The FBI provides qualified instructors to conduct training sessions for local police departments at no cost, and professional police associations, such as the International Association of Chiefs of Police, and the International Association of Campus Law Enforcement Administrators (IACLEA), sponsor a wide range of training workshops, seminars, conferences, and programs. In addition, training bulletins, both in-house and external, are excellent to keep officers abreast of professional development, innovative techniques, and changing law.

Coach-pupil training, if planned and done correctly, can also produce rewards for the small department. For example, a supervisor may ride with a subordinate during a shift and teach vehicle stop techniques or patrol techniques. Staff meetings or general department meetings are often a convenient means to provide special training for personnel as are seminars, conferences, and workshops. The latter may involve travel and leave time but will prove rewarding as a motivational factor.

Many departments use their own institution's criminal justice departments as resources, while others pool their resources and establish joint training sessions with neighboring police departments. Campus police sponsor training programs to complement minimum standards training. In 1980, the Alabama Association of College and University Police

Administrators sponsored the first statewide training seminar for campus police/security officers.

A relatively new training technique, which works especially well for smaller departments, is the use of the video recording system. Many educational films and materials are available through state and regional film libraries for a nominal fee. The time spent viewing the tape, films, etc., is minimal and can be done on duty or roll-call time, thus avoiding both overtime costs, travel, lodging cost, etc. A positive feature of this approach is the ability of the small department to produce its own training programs as well as public relations materials.

The application of computer technology is constantly expanding. So why not use this medium for in-service training? This departs from the traditional teacher-learner method and offers some advantages. The courseware can be developed by the department and adapted to the specific needs of the individual. This has already proven effective in college criminal justice courses. While the initial costs may be somewhat high, they are minimized by the long-range benefits. This is also the least expensive medium when considering the cost of training personnel.[20]

Most campus public safety departments have many resources within their institution which can afford equipment and personnel to assist in computer-based training.

There are certainly other innovative techniques for in-service training programs. In fact, the possibilities are as broad as the creativity of the chief administrator and the instructional staff. Many methods and techniques can be adapted or developed by the small department to meet its own needs. What is important is to maintain an effective in-service training program beyond minimum standards requirements.

In the 1970s, universities responded to the needs of the police by initiating academic programs where none existed. These universities have become more flexible in providing undergraduate programs to meet the needs of these "student" cops.

Today, numerous university programs for educating and training police officers are available. Police training at this educational level reduces to a very marked degree the load on in-service training but does not take its place. Both are necessary. Since many campus police officers now enter the law enforcement profession with college degrees, other officers are influenced to continue their education. They recognize the importance of higher education in a society where the level of education is steadily rising, especially within the academic community.

Higher education can also develop qualities of leadership and executive potential. It will give officers a long-range perspective of the role of the police in modern society. College training is important for competitive reasons, and this is becoming increasingly true in the area of law enforcement.

Staff development in campus police and security departments often focuses on training, educating, and improving the rank-and-file patrol officers while overlooking the continuous improvement of supervisors and managers. The challenges of managing police departments can be met only by dedicated professionals who possess the knowledge and experience to participate in the broad issues of the day. Because campus public safety managers are now held to a higher degree of accountability, they must improve their command of management skills and techniques. Campus police/security managers must be given adequate tools if they are to perform properly, and the inclusion of executive education in developing managerial skills can make a special contribution to the management capacity of police executives. "Police schools" are not enough to prepare campus public safety managers to meet the challenges of their jobs. It is important to give these managers and potential managers the opportunity to grow professionally by taking advantage of courses in management and supervision.

Staff development for the campus police/security department should be viewed as a comprehensive approach which goes beyond in-service training and college police education programs. The development of the officers in other areas will enhance their total effectiveness. Often, training and education do not provide the job satisfaction and motivation that all employees need. There are other approaches which can improve personnel.

Personnel rotation is an effective means of employee development. In smaller departments, rotation may be limited to geographic areas of varying crime incidence and major functional assignments. This offers employees new and valuable perspectives on work and responsibility. Lateral transfers to other job assignments may also be an incentive, as well as a method for further developing the employee's experience, knowledge, skills, and perspective. Promotion is an ideal method of developing an employee as they grow professionally and become proficient at each level.[21]

Special assignments and/or extra responsibility are often good methods for improving and developing an employee. This shows the employee the administrator's confidence in him/her and affords the employee the opportunity to demonstrate skills and abilities. This is particularly feasible in a small department where responsibilities can be shared among rank-and-file employees due to the lack of organizational specialization.

Another area which merits attention is personal counseling for campus police personnel. Stress is a proven factor relating to performance among police officers. Special sessions could be held, collectively or individually, to address such issues as conflict resolution, marital difficulties, anxiety, stress, etc.

Minimum standards requirements represent only the tip of the iceberg. It is essential that campus public safety administrators recognize the significance of a continuous, comprehensive staff development program for their department, no matter how large or how small. To fail to recognize this and respond effectively will result in a stagnant, ineffective organization full of disgruntled, non-productive individuals. Staff development need not be limited to officers but should include all employees (i.e. radios dispatchers, secretarial/clerical, and student employees). Surely, a well-trained force will be more motivated than an ill-trained one. To be committed to quality training and staff development will yield bountiful fruits of a motivated and productive department.[22] Above all, the organization will gain support within the campus community because the clientele will recognize the results in terms of improved performance, motivated officers, and a more professional posture.

PERFORMANCE EVALUATIONS

All of the good intentions and extensive efforts to recruit, select, train, and continuously develop employees would be of little worth without an ongoing evaluation process to determine if employee performance is satisfactory. The results of the performance evaluation will indicate to the administrator whether or not the employee is progressing and performing up to par, if more training, guidance, and development is required, or if the employee should seek employment elsewhere.

Performance evaluation is often viewed negatively by employees. The campus public safety administrator should communicate and stress to all organizational members the positive aspects of performance evaluation. It provides the administrator or his designate with the opportunity to sit down and review and discuss the employee's job performance, working conditions, policy, procedures, and other areas relating to the organization and the personnel function. It should be viewed as a "two-way street" approach with feedback coming from the employee. The performance evaluation is also a valuable tool to enhance employee development by identifying performance problems and special employee needs which may have been overlooked by the administration. The end result of the performance evaluation should be improved performance.

Many institutions' personnel departments formulate performance evaluation instruments for the entire institution. In some cases, one type of form is used to evaluate all employees, regardless of their job classifications or status. In essence, the same criteria is used to evaluate significantly different positions and tasks. While this affords uniformity for employee evaluation on an institution-wide basis, it places certain constraints on administrators' efforts to evaluate performance in specific job-related tasks. General performance criteria for evaluation often include in these evaluation instruments:

1. Quality of work
2. Quantity of work
3. Cooperates with others
4. Personal appearance
5. Punctuality
6. Attitude
7. Initiative

Certainly, these criteria have some general application to campus public safety employees. In many situations, the campus public safety has no recourse but to use the institutional performance evaluation instrument. It must be noted that these performance criteria are based on institutional policy, regulations, and procedures, whereas the campus public safety department will have additional standards by which their employees should be evaluated. Therefore, where possible, the campus police chief should include specific job-related criteria, either by designing his own performance evaluation instrument or getting approval to add supplemental criteria to the institutionally designed instrument. Such specific task-related criteria would include but not be limited to the following:

1. Personal equipment display and maintenance
2. Court appearance demeanor
3. Case follow up
4. Investigative efforts

Whatever instrument and criteria is decided upon, it is important to ensure that the employee understand the basis or criteria on which he is being evaluated and have the opportunity to discuss the performance rating with the evaluating supervisor. The performance evaluation process should include a well-defined, written purpose and plan outlining the steps within the process to include an appeals process. Due process should be adhered to at all times. The overall purpose of the performance evaluation process is to improve the individual employee, thus improving the effectiveness and accountability of the campus public safety organization.

Any performance deficiencies identified should be complemented with a mutually agreed upon plan for improvement. The campus public safety administrator should view the performance evaluation interview as an opportunity to identify the employee's performance deficiencies, discuss possible approaches for improvement, and encourage the employee to become a better, more productive member of the organization. Constructive criticism with a word of praise will be well received by the good-intentioned employee; subsequently, he can become a contributing component of the organization.

EMPLOYEE DISCIPLINE

As with any organization, the campus public safety department will need a disciplinary process as part of the personnel management function. While discipline carries negative connotations, it is necessary to maintain control of employees' conduct and ensure compliance with policy, regulations, and procedural guidelines. While campus police/security departments are quasi-military organizations which often conform to rigid standards for officers, the campus community setting with its spirit of academic freedom should temper strict military-like discipline standards within a reasonably humanistic approach. College and university central personnel departments maintain disciplinary procedures for all the institution's department. While these procedures may suffice, some are vague and have only general application. In such cases, it is essential for the campus public safety director to formulate disciplinary policy and establish a comprehensive disciplinary process. There are three basic elements which should be included when developing this policy and setting up a suitable process. These are:

1. **Written policy and regulations.** These should be clearly stated and disseminated to all employees. They should include the disciplinary procedures, and penalties for violating department policy and regulations. These departmental disciplinary procedures should not conflict with or contradict the institution's policy and procedures.

2. **Uniform application.** The campus safety administrator should ensure that the application and enforcement of disciplinary penalties are uniform and reasonable. Otherwise, the administrator and the entire process will have no credibility with employees. When penalties are applied uniformly and equitably, employees will respect the procedures and accept disciplinary action in stride.

3. **Grievance procedure.** Every employee being disciplined, whether a simple written reprimand or an extended suspension, should have the right to appeal his case to a higher administrative level. Usually, this is included in the institution's disciplinary procedures. Due process must be afforded every employee. This includes a hearing to inform the employee of the complaint against him and give him an opportunity to respond.

It should be pointed out that not all infractions of departmental standards require application of formal disciplinary procedures. Often, a verbal reprimand will suffice to correct a minor misconduct or negligent performance. For example, if an officer is two minutes late for the first time in his eighteen months in the department, a simple verbal reprimand and warning would be sufficient. If this becomes a habit, more formal written disciplinary action would be required. Another informal approach is the use of the memorandum to remind employees that certain infractions of departmental policy have occurred (e.g. littering patrol cars, spending too much time in the office) and should cease immediately. This approach is especially appropriate when there is a widespread minor problem which may or may not be officially reported. A memorandum will usually get the attention of the guilty culprits and alleviate the problem without formal disciplinary proceedings. The key to such informal discipline is reasonableness and uniformity. It would be unwise to verbally reprimand one officer and suspend another for the same first-time violation.

While it is the intent of a sound discipline plan to correct employee deficiencies and, thus, improve and development employees for better service to the organization, the campus public safety administrator must be willing to dismiss unsuitable employees who cannot conform to departmental standards and rules of conduct. Valid documentation of all significant infractions and performance negligence is very important. Too often, administrators allow themselves to be plagued by problems from an employee over a long period of time, because they feel that termination of the employee will result in a complicated grievance procedure and, ultimately, litigation. Therefore, they avoid taking decisive action and, subsequently, erode their credibility with other members of the organization. Close supervision, written documentation of performance deficiencies, discussions with the employee, and accurate performance evaluation ratings will provide the necessary support to dismiss unsuitable employees. While internal transfer to another area or assignment may be considered, it may also simply move the problem instead of solving it. Failure to remove these employees from the organization will be detrimental to the mission and morale of the organization.

SUMMARY

Since higher education is essentially a "people business," it imperative that campus public safety directors select, develop, and put in service personnel capable of responding to the needs of people within the campus community. Despite some prevailing perceptions, this is no easy task. It involves much more than hiring and firing employees. Personnel management requires a comprehensive plan to include continuous efforts from the selection process through termination of employment. An effective personnel system should include policy, procedures, and records.

More emphasis must be placed on the professional development of personnel. Minimum standards for campus police/security officers will no longer suffice in an era of frequent litigations involving the actions of officers. Opportunities for continuing education and training should be afforded for all employees with the campus public safety department.

The most important consideration of any organization is its people. While this should be apparent, far too many administrators fail to focus on the individual employee. Each person within the campus public safety department must be given the opportunities to improve and progress if he/she is expected to perform to their capacity. Each individual should always be treated with respect. The campus public safety director should strive to make every individual employee feel like they are an important part of the organization and encourage their contribution to the department. By doing so enhances the morale of all employees and, consequently, improves performance.

NOTES

1. Larry Slamons, *The University of Arkansas' Public Safety Annual Report, 1985.*

2. President's Commission on Law Enforcement and Administration of Justice, Task Force Report: The Police (Washington, D.C.: U.S. Government Printing Office, 1967), p. 167.

3. Civil Rights Act of 1964, Title VII.

4. George C. Schowengerdt and Debra A. Robinson, "Officer Selection: An Important Process for Small Departments." *FBI Law Enforcement Bulletin,* 1983, 52, pp. 10–12.

5. Diane C. Bordner and David M. Petersen, *Campus Policing: The Nature of University Police Work* (New York, New York: University Press of America), 1983.

6. Robert J. Meadows, "A Study on the Relationship Between Demographic Characteristics of College and University Safety Officers and Their Role Orientation Toward Service or Law Enforcement. Unpublished Doctoral Dissertation, Pepperdine University, pp. 155–158.

7. Ibid., p. 158.

8. James A. Telb, "The Relationship Between Personnel Characteristics of Campus Security Officers and Their Role Orientation" (Doctoral Dissertation, The University of Toledo, 1980), *Dissertation Abstracts International,* 41, 1337A.

9. John W. Powell, *Campus Security and Law Enforcement* (Boston, Massachusetts: Butterworth, Inc.), 1971, p. 55.

10. Swen C. Nielsen, *General Organizational and Administrative Concepts for University Police* (Springfield, Illinois: Charles C Thomas), 1971, p. 55.

11. James A. Telb, *Personal Characteristics of Campus Security Officers,* p. 161.

12. Paul B. Weston and Preston K. Fraley, *Police Personnel Management* (Englewood Cliffs, New Jersey: Prentice-Hall), p. 88.

13. L.A. Giddings, M. Furstenberg, and H.J. Noble, *Manual for Training Sheriffs* (Washington D.C.: U.S. Government Printing Office), 1969.

14. T.S. Crockett and A.F. Kelly, *Police Reference Notebook* (Gaithersburg, Maryland: International Association of Chiefs of Police), 1970.

15. James V. Cotter, Commission on Accreditation for Law Enforcement Agencies. Presentation at the Alabama Association of Chiefs of Police Conference, February 13, 1984, Birmingham, Alabama.

16. Ibid.

17. J.H. Auten. *Training In the Small Police Department* (Springfield, Illinois: Charles C Thomas), 1973, pp. 5–6.

18. Florida State University Department of Public Safety, Department Philosophy: 1985.

19. Victor A. Lubans and J.M. Edgar, *Policing By Objectives* (Hartford, Connecticut: Social Development Corporation, 1978), p. 178.

20. Robert O. Walker, "A Rational Supporting Computer-Based Instruction." *The Police Chief,* 49, pp. 60–64.

21. Paul B. Weston and Preston K. Fraley, *Police Personnel Management,* pp. 116–117.

22. George R. Gallagher, "Productivity and Motivation In Training: It Is Up To You, Boss," *The Police Chief,* 50, 1983, pp. 101–102.

Part III

OPERATIONS: THE DELIVERY OF SERVICES

U niversity and college administrators responsible for campus public
safety operations must recognize the multiplicity and diversity of
services required to meet the needs of today's campus community. The
past three decades have witnessed increased enrollments, expansion of
building construction, increases in vehicles on campus, a rise in crime,
increased liability and litigation, and a departure from the *in loco parentis*
doctrine. Subsequently, public safety needs have undergone a major
shift from a watchman concept to a comprehensive approach providing a
wide range of services to include: law enforcement, building security,
parking, traffic, fire safety, environmental safety, civil defense, and other
public services. Many high-level university officials and public safety
directors have failed to understand the need for such a comprehensive
approach. On many campuses, public safety services are fragmented,
with some functions being provided by departments totally unrelated to
public safety. For example, the provision of fire alarm systems is often
the responsibility of the physical plant department with decisions made
by those unfamiliar with fire safety codes and current safety standards.
Also, on some campuses special security officers are selected and employed
for special events (e.g. athletic events, concerts) by campus officials
other than the director of public safety. Key control is still another
example of a function which is often administered by officials not directly
responsible for the safety of persons and security of buildings and
property.

It is encumbent on the campus public safety director to make every
effort to establish a comprehensive public safety program centralized
under a single department head. This will enable the director to conduct
a comprehensive plan, set institution-wide goals and objectives, and
effectively deliver all of the public safety services needed by the campus
community. Certainly, open lines of communication and cooperative
efforts must exist between the campus public safety department and all
other departments in order to accomplish objectives and serve the cam-

pus community. Ultimately, the effective and efficient delivery of services is the main concern of the campus public safety director. The accomplishment of this will create a safe environment conducive to the mission of the higher education institution.

Chapter 8

LAW ENFORCEMENT SERVICES

M ost universities, public and private, provide some law enforcement-related services. Even though some institutions are not authorized to employ sworn officers, their security forces usually provide at least quasi-law enforcement services (e.g. enforcement of minor violations of the law, detaining trespassers and other law violators). For example, a non-sworn security officer at a private institution may apprehend a non-student for criminal trespassing, detain him until local police officers arrive, and obtain an arrest warrant. Whatever the type of institution, few are immune from circumstances and incidents that will require a law enforcement response by public safety officers. Criminal activity exists on all campuses. University administrators cannot ignore this fact and must be willing to respond accountably. It is important, therefore, that university officials recognize the need to provide an effective public safety operation capable of performing law enforcement tasks when required to do so.

THE PATROL EFFORT

The most important component of any law enforcement agency is the uniformed patrol division. In many small departments uniformed officers are the only full-time personnel within the agency, except, perhaps, a secretary or clerk-typist. To the general public, the uniformed patrol officer represents the department and all it stands for. Therefore, the organization and implementation of the uniformed patrol operation should be a major consideration and top priority for the campus public safety administrator. He must ensure a degree of quality in those who wear the badge and effectiveness in their delivery of services.

The success of any organization depends on the quality and effectiveness of its members. This is no less true for campus public safety departments. The director must afford the campus community well-trained patrol officers who demonstrate a professional demeanor. The patrol officer

137

should be trained as a generalist to handle the wide variety of problems and crimes which occur in a campus community. They must be service oriented with a special appreciation for students and higher education. They should understand their role within the mission of the institution and fulfill their responsibilities accordingly. The director must ensure that every patrol officer's appearance conforms to high standards and reflects the professional philosophy of the department. Regular and unscheduled inspections of patrol personnel by the director and/or supervisors is important in order to assure consistency and excellence in personal appearance.

In order to provide dependable and effective law enforcement service, the campus public safety administrator must maintain adequate patrol vehicles. As with the patrol officers, the vehicles should perform effectively as well as look good. Too often, campus police/security vehicles are old, dirty, and operate like they look! This is often the result of top administrative officials placing public safety needs low on their list of priorities. This could be due to perceptual differences or the inability of the campus public safety director to articulate his needs. Sometimes, however, it is due to a lack of effort or inadequate management on the part of the public safety director. The accountable director will recognize the impact that the appearance of patrol vehicles will have on the morale of his officers, the perceptions of students and other publics, and the confidence of the institution's administration.

While many institutions are small in terms of enrollment and the physical plant, uniformed patrol services should be provided on an around-the-clock basis. To support such coverage a minimum number of officers must be on staff. The author recommends a minimum of six uniformed patrol officers, which does not include the chief administrator. Figure 12 provides a sample shift schedule illustrating how six uniformed officers and a director can adequately provide around-the-clock coverage.

Many small institutions with an enrollment of 1,000 or less will require most of the same law enforcement services as institutions with larger enrollments. It is often difficult to determine at what point more than the minimum of six officers would be justified. Generally speaking, six uniformed patrol officers can appropriately serve an enrollment of 2,500. Beyond this enrollment, the author recommends adding one officer per each additional 500 students. Factors to be considered when determining appropriate manpower include: the location of the campus, other func-

FIGURE 12
UNIVERSITY POLICE DEPARTMENT
OFFICERS' SCHEDULE

	SUNDAY	MONDAY	TUESDAY	WEDNESDAY	THURSDAY	FRIDAY	SATURDAY
7AM-3PM	King	Jones Smith	Jones Smith	Jones Smith	Jones Smith	Jones Smith	King
3PM-11PM	Williams Adams	King Williams	King Williams	King Williams	Roberts Williams	Roberts Adams	Roberts Adams
11PM-7AM	Roberts	Roberts	Brown	Brown	Brown	Brown	Brown
6PM-2AM				Adams	Adams		

NO CHANGES OR SUBSTITUTING SHOULD BE DONE WITHOUT THE APPROVAL OF THE CHIEF.

tional areas of assigned responsibilities, whether the institution is residential or commuter, the surrounding community, and special security concerns. Currently, a wide disparity exists between institutions with varying circumstances. For example, Birmingham Southern College, a small private institution located in an urban setting in Birmingham, Alabama, has a security patrol force of 20 patrol officers to serve approximately 1,800 students. In contrast, Livingston University, a small public institution located in Livingston, Alabama, has a police department with five patrol officers to serve approximately 1,500 students.

The patrol effort must be conducted in clearly marked vehicles on an almost consistent basis, yet with no obvious patrol pattern. The author recommends that a zone approach be used to ensure that all areas of the campus are patrolled and to know when and by whom a particular zone was checked. This approach entails dividing the campus into logical geographic areas or zones and designating each zone with a letter or number. This is useful in patrol techniques as well as keeping statistics on crime and other incident calls. An effective patrol unit will drive through all areas of each zone checking buildings and observing pedestrian and vehicular movement. During nighttime hours the patrol officer should occasionally get out of his vehicle and perform security checks on foot. All such patrol activities should be communicated by two-way radio to a central dispatch and entered on a permanent log. This will serve to substantiate patrol activities and may be useful in evaluating employee performance as well as documentation in court proceedings.

JURISDICTION

A point of contention between top administrative officials and campus public safety personnel over the years has been the issue of jurisdiction. It should be made clear that the extension of jurisdiction will vary from institution to institution, depending on state legislation, municipal ordinance or agreement, and the policy of the college or university. Most campus police/security jurisdictional authority is limited to the property of the institution and, in many cases, adjacent or contiguous streets of the campus property. The first and foremost concern of campus public safety should be the campus community, the security of its property, and the safety of its people. In most cases police/security officers should limit their patrol efforts to campus property. However, there are many circumstances which warrant some reasonable extension of jurisdiction beyond the confines of the campus property lines. Often, streets or highways may pass through the middle of the campus, thus affecting students' safety and the institution's pedestrian and vehicular traffic flow. Some institutions may not be located on one main campus but may be scattered over a wide geographic area within a city connected only by city streets. Occasionally, a crime will occur on campus and a fleeing suspect will get off campus before campus patrol officers can apprehend him. This extenuating circumstance, along with other special situations, justify some jurisdictional authority beyond the campus borders. The campus public safety director should communicate such procedures to his/her officers and issue an appropriate policy thereto. He/she should iron out any differences of opinion between himself and his supervisors regarding jurisdictional authority and establish a mutual agreement if exceptions are acceptable in extenuating circumstances. A reasonable policy followed by the reasonable exercise thereof by officers is the best approach.

The patrol effort should focus on several functional areas: (1) crime prevention, (2) law enforcement, (3) vehicular traffic control, (4) service, and (5) public relations. While a formal crime prevention program may be assigned to a special division or designated personnel, one of the uniformed patrol officer's objectives is to prevent crime and the opportunities for crime. This is done through what is commonly called "preventative patrol." The presence of marked patrol vehicles constantly patrolling the campus may discourage would-be perpertrators from coming on campus to practice their trade. It also serves as a reminder to would-be student violators that "the law" is present and may reduce their inclination to commit crimes on campus. The alert patrol officer will notice circumstances which could provide opportunities for crime (e.g. dark areas, unsecured valuable property, open windows, unlocked buildings). The patrol officer will also serve as the "eyes and ears" of the department by observing any potentially illegal activity such as illegal sales of controlled substances (drugs) and suspicious behavior of would-be sex offenders loitering on campus. The campus public safety director should stress on-patrol crime prevention strategies to all patrol officers.

Actual law enforcement functions of the campus patrol officer normally claim less than 5 percent of his/her time on duty. However, when law enforcement efforts are needed, they must be delivered appropriately and effectively. While a strict law enforcement approach is not encouraged, the patrol officer must be just as well trained and prepared to respond to exigent circumstances as his municipal counterpart. The campus public safety director must orient officers as to proper enforcement procedures in a variety of circumstances. Discretion of authority must be stressed. Good judgment must be exercised by patrol officers when determining the difference between student misconduct and a criminal act. This will be discussed in greater detail in a later chapter. When a crime is committed, officers must be prepared to respond appropriately. This may include calling for the assistance of local law enforcement authorities. As mentioned in a preceding chapter, crime on campus varies from petty theft to murder. Normally, the uniformed patrol officer is the first official to arrive at the scene of a crime. The patrol officer must apply his knowledge and training to whatever situation arises. The initial action and performance by the patrol officer at the scene of a crime or when taking a complaint will have a direct effect on the victim, the apprehension of a suspect, the investigation, and the success of the adjudication process. An accurate written report must be taken by the patrol officer describing the circumstances surrounding the incident. In crimes against persons, the victim must be afforded immediate medical or other types of assistance and support. The apprehension of the perpetrator or suspect is the responsibility of the patrol officer. In most cases the city or county jail facility is utilized for incarceration of prisoners. If the institution's patrol officers are not authorized with arrest powers, they should assist local law enforcement officers in every phase of the arrest. The campus public safety director should establish a mutual agreement of this type with local law enforcement chief administrators.

Vehicular traffic control is another functional area on which the patrol effort should focus. Every campus community has streets, parking lots, and regions of vehicles. On almost every campus today, traffic flow, speeding, and other vehicular violations are formidable problems for the campus public safety administrator. Many campuses were built in the nineteenth century and were not designed for current volumes of vehicular traffic. Most streets were planned and constructed for automobiles prior to the major growth in enrollments and expansion of higher education which occurred during the 1960s and 1970s. Thus, the campus public safety patrol officer is charged with the responsibility of maintaining and controlling a large volume of traffic on streets inadequate to handle it. It is, however, an important responsibility. Not only is it important to maintain an orderly flow of vehicular traffic, it is important to control this traffic for the safety of pedestrians and other drivers. While traffic signs and control devices are helpful, some enforcement efforts are needed. Otherwise, some drivers would ignore traffic laws and regulations and flagrantly violate these rules, thereby endangering themselves and others. Some administrative officials, on the one hand, frown on any effective enforcement efforts by campus patrol officers (i.e. the issuance of traffic citations) and, on the other hand, expect adherence to traffic laws and presume no serious accidents can happen on their campus. Death and injury due to traffic accidents is no longer uncommon on many campuses across the country. No longer can institutions ignore the liability risks which may result from the institutions' negligence of effective traffic control and enforcement. It is encumbent on the campus public safety administrator to apprise university officials of traffic problems and potential hazards and seek their support for efforts to effectively deal with these problems. Many campuses use radar devices to control speeding on campus and on streets adjacent to campus which affect students. Many public institutions use the same uniform traffic citation as do municipal and state law enforcement agencies. These are usually utilized in enforcing city and/or state traffic laws on and around campus. Other institutions continue to use campus traffic tickets with ultimate adjudication of the violator at a campus judicial traffic hearing. The disadvantage of this approach is that many serious traffic violators are not students or in any way affiliated with the institution and thus are immune from institutional regulations and procedures. The campus public safety director must identify traffic problems on his/her campus and determine the best comprehensive approach to deal with them.

The largest portion of the campus patrol effort is devoted to service. This is also true in all other law enforcement agencies which provide a uniformed patrol operation. It is important that the campus public safety director recognize the significance and scope of service to the campus community and direct his patrol officers toward a service-oriented approach. Service covers a wide variety of activities. Generally, service activities are all those except law enforcement functions. It should be noted that in some larger campus public safety departments, specific service areas may be assigned to special units (e.g. environmental health services performed by an environmental specialist). Within the context of this discussion, service includes primarily the following activities: unlocking car doors, physical security, assisting motorists, parking enforcement, fire safety, emergency medical response, environmental health, and other general services. Some of these areas are covered in greater detail in separate discussions in this text. Many of the routine service activities comprise the majority of the tasks performed by a patrol officer on an average workday. For example, on an average day some campus patrol officers may issue in excess of fifty parking citations, unlock a dozen car doors, lock or unlock eight to ten office doors for faculty members, provide assistance to four stranded motorists, and respond to two or three non-law enforcement incidents. Any time left within an eight-hour shift would be almost negligible after meal and coffee breaks. It is clear that service consumes the majority of the patrol officer's time. Therefore, patrol officers must be keenly aware of the importance of the service role and perform these tasks with the same professional demeanor and effectiveness as afforded law enforcement responses.

Public relations is an area of the patrol effort that warrants special attention. Public relations may be in the form of structured programs and approaches or it may be an integrated part of all other functional areas and routine activities. A well-planned and directed public relations program within the campus public safety department will certainly include the uniformed patrol officers. They may participate in various presentations such as crime prevention, self-defense, and drug awareness. They may assist in distributing public relations pamphlets and brochures. But the most common and, perhaps, the most effective public relations efforts by uniformed patrol officers are performed during the delivery of services. The attitude, dedication to serve, and the manner in which a service is performed best demonstrate positive public relations. The friendly, helpful demeanor of patrol officers while on routine patrol will have a far-reaching influence on students who may come to respect and appreciate "the law." Patrol officers who stop to chat with students will have a greater public relations impact than costly programs aimed at bridging the gap between students and police.

INVESTIGATIVE SERVICES

The investigative function is an important component within law enforcement services. In many small campus police/security departments this function is performed by regular uniformed patrol officers who are usually generalists rather than investigative specialists. Even in departments which have specially designated criminal investigators, the uniformed patrol officer will always perform some investigative functions when he/she responds to a criminal incident. Regardless of who is responsible for investigations, this special area of law enforcement should receive the full support of the campus public safety director. He/she should provide special training to develop investigative skills and techniques among all officers, provide special investigative tools and supplies, and ensure proper, thorough investigation of all crimes committed on campus. The director should recognize the uniqueness of investigative work and understand that it involves long hours of painstaking efforts by investigating officers and a certain amount of freedom from other routine tasks during the investigative process. The investigation of crime involves a number of distinct processes, including the following:

1. the initial gathering of information and evidence from the crime scene, from witnesses, and from the victim(s).
2. identification, preservation, and analysis of physical evidence
3. extensive interviews with victim(s) and witnesses

4. communication with and assistance from other law enforcement agencies

5. utilization of modern investigative techniques to identify and determine suspects (e.g. National Crime Information Center files, local criminal files, criminal profiling techniques, etc.)

6. apprehension, processing, and prosecution of suspect(s)

7. preparation of case and presentation in court

Investigations is a complex area of campus law enforcement, in that it may involve sensitive matters involving suspects ranging from students to top administrative officials. It may involve the theft of a stereo from a student's room, a series of burglaries involving thefts of tests from faculty offices, or embezzlement of large sums of money by an administrative official. It is very important that a strict chain of command and lines of communications be established within the public safety department which ensures that the director be informed of any special investigation which might have a significant campus-wide impact. Confidentiality of all investigations must be maintained. Otherwise, the effectiveness of the investigative process will be diminished and the credibility of the department will suffer.

The campus public safety administrator should obtain the full support of his superior and all top administrative officials regarding the investigative effort. Many top university administrators oppose the investigation of internal crimes committed by the institution's employees. For example, the campus public safety director of a medium-sized institution discovered, through his own investigative efforts, that the director of the physical plant had illegally taken significant amounts of university-owned building materials which were used to remodel and expand his home. When the public safety director presented his findings to the president of the university, he was told to keep it to himself and take no legal action. The president discouraged his investigative efforts and informed him that it was an administrative matter to be handled by the president's office. This kind of situation is not uncommon on campuses across the country. Therefore, it is the responsibility of the campus public safety administrator to take steps to preclude such lack of support by communicating to his/her superiors the significance and potential negative ramifications of neglecting the investigation of crimes against the institution and the state.

POLICING STUDENTS: DISCRETION AND ALTERNATIVES

The most striking difference between campus law enforcement and other more traditional types of law enforcement is the clientele. As mentioned in a previous discussion, the campus community's population is made up of predominantly young single adults who are in the pursuit of educational goals. Many of the students are away from home for the first time and are experiencing freedom from parents and other authorities. The other major portion of the population is composed of faculty and staff members who, in one way or another, are also in pursuit of or supporting educational goals. Generally speaking, the campus community lacks such groups or individuals as the low socioeconomically deprived, hard-core criminals, juvenile delinquents, high school dropouts, and the unemployed which are usually found in the average municipality. Certainly, there are exceptions to this otherwise ideal situation. Since most campus communities are relatively accessible to anyone who wishes to enter, the criminal element can intrude. And it would be unrealistic to pretend that some students do not commit crime. But generally, the unique clientele within the campus community does not generate a large number of serious criminal activities. By far, it is students, not common criminals, with whom the campus law enforcement officer comes into contact on a routine, daily basis. Policing students requires a special understanding and philosophy on the part of the campus public safety administrator, who must direct his/her staff toward a law enforcement approach compatible with this philosophy. This philosophy embodies an emphasis on police discretion and the use of alternatives to arrest in some situations. This emphasis centers around the question: What determines whether a specific action constitutes student misconduct or crime?

Many traditional student activities and their behavior include mischievous conduct and pranks, often resulting in damage to or loss of property, personal injuries, and disruption of public order. Prior to the demise of *in loco parentis,* almost all infractions of campus rules and/or violations of the law on campus were handled by campus administrative procedures. However, since the decade of the sixties there has been a trend toward treating these incidents as they would be treated in a municipal setting. Today, some so-called student pranks are dealt with harshly by campus police/security officers, often resulting in formal arrests and adjudication in a local municipal or county criminal court. For example, a student caught with marijuana in his room in the 1950s would have probably been immediately expelled from the institution without any criminal charges being filed against him. Today, the same student would be arrested first and then, perhaps, face disciplinary action by a student judicial board. A similar response might occur today if a fraternity defaced the institution's founding father's bronze statue. Does this mean that all acts of misconduct and all violations of the law by students should be dealt with through the criminal justice system? The answer is an emphatic no.

Police Discretion

As with their municipal counterparts, campus police/security officers must exercise discretion when determining whether or not to arrest an individual. Police discretion has been discussed at length, debated and criticized, but no feasible alternatives have been offered. Therefore, it is still the campus patrol officer who must decide what constitutes a prank and what constitutes a criminal offense—he has that authority and responsibility. It is the responsibility of the campus public safety director to assist him/her in the exercise of that authority. Since this obviously cannot be done at the scene of the incident, it must be done through in-service training, role orientation, and policy and procedures. Campus patrol officers must be guided toward a "temperance of authority."[1] They must develop proper role perceptions, have a clear understanding of the administration's philosophy toward student offenses, know what alternatives to arrest are available, and cultivate decision-making skills in crisis situations. Yet, the discretionary powers are an awesome responsibility for a campus patrol officer. No two situations are identical. He/she must approach every incident without the benefit of a preview or instructions.

While it would be impossible to develop specific criteria for determining which student offenses should warrant arrests and which should result in student disciplinary action, some general considerations can be used to assist in making these difficult decisions. While these are not all inclusive, they offer some guidelines for assessing most situations:

1. Is the offense a major violation of the law? If yes, an arrest would be appropriate. Major violations of the law include but are not limited to all felony offenses, theft, assault resulting in injury, etc.
2. Was criminal intent present? If yes, an arrest would be appropriate.

For example: If a group of fraternity members illegally enter a building and remove the campus chimes speaker with the intent to sell it or give it to an associate fraternity on another campus, this would constitute criminal intent. It might be a prank if they kept it for a while and later placed it on the front porch of the president's mansion.

3. If there is a victim, does he/she wish to press charges? In situations such as simple assault, petty theft, vandalism etc., victims may not wish to file charges. If this is the case, the officer may refer the matter to the campus administrative process.

4. In minor offenses, would an arrest be in the best interest of the institution, the public, and/or the offender? For example: If an intoxicated student is seen by campus police staggering across the campus, would arresting the student accomplish more than turning him/her over to the dormitory director for "protective custody"? Probably not. An arrest would not be in the best interest of the institution, the public, or the students in this situation.

5. Are reasonable alternatives to arrest available? In a case where a group of students paint the windows of the administrative building, an institution-imposed penalty of cleaning the windows and probationary status for the participants would be a reasonable alternative to arrests for vandalism. The student affairs division on most campuses provides the vehicle by which these alternatives can be adjudicated.

6. Was the offender a repeat offender? In some cases, this might be justification for an arrest, depending on the nature of the second offense.

While these considerations are applicable for student offenders, non-students and those not associated with the institution who commit offenses on campus are usually viewed in a different light. Normally, they are dealt with more severely using a more strict law enforcement approach. For example, a male, non-student trespasser caught visiting a friend unlawfully in a female dormitory would likely be arrested on the first offense, whereas a male student trespasser in the same situation would probably receive a warning the first time. Perhaps the only explanation for this is the proprietary attitude of administrators which encourages differential enforcement.[2] The institutional atmosphere in which institutional members, to include faculty and staff, are afforded special treatment permeates the campus community and is an unwritten policy of the campus public safety department. This is evidenced by the attitudes of students toward campus police and local city police. Most students prefer campus police over city police because they feel they will be treated more leniently by campus police.

Alternatives

There are a number of alternatives to arrest for minor offenses by students. Perhaps the most traditional campus agency charged with dealing with student misconduct is the student affairs division. The dean of students still exercises a good deal of authority over the conduct of students. Student offenses which are not considered serious enough to warrant arrests may be referred to the dean of students. He usually has several options at his disposal, all of which must ensure the student the right of due process. He may reprimand the student offender and assign a penalty or place the student on probation. He may temporarily suspend the student until a hearing is set. Some institutions provide for an administrative hearing in which temporary or permanent action may be taken by a committee comprised of key administrative officials and faculty/staff members. Other institutions have a judicial board to make determinations of guilt or innocence and have the authority to set penalties to include expulsion from the institution. Some judicial boards include student members along with administrative officials and faculty/staff members. It is usually the dean of students who directs the adjudication process on campus.

It is very important that the campus public safety administrator develop and maintain good communications with the dean of students. He should establish routine procedures for communicating appropriate information regarding police/security contact with student offenders and/or victims. Regular reports should be submitted to the dean's office regarding incidents in which students were involved. The dean of students should reciprocate this procedure by keeping the campus public safety director apprised of problems with students and, especially, potentially explosive situations. By establishing such a two-way communication, the dean of students and the director of public safety can better serve the students.

Another key administrative agency which may serve as an alternative to arrest is the housing office. Often, this may be under the dean of students. If not, the director of housing can handle student misconduct when violations occur within dormitories or apartments on campus. Vandalism, trespassing, and disorderly conduct are examples of offenses which may be referred to the housing office instead of making arrests. As with the dean of students, the director of housing may reprimand the student offender, impose a penalty, suspend the offender from campus housing, or take the offender to a judicial body for adjudication. It is important for the campus public safety director to maintain open lines of communication with the housing offices. In many large residential institutions, a considerable number of criminal incidents and offenses of all types occur in dormitories and campus-owned apartments. When the police/security officers respond to such incidents in campus housing, a report should be submitted to the housing office notifying the director of housing of the date, time, and nature of the incident.

Some institutions maintain a student court under the auspices of the student government association. This court presides and has jurisdiction over most student misconduct on campus, with their decisions appealable to an administrative board. In some situations, the campus public safety officers may appropriately refer student offenders to this court for adjudication as an alternative to formal arrest and adjudication through the criminal justice system. This would be applicable only in cases of minor violations. The success of this would depend on the effectiveness and credibility of the student court. Again, the campus public safety director should have open lines of communication with the SGA and the student court.

LAW ENFORCEMENT RESPONSE TO SPECIAL CIRCUMSTANCES

Student protests and illegal demonstrations, cults on campus, potential terrorist activities, and hazing all pose a threat to the campus community. While these incidents are not usually included in most discussions of crime on campus, they do occur and may be on the rise. It is essential that the campus public safety director be aware of the possibility and, perhaps, the existence of one or more of these activities. When these incidents occur, a law enforcement response may be required and it is usually campus public safety personnel who must deal with the problems head-on. Certainly, a well-established rapport with all members of the campus community, to include student leaders, will increase the possibility for success during these special circumstances. Preparedness and good judgment are prerequisites for a peaceful resolution and acceptable outcome.

Such special circumstances within the campus community further justify and, in fact, demand the presence of well-trained, highly competent campus law enforcement personnel capable of responding to any threat or exigent situation. Negligence in providing adequate law enforcement service may well result in serious complication of the incident as well as significant liability risks on the part of university officials to include administrators and boards of trustees. In the absence of effective campus law enforcement services, local, county, and/or state law enforcement agencies may assume responsibilities as well as full control. This may be to the dismay of university officials when they discover that major decisions requiring the law enforcement response, treatment of students, and resolution of the problem are made by these off-campus law enforcement officials. Of course, this is not to say that local, county, and/or state law enforcement agencies may not be needed to provide backup assistance. Such mutual-aid arrangements are much appreciated by most university officials and, in particular, campus public safety personnel. This is to say, however, that, where feasible, viable law enforcement services should be provided by the university in order to effectively respond to and control special circumstances when they occur within the campus community.

Demonstrations

As mentioned in a previous discussion, campus protests and radical demonstrations, which were thought to have passed with the 1960s, have reappeared on campuses across the nation. Student demonstrations and radical activities protesting racial inequality in South Africa occurred on many campuses during 1985 and 1986. Fortunately, most of these universities' campus public safety departments were prepared with high-caliber law enforcement responses. A case in point is the University of Kansas Police Department's response to a series of radical activities in the spring of 1985. The issue was South Africa's apartheid. During the nearly two-week anti-apartheid civil disobedience protest, the university endured one long-term building occupation and two abortive attempts at occupation, numerous marches and rallies, and an incursion into the chancellor's office. The University of Kansas Police Department (UKPD) arrested 65 people for various forms of criminal trespass. Yet, there were no injuries, no property damage, and no necessity for the use of force. The answer to the commendable job done by the UKPD was *communication.* There were excellent communications between police and UK administration and between police and demonstrators throughout the entire protest period. Of particular importance was the excellent rapport established between UKPD officers and members of the anti-apartheid group.[3]

The law enforcement capability afforded the UKPD, coupled with preparedness and good judgment on the part of the director of the UKPD, made it possible for the university to handle its own problem and maintain control until its resolution. This incident which occurred at the University of Kansas could be a reality on other campuses previously thought immune from such circumstances. It is, therefore, recommended that all university administrators and campus public safety directors give due consideration to such possibilities and ensure that an adequate law enforcement response is a reality.

Cults

Another special situation facing campus law enforcement is much less obvious than radical protests and demonstrations and is quietly deceptive. In fact, its effects often go unnoticed by university administrations and campus law enforcement officials. This may be due, in part, to ignorance of the problem and/or failure to admit that the problem exists. This special problem is cults on campus. William Goldberg, a clinical social worker in New Jersey, suggests that the campus community is a "spiritual supermarket" where the chief recruiting centers of most destructive cults operate.[4] He says that virtually every college campus in the country has been and continued to be visited by their organizations. According to Goldberg, these cults pressure the students to abandon their families, friends, and future in order to follow an individual who claims to have discovered the path to perfection. Although college students are not the only ones vulnerable to the appeal of cults, they are in a circumstance that is particularly condusive to its appeal.[5]

Certainly, it is often difficult to define a cult. Since it is often associated with religion, many universities avoid addressing the issue due to the controversy that would be created in any attempt to restrict freedoms guaranteed by the Constitution. However, university administrators and campus police directors need to weigh the rights of individuals against what is best for the campus community. When these so-called "religious" cult activities harm unsuspecting people, disrupt peace and safety, and violate the law, they must be dealt with forthwith. Dan Martin, former chief of police at North Texas State University, states: "As long as cults are using deceptions in recruiting and using mind-control to convert followers, university administrators have a responsibility to warn students what to expect."[6]

To assume that cults are harmless and not a threat to the campus community would be unrealistic. There are numerous accounts of innocent students who have been deceived by cults and have had their minds and bodies irreparably damaged, all in the name of a so-called religion. It behooves campus officials to remember the 913 Americans who died on November 18, 1978 in Jonestown, Guyana in a mass suicide-murder ritual. While this is an extreme case, similar results could occur within a campus community if responsible campus law enforcement officials fail to respond to cases where evidence of cultism exists.

Dan Martin supports cult awareness and education efforts. Cult awareness is important to campus police officials, residence hall staff, deans of students, student counselors, and college presidents. He states:

> Universities need to serve their campus communities much in the same way the Better Business Bureau serves their community: Unscrupulous organizations should be screened and documented for the benefit of the students. Even then, be prepared to explain to distraught parents how their son or daughter could mysteriously disappear from campus without notice.[7]

It is the campus public safety's law enforcement responsibility to monitor any organization which may threaten the tranquility and safety of students and respond appropriately. In some cases, cults have been involved in illegal activities and have been investigated by the FBI and IRS.[8] Usually, the campus public safety department provides the only investigative service within the campus community. Campus public safety officials should directly encounter the cult recruiter(s).[9] Also, campus law enforcement efforts should include enforcing rules regarding registration of outside groups on campus, loitering status, trespassing, solicitation ordinances, etc. It is essential that this effort be conducted wisely and discreetly.

Terrorism

A relatively new problem facing modern-day law enforcement personnel in this country and around the world is terrorism. While terrorism has not been felt in the United States as it has been in Europe and the Middle East, its threat here is very real. The U.S. involvement in so many controversial international issues affecting countries and radical groups sets the stage for reprisal and militant opposition in the form of terrorism. Already, U.S. citizens have been targets of terrorist attacks in foreign countries. The fear that such terrorists' incidents will strike at home is not without validity.

One characteristic of terrorism is the importance of news coverage. The best way to get the attention of the media, government officials and the public is to resort to violence and to stage such an incident in a location, at an event, and with the people present that will merit worldwide news coverage. Our campus communities provide the ideal ingredients for such an incident of terrorism.

Colleges and universities, by their very nature, are bastions of academic freedom and free speech. Consequently, controversial issues are often discussed, debated, and protested. Frequently, controversial national and international figures will visit campuses to espouse their ideological or political views on dissentient issues. In many cases such events attract local, state, and national news media as well as opposing visitors, radical groups, and VIP's to include government officials and leaders of various groups. This type of setting provides radicals and terrorists with the optimum circumstances to stage an act of violence in the name of their particular group or cause.

At a meeting of the Alabama Association of Campus Law Enforcement Administrators in Tuscaloosa, Alabama in June 1986, Mr. Steven Brannon, a special agent with the FBI, discussed the significant role campus law enforcement plays in meeting the threat of terrorism within the campus community. He stressed the real potential for problems for colleges and universities. In addition to the aforementional conditions, Mr. Brannon pointed out that most universities have significant numbers of foreign students with some representing countries which are associated with terrorist activities. During the 1986 attack on Libya by the U.S., several universities reported a noticeable change in the behavior of Libyan students on their campuses. Some of these students made clear their loyalty to Libya, its leaders, and their actions. This was reported by several local news agencies.

It behooves the campus public safety directors to prepare for terrorist activities. It is important to stay informed as to the number and kind of foreign students and/or foreign residents in and around the campus community. The campus public safety director attempts to be aware of any potential radical groups and current issues of concern to these groups. Preparation for special activities involving controversial visitors and/or events on campus is essential. Communication with other law enforcement agencies having vital information regarding radical individuals and groups is important. For example, the FBI, CIA, and the U.S. Immigration Service Enforcement Division may have information on certain foreign students who are known to have ties with radical groups. While these agencies have often been reluctant to share such information, it is encumbent on the campus public safety director to persuade these officials to share this information based on its relevancy to the safety and the campus community.

The campus public safety director must ensure that his "bases are covered" and have a plan to provide an effective law enforcement response to the threat of terrorism. It could happen on any campus at any time. As international issues are increasing by being brought to the campus, the possibility for a terrorist incident increases.

Hazing

Perhaps one of the most common special circumstances on the college campus is hazing. This ritual is practiced by many fraternities. Since 1978, 29 college students have died in hazing incidents across the country.[10] Many more have been injured. All national fraternities and the National Interfraternity Conference have rules strictly prohibiting hazing in initiation rites. Eighteen states have statutes making the practice illegal. Yet, these efforts have not stopped the practice.[11] It continues to be a problem and should be of concern to campus law enforcement officials, since it may affect the safety of students and, in many cases, may involve criminal negligence.

The difficulty many top administrators and campus public safety officials face is the nature of hazing. It is usually voluntary. In most cases, the pledges or inductees are sworn to secrecy. A particular hurdle for some campus public safety directors is the attitudes of university administrators who choose to ignore the problem for fear of harming the reputation of their institution. Fortunately, many institutions are taking strong stands against hazing.[12]

The appropriate approach to hazing for campus law enforcement includes identifying any specific hazing problems among fraternities. Such information should be communicated to campus officials responsible for fraternity activities. The campus public safety director should request the opportunity to meet with fraternity leaders to discuss the legal ramifications as well as the dangers of hazing activities. When dangerous or illegal hazing incidents are reported or known by campus public safety officials, they should take appropriate steps to stop these activities. Most states have statutes which can be applied to hazing incidents (e.g. criminal mischief, menacing, criminal tampering, reckless endangerment). Whenever possible and appropriate, these kinds of laws should be utilized in prohibiting harmful hazing incidents. While this may seem as a hard-line approach, it is the responsibility of campus public safety officials to protect students and respond to it in a law enforcement approach when necessary to maintain the peace and safety within the campus community.

SUMMARY

Law enforcement services are relatively new to the campus community. While student unrest and disorder during the sixties launched the movement to have cops on campus, crime in the seventies and eighties has demanded the growth in quantity and quality of law enforcement services to virtually every campus in the country today. It has been a short, yet exciting and challenging history. Campus law enforcement has been the recipient of modern police techniques, a new emphasis on quality in law enforcement, and growth in higher education to include the expansion of institutions and increased funding. Generally, campus law enforcement departments have been free to experiment and "do their own thing" unhampered by the deep-rooted police traditions followed by many small municipal police departments. Today, both public and private institutions all across the country have developed first-class law enforcement operations designed to meet the particular and unique needs of their campus communities. Collectively, they represent a very significant segment of the law enforcement community. Individually, they are vital components of the respective institutional organizations.

They enhance the academic goals by providing the kind of law enforcement services needed in this special environment.

NOTES

1. Diane C. Bordner and David M. Petersen, *Campus Policing: The Nature of University Police Work* (New York, New York: University Press of America, 1983), p. 221.

2. Ibid., p. 211.

3. John T. Brothers, "Communications is the Key to Small Demonstration Control," *Campus Law Enforcement Journal* 15, No. 5, (Sept./Oct. 1985), pp. 13–16.

4. William Goldberg, "Cults on Campus: How Can You Help?" *Campus Law Enforcement Journal,* 16, No. 2 (March/April 1986), p. 7.

5. Ibid., p. 15.

6. Dan Martin, "Cult Awareness On Campus," *Campus Law Enforcement Journal,* 16, No. 2 (March/April 1986), p. 7.

7. Ibid.

8. Ibid.

9. William Goldberg, "Cults on Campus," p. 16

10. Thomas J. Meyer, "Fight Against Hazing Rituals Rages on Campus and In State Legislatures," *The Chronicle of Higher Education,* 32, March 12, 1986, p. 34.

11. Ibid.

12. Ibid.

Chapter 9

SECURITY AND SAFETY SERVICES

All non-law enforcement services, to include security, safety, and special services, comprise from 90 percent to 95 percent of the functions of the campus public safety department. While the majority of services provided by municipal police agencies are also non-law enforcement in nature, they do not include the wide variety of public safety services as do campus public safety agencies. In municipalities, such services as fire safety, medical emergencies, parking enforcement, and civil defense procedures are not usually provided by a single department but are assigned to separate departments whose mission, goals, and objectives are usually focused on one of these service areas. All of these services plus law enforcement responsibilities are usually found in one department within the campus community, whether it be called police, security, traffic and safety, or public safety.

As pointed out in an earlier discussion, the service role of campus public safety should receive the greatest attention and effort. The campus public safety director should lead and direct his program with emphasis on quality in the delivery of non-law enforcement services. This is often not accomplished by many campus public safety directors. Some directors are more law enforcement oriented in their perception of the role of public safety and, subsequently, neglect the effective delivery of the non-law enforcement services. The result is often seen in inadequate fire safety programs, neglected dormitory security, and a complete lack of plans for civil defense and medical emergency procedures.

SECURITY SERVICES

Every institution of higher education should have an effective security system to protect its property and clientele. As mentioned in an earlier discussion, colleges and university campuses have millions of dollars' worth of facilities, equipment, books, and valuable items. More importantly, many campuses house students in dormitories and apartments.

All of these require protection. The major goal of a security system should be the early detection and prevention of criminal activity. Physical plant security should be the early detection and prevention of criminal activity. Physical plant security should include both security personnel and security devices. A surprising number of small institutions provide neither. The author recently consulted with an institution with a residential population of 800 which had no security personnel on the premises nor any electronic security devices!

The use of electronic security system has increased in recent years as technology has advanced. Many campus administrators have resisted the implementation of such electronic, security systems, choosing instead to rely on security personnel to lock and physically monitor buildings. Such an approach fails to recognize the benefits that a technologically advanced security system can provide. Despite the initial high costs of purchasing and installing electronic security systems, their effectiveness in complementing other security efforts will be cost effective in the long run. In fact, electronic security systems are much less expensive than providing sufficient manpower to cover the same areas and afford the same security surveillance of buildings. This is not to say that electronic security systems should eliminate the need for police and security officers. Security personnel are needed to activate alarm systems, monitor them, and respond when an intrusion is indicated. Since few electronic security systems are immune to malfunctions and the "professional" burglar, patrol officers must continue routine spotlight checks of buildings and security checks.

A multiplicity of electronic security systems are available on the market today. It is the responsibility of the campus public safety director to be familiar with these and be knowledgeable as to their effectiveness and applicability to his/her unique circumstances. There are a number of security publications and associations which can provide abundant information regarding electronic alarm devices. A variety of types of devices are available such as photoelectric systems, closed-circuit television (CCTV), ultrasonic motion detectors, microwave motion detectors, magnetic contacts, and passive infrared intruder detectors. Even among these types of systems there is a wide variety of uses and applications. For example, the building alarm may be audible within the building or silent and a signal received at a central monitoring station. The latter is recommended. Computerization of these systems has further sophisticated electronic security systems. Some campus public safety departments now have elaborate computerized consoles with audiovisual alarm indicators and CCTV monitors manned around the clock.

Building security is the responsibility of the campus public safety department. Therefore, the director of campus public safety should be involved in every phase of the acquisition of electronic security systems to include the planning, selection, and installation of the system(s). The system(s) should be connected to the campus public safety facility and be monitored by security personnel on a 24-hour basis. The director should ensure that written procedures for monitoring and responding to alarms are formulated and disseminated to all employees who may be involved. Accurate records must be maintained regarding alarms and/or malfunctions. A prearranged agreement between the campus public safety department and those responsible for repairing faulty electronic security devices must be established to ensure quick response in order to reduce the time that a system is inoperative.

ACCESS CONTROL

Access control of campus buildings is a problem that has existed as long as campus buildings themselves. Most every institution of higher education has experienced the problems of unauthorized entry of buildings and the collateral effects thereof. These problems include students entering closed buildings for the purpose of stealing tests and/or other material, off-campus intruders attempting to steal valuable equipment, or other illegitimate reasons. Therefore, an access-control system must be considered of utmost importance to the overall building security system. Building access and control should be the responsibility of the campus public safety department.

Existing access-control systems vary from institution to institution. Most colleges and universities have basically the same type of system as was originally installed and are reluctant to consider updating their system due to high costs. Yet, a few have installed new and more effective access-control systems because security problems and property loss demanded improvements. Regardless of the type of system used, the entire campus community must be educated as to the importance of access control and cooperate in the use of the system. As Powell points out, "Access control systems on college campuses are only as effective as the people using them want them to be".[1] An ongoing crime awareness and security-conscious program aimed at all segments of the campus community will enhance security efforts.

The most common access control system is the traditional lock-and-key type. This is also the most abused system and the most difficult to control. On most campuses using this system, unauthorized keys are abundant to include great grand master keys which access almost every door on campus. The author was recently involved in the investigation of a burglary incident of a campus building by students which resulted in the confiscation of a key ring with seven great grand master keys. It is recommended that key control be under the direction of the campus public safety director. Where feasible, locks should be changed periodically and keys reissued under strict control measures. It is also recommended that traditional key-access systems be supported with an additional system (i.e. a cipher locking system or an alarmed access-control system).

The card-key access system is a relatively new approach to building security on college campuses. It utilizes ID cards which are programmed to permit entry into designated approved areas. These ID cards are inserted into readers, usually located at building entrances and room doorways. The cards can be programmed to allow the holder entry into a number of different areas or they may restrict the holder to one specific door. For example, an academic dean's card may permit him/her entry into every area under his direction to include building entrance doors, all office doors, classroom doors, equipment rooms, etc. A faculty member's card may permit him/her entry only to his/her office and classrooms. Card-key systems are particularly applicable to dormitories. This type of system is used extensively and effectively at the University of Alabama in Birmingham (UAB), an urban campus with extensive research facilities. UAB's card-key system is centrally controlled and monitored from the communications center. From here, every access door equipped with a card-key reader is monitored by a computer. The computer indicates, via a readout and printout, when a card key is being used, the exact location, and which card key is being used. Another feature which UAB's system has is that all doors connected to this system can be locked or unlocked from the central control computer. This precludes the need for security personnel to manually lock or unlock doors.

The cipher locking system is another access control system. It employs the use of keys pads with numbered or lettered keys that must be pressed in predesignated order, commonly called a code, to gain entry. The system may be monitored by a central control panel or it may be a local system. This type of system is often found in dormitories. As with key control, the control of codes is often a problem. It is recommended that this system be combined with the traditional key system.

While there are other access-control systems, these represent those most commonly used and accepted. Certainly, with the use of sophisticated remote-control locking devices from a central monitoring station, CCTV, and computerized individual remote hand-held devices, more control can be obtained, but they may not be economically feasible and/or operationally justified. Again, the key ingredient is the full cooperation of all members of the campus community. Coupled with an effective electronic security system, educated community members can ensure the highest level of building security.

The University of Alabama in Birmingham (UAB) implemented a sophisticated security access system which involves the use of card-key access. Faculty and staff members are issued card keys which permit them entrance to their respective buildings or areas of work. Certain areas are accessible by designated faculty/staff members whose card keys are programmed to allow them this access. The entire system is monitored at a central control panel located in the university police department.

A note should be made regarding the importance of adequate lighting to enhance any security system, whether indoors or outdoors. Adequate lighting may well reduce the opportunity for criminal activity and discourage unauthorized persons from intruding on campus. A lighting survey should be conducted to determine which areas need additional light and how much and what type. The campus public safety director should be directly involved in this process. He/she may wish to use the consultation services of a campus engineer or outside consultant who has special expertise in the area. (Not only will adequate lighting reduce the likelihood of crime and trespassing, it will also create a sense of safety and security among campus community members.) Lighting in building corridors, stairwells, entrance ways, and porches should receive special attention. Lighting around buildings, particularly around trees and shrubbery, should receive special attention. These areas should be routinely monitored so that burned out or broken lights can be replaced as soon as possible. All walking areas should be well lit. Parking lots and decks must have adequate lighting. Recreational areas and facilities must be well lit to discourage trespassers and would be perpetrators.

Lighting up a campus can be expensive. Many top administrators resist expenditures for this area and place lighting low on their list of priorities. One lost life or a million-dollar lawsuit usually persuades college presidents to find adequate funds and exert whatever efforts necessary to light up the entire campus. Adequate lighting on campus is a responsibility of the institution as well as good liability protection. It is the responsibility of the campus public safety director to inform the administration of lighting deficiencies and recommend the necessary efforts to correct them, thus providing the institution with a safe and secure nighttime environment.

RESIDENTIAL SECURITY

Residential security is a special area of concern for the campus public safety director. While residential security responsibilities may be shared with the dean of students, director of housing, and/or director of apartments, the safety and security of campus residents should always be the concern of the campus public safety director. This area focuses on personal safety and security rather than building security which is primarily concerned with property loss and destruction. There are primarily two types of residential facilities on most campuses: dormitories and apartments. Dormitories come in all shapes, sizes, and living arrangements. They may be high rise, clusters, single level, coed, and/or a variety of other arrangements. Apartments may include duplexes, multi-units, high rise, and/or various other configurations. Some dormitories and apartments have central access with exterior entrance/exit doors and also interior living unit doors opening into a corridor. Others are designed with each living unit's door opening to the outside. Whatever the design, special security measures should be taken to ensure the safety of residents. It is important to note that there are two approaches to residential security: (1) security systems and (2) awareness and prevention efforts.

SECURITY SYSTEMS AND APPROACHES: DORMITORIES

Dormitories represent the traditional college residential living facilities for students. In fact, many existing dormitories built in the late 1800s and early 1900s are still used to house students today. Many dormitories were constructed on campuses during higher education's major growth era during the 1960s and 1970s. The tremendous increase in student enrollments, resulting in part to the baby boom generation, demanded more living accommodations. During this period the high-rise dormitory became popular. It was not uncommon to see nine- to twelve-story dormitories being constructed on campuses. One characteristic which both the existing "ancient" dormitory and the new dormitory had in common was that neither were designed and constructed to include adequate security systems. Fire safety systems, which will be discussed later, were also not included in many of these buildings.

Electronic security systems as presented in the previous discussion offer the campus public safety director a wide range of options from which to select the most appropriate one for dormitories. It is recommended that an effective electronic security system be utilized at all entrance doors and at each living unit. This ensures double protection. For example, a card-key access system installed at exterior entrance doors to the building reduces the chances of unauthorized entrance and allows only those with card keys to enter. Such a system should be connected to a central monitoring station which is alerted in the event of a security violation. Once inside, each living unit should have a cipher-locking device which permits only the residents of that particular room to have access. The codes on these devices should be changed periodically to enhance privacy and increase the integrity of the security system. While this type of system is the one recommended, the traditional key system can be used with some degree of effectiveness under close supervision and with periodic changes of locking hardware.

There are many types of systems which can be effective and they can vary in their application.

There are other security devices which can be effective and should be carefully considered. Peepholes in entrance doors of each room provide the resident a look at his/her visitor and precludes an open door for an intruder. Safety latches and chains are also recommended to allow the resident to open the doors and yet be assured some safety and security from a potential intruder. Electronic monitoring cameras such as the CCTV system, as mentioned in a earlier discussion, can be utilized to monitor all activity in hallways of dormitories. These can be connected to a central monitoring station either in the dormitory or in the campus police/security department. Adequate lighting both in hallways and stairwells and around the outside of the dormitory is important in removing the opportunity for a would-be trespasser.

A relatively new approach adopted by a number of institutions is the use of dormitory guards in and around dormitories. While this approach is often used in the absence of an electronic security system, it is recommended that it be used in conjunction with it. This method involves dorm guards or monitors who are assigned security duty to one or more dormitories. Their responsibilities include routine checks of all entrance doors, monitoring and controlling access to dormitory entrance doors, security checks around the outside of dormitories, and reporting all security violations either to the dormitory officials or public safety officers. Of those institutions using this approach, most employ responsible students as guards or monitors. This has proved effective on many campuses.

SECURITY SYSTEMS AND APPROACHES: APARTMENTS

University-owned apartments require basically the same physical security systems and approaches as do dormitories. However, apartments and apartment complexes often present unique security problems to the campus public safety director due to their locations, design, and management arrangements. On some campuses, apartments are located away from other residential facilities and, often, away from the main campus. This often requires special patrol efforts by police/security officers. Apartments are usually designed differently from dormitories, in that apartments are less restrictive in terms of access. On some campuses, apartments are not under the jurisdiction of the housing director but may be administered by the business manager, since many apartments are used to generate revenue for the institution. The residents of apartments may include more non-traditional students and, in some cases, non-students. Married couples often reside in campus apartments as do older students and adults. This creates an atmosphere of more freedom than found in most dormitory settings. Many apartments provide a pool and/or other recreational facility which often attracts non-residents and trespassers. Visitors to apartment dwellers are usually less scrutinized and such practices as quiet hours, visitation periods, etc., are not found in apartments. All of these characteristics requires special security considerations and, usually, different approaches to apartment security than that used for dormitory security. Since there are fewer security restrictions on apartments, it is more difficult to control access in and around the apartments. However, within these constraints electronic security devices should be employed as well as close monitoring by security personnel. As with dormitories, exterior lighting around apartment units and buildings should be adequate.

AWARENESS AND PREVENTION EFFORTS: DORMITORIES AND APARTMENTS

While security systems and approaches are certainly necessary, they will be completely ineffective without the cooperative efforts by all residents, whether dormitory students or apartment dwellers. Awareness of potential intruders and crime on the part of all residents is very important. Their subsequent efforts to prevent crime and the opportunity for crime is the key ingredient in making a residential facility safe and secure. Lending a key, propping a door open, or leaving a room door unlocked are examples of careless and thoughtless actions by residents which diminish the integrity of the security system. It is the responsibility of the campus public safety administrator to work with the various departments and groups on campus to promulgate security and safety awareness. This will be covered more thoroughly in a later section on campus crime prevention which will include residential facilities.

COMPUTER SECURITY

With the proliferation of computers in the campus community since the early 1980s, personal computers and microcomputers are now commonly found in almost every office on campus, not to mention in many classrooms and those located in computer labs. There have also been a growing number of computer thefts on most campuses. These computers are small, easy to carry, and valuable. They are "hot items," both for use by the perpetrator and for sale on the black market. A major contributing factor to this problem is that these computers simply are not properly secured. Administrators and faculty members are often unaware of the vulnerability of these computers and neglect to adequately secure them. Today, there are several commercial computer security systems which can be implemented and be effective in property-loss prevention. Some campus maintenance personnel can provide adequate locking hardware which makes it difficult for computers to be taken. While these efforts certainly should be made to secure computers, the campus public safety department should be involved and serve as the controlling and coordinating agency for computer security. The selection of an approved and effective computer security system should be of paramount concern. The campus public safety department should be notified when these computers are acquired and of the location(s) they are to be used. It should be the responsibility of the campus public safety department to ensure that approved security systems are installed. Each computer should be properly marked with permanent identifying numbers and a record kept indicating this number, the type of computer, and the exact location. To complement this system, routine computer security inspections should be conducted by campus public safety officers to maintain an up-to-date status on the security of personal and microcomputers on campus.

OTHER SECURITY CONCERNS

Campus security efforts certainly extend beyond the walls of campus buildings. Special consideration should be given to the safety and security throughout the campus to include parking lots and decks, recreational facilities, streets and sidewalks, and all grounds of the institution. Again, adequate lighting is extremely important to illuminate otherwise dark areas of campus in order to reduce the opportunity for crime. The use of emergency telephones or radio call boxes located in strategic areas is an approach which has had a good deal of success on some campuses. Their purpose is to provide assistance to those in need of emergency response or other urgent help. The University of Houston uses a radio call box system. This system includes fifteen radio call boxes strategically located throughout the campus community. Each of these boxes is connected by radio signal directly to the campus public safety's communication center and, when activated, indicates the location of the box. When a box is activated, the central radio dispatcher sends an officer to the box to render assistance.[2]

The use of CCTV around parking lots and recreational facilities provides around-the-clock monitoring to increase the safety of persons and security of property in these areas. This system should be supported by frequent security patrols and checks by public safety officers. In some cases, these areas demand a security officer or attendant on the premises to monitor access and watch property (e.g. vehicles, equipment).

Many campuses have electronic card-key accessed control devices for parking lots and decks. These "arms" prohibit the entrance of unauthorized vehicles into these areas by blocking the entrance way. Authorized persons must have a coded card key, which is inserted into a slot in order to gain entrance to the lot or deck parking.

Another novel approach to security is the use of whistles by students and other members of the campus community. This usually involves females on campus. For example, female students are issued regular plastic whistles which may be attached to their key ring. In the event of an emergency, they can blow the whistle loud and furiously to summon help. Of course, an extensive awareness program must precede such an approach to ensure everyone understands the significance of the whistle.

The security of property located outside of buildings (e.g. bicycles, vehicles, statues, signs) is still another concern for the campus public safety director. As part of the crime prevention program a special effort should be made to gain support and cooperation from all members of the campus community. Special locations and locking devices are recommended for parking bicycles. Vehicles should be monitored and those found unsecured by public safety officers should be cited with a friendly warning to apprise the owner of his/her carelessness and the potential for loss. Statues and signs should be well lit where feasible and, in some cases of expensive property, be electronically secured by an alarm that is monitored by a central monitoring station.

There are many special security considerations and a host of innovative approaches. The campus public safety administrator should devote a significant portion of manpower and money to security efforts. Time and money spent in this way may reduce time spent investigating criminal activity and loss of life and property. A comprehensive approach to include security systems and awareness and prevention efforts should be launched and directed by the campus public safety department. Campuswide participation by all appropriate departments, groups, and individuals will increase the potential for success.

SAFETY SERVICES

Fires, vehicular accident injuries, drug overdoses, hazardous chemical spills, and job-related injuries do occur on the college campus just as they do in any community. As with a municipality, the campus community should expect effective responses to these types of emergencies by qualified personnel. In addition, the campus community deserves a comprehensive program aimed at safety education, prevention, protection, and service. It is apparent that not all institutions of higher education can afford to provide all safety services. However, it is just as apparent that all institutions are responsible and may be held liable for the safety of its community members. Therefore, even though an institution may not operate its own fire department or ambulance service, it must make provisions for the delivery of these emergency services. On the other hand, safety concerns (e.g., fire detection systems, occupational safety) are the direct responsibility of the institution.

FIRE SAFETY AND PROTECTION

Fire safety and protection is a major area of campus public safety. Many institutions experienced the tragedy of fires on campus to include fires in dormitories resulting in loss of life. In his early years as a campus public safety administrator, the author found himself faced with a life-threatening dormitory fire and totally unprepared with no fire safety plan. From that incident, the importance of fire safety and protection has become paramount in promoting a comprehensive campus public safety program. A frightening number of institutions have given little attention to this vital area of public safety. It affects virtually every individual who attends classes, works, or visits on the campus. It includes fire prevention, fire detection, fire suppression, evacuation, and well-planned communications and procedures.

As with any major program, a fire safety program must begin with a comprehensive plan to include an assessment of needs, goals and objectives, and strategies to meet these goals and objectives. It should be the responsibility of the campus public safety director to direct and implement such a program. He must have the support of the president and other top administrators. He must get the cooperation of local and state government officials, key campus officials, and all affected groups and individuals throughout the campus community. He must draw on the expertise of fire department personnel, fire safety consultants, and other campus public safety leaders.

While a comprehensive campus fire safety program demands a multiplicity of approaches and applications, the following basic components are recommended:

1. A comprehensive fire safety and protection plan should be developed by the campus public safety department with the assistance of outside agencies and campus officials.
2. Mutual agreements and procedures should be developed between the institution and the local fire department regarding responsibilities, jurisdiction, and response procedures.

3. An effective radio and/or telephone communication network and procedure should be established between the campus public safety department and the local fire department.
4. All buildings on campus should be equipped with fire-detection equipment (smoke detectors) and fire alarm systems which are connected to a central communication center and monitored around the clock. Sprinkler systems are recommended, especially in residential facilities. The equipment and devices must meet all federal, state, and local fire safety standards.
5. All buildings should be equipped with approved fire extinguishers located at specified intervals and sites.
6. Special consideration should be given to residential facilities to ensure the safety of residents.
7. Evacuation procedures and routes should be developed and posted in each building in several strategic locations.
8. Regularly scheduled inspections of all fire-detection equipment, fire alarm devices, fire extinguishers, and monitoring equipment should be conducted.
9. Emergency telephone numbers should be disseminated to all living units, offices, and other areas throughout the campus community.
10. A well-planned and extensive fire prevention program should be developed and implemented. It should emphasize awareness and fire safety measures on the part of all campus community members.

Generally, most colleges and universities depend on local fire departments for fire-suppression services. The campus public safety director must work to keep open lines of communication and a good relationship with local fire department officials. Regular meetings between campus safety officials and local fire department officials are recommended to discuss concerns, potential problems, and cooperative efforts. In many cases, the municipal fire department may be small and may be a volunteer organization. In such situations, these departments may need financial support from the college or university. Sharing responsibilities often means sharing financial resources. Some institutions purchase equipment for the local fire department (e.g. fire trucks, ladders, radio communications systems).

Some institutions have their own fire department. Clemson University in Clemson, South Carolina, is one such institution with a fully equipped and manned fire department on campus. It serves the campus community and the city of Clemson. However, this is the exception rather than the rule.

EMERGENCY MEDICAL SERVICES

Since no campus is immune to life-threatening emergencies, an effective emergency medical response is needed. Most campuses do not provide their own ambulances or emergency medical technicians but rely on local agencies for these services. Yet, it is the responsibility of the campus public safety director to ensure that this emergency service is available and adequate to meet the campus community's needs. The following recommendations are considered essential in providing such a program:

1. Develop a plan to include needs, communication procedures, response procedures, transportation decisions, and cooperative efforts.
2. Establish and maintain clear lines of communication with local emergency medical/ambulance personnel and hospital officials regarding emergencies on campus.
3. Encourage and support the training of campus public safety officers in basic first aid and CPR, since these individuals are usually first responders. Basic state-certified emergency medical technician training should be provided for officers and other interested volunteers on campus in order to assist in medical emergencies.
4. Work closely with campus nurses, physicians, and health officials to determine what services may be available and appropriate on campus in the event of an emergency.
5. Disseminate an emergency telephone number campus-wide for medical emergencies.

Emergency medical services can be shared between the college or university and the local government agencies through joint funding and/or through cooperative efforts such as the institution providing emergency medical technicians to work on ambulances or the institution providing its own ambulance and response team for both campus calls as well as assisting the local agency with its emergency calls. There are many institutions which fail to recognize the importance of supporting this vital service provided by a local agency. The campus public safety director should act as a liaison between the institution and the local agency to promote a good relationship and improve services.

ENVIRONMENTAL HEALTH AND SAFETY SERVICES

The storage of chemicals, hazardous materials, and gas cylinders is common on most campuses today, particularly on campuses engaged in scientific research. Occupational safety and health concerns for employees should be as important to an institution of higher education as it is to factories and industries. Environmental health and safety is a relatively new area of concern in higher education brought on by an increase in scientific research done by many universities as higher education continues to provide government and industry with scientific and technological knowledge and developments. Within the past decade more and more institutions have recognized their liability and responsibility for ensuring the safety of all members of the campus community.

The University of Georgia serves as a model for providing effective environmental health and safety services. Operating a comprehensive public safety program, the University of Georgia places its Environmental Safety Services Department (ESSD) within the Public Safety Division. The ESSD is responsible for laboratory safety, radiation safety, fire safety, and hazardous materials. The ESSD is concerned with the proper storage of chemicals, control of radioactive materials, equipment safety in all work areas on campus, safety at construction sites, and the control of all hazardous materials. Highly qualified personnel direct these services and maintain regular inspections and accurate records. Federal, state, and local safety standards are adhered to by the ESSD to ensure the safety of all campus community members.

Michigan State University's Public Safety Division contains an Occupational Safety Section which involves two primary areas. The first concerns how people perform their work or educational tasks. This involves public safety personnel who are specialists in their field who are responsible for inspections of work places, presentations of safety education programs, and the investigation of accidents. The second area concerns the safety equipment located about campus (e.g. fire extinguishers, evacuation alarms, sprinklers).

Regardless of size, virtually every college campus has some chemicals, hazardous materials, dangerous structural faults, and/or dangerous equipment. On most small campuses and on many large ones these have been a neglected area of concern. Environmental health and safety services on some campuses are fragmented, with various departments responsible for their area's safety but all operating with no comprehensive plan or guidelines. Safety hazards such as exposed wiring, faulty electrical circuits, broken stairs, and other structural dangers often go unattended. Subsequently, some areas completely neglect safety and dangerous situations exist just waiting for a tragedy to occur. It is essential that every institution regardless of its size accept the responsibilities of environmental health and safety. Certainly, there are a variety of approaches depending on the factors such as the size of the institution, its organizational structure, its location, and the availability of outside assistance (e.g. a local fire department or a state safety inspection agency). Whatever the circumstance, the following basic elements of an environmental health and safety program are recommended:

1. Develop a campus-wide plan for environmental health and safety to include a complete assessment of all potential environmental hazards to include work areas, laboratories, and chemical storage areas.
2. Establish an environmental health and safety unit or appoint a campus official with these responsibilities to be placed within the campus public safety department.
3. Provide adequate training for environmental safety personnel.
4. Enlist the support and cooperation of all administrators, faculty, and staff concerned in affected areas.
5. Conduct regular inspections of all areas and maintain adequate records. This includes inspections of machinery, equipment, hazardous materials, and building/electrical conditions.
6. Identify and follow all federal, state, and local safety codes and standards.
7. Establish open lines of communication and operational procedures with state and local environmental safety officials to include those agencies which will respond to emergencies on campus.
8. Provide a complete listing of all areas containing hazardous materials and explosives to the local fire department in the event of a fire in that area.

As the top university administrator, the president should ensure that the environmental health and safety of the campus community is attended in an effective way so as to protect campus community members and relieve the institution of serious liability risks. The campus public safety director should be aware that his responsibilities to ensure a safe campus environment include these areas of environmental health and safety. He should view this as being just as important as security and law enforcement, since all of these service areas concern the safety and protection of campus community members.

CIVIL DEFENSE SERVICES

Campus communities are just as susceptible to such emergencies as blizzards, earthquakes, floods, hurricanes, tornadoes, explosions and even terrorist attacks as are cities. Major civil disorders resulting in widespread injuries and death have been known to completely disrupt campus communities requiring emergency assistance. Student unrest and rioting during the 1960s created serious safety problems for campus public safety officials. The 1980s have witnessed significant disruptions and violence on many campuses over the apartheid issue as discussed in an earlier chapter. All of these critical situations may demand assistance and relief for victims. Most campus law enforcement, fire safety, or medical emergency services are not normally prepared or equipped to respond to and handle such large-scale emergencies. Yet, if it happens, it should be the responsibility of the campus public safety director to direct, control, and provide assistance to these emergencies on campus. This kind of assistance is commonly referred to as civil defense. Traditionally, civil defense is concerned with saving lives and property in the event that our country is attacked by an enemy. But during peace time, civil defense provides assistance in a wide variety of natural and manmade disasters as described above.

Federal, state and local governments share the responsibility for civil defense. Local agencies develop and carry out civil defense plans for their communities with the guidance and assistance of state and federal agencies. There are four primary tasks of a civil defense program: (1) warning, (2) evacuation, (3) shelter, and (4) emergency services.

It is somewhat disconcerting to realize that many municipal, county, and state civil defense programs do not include the campus community nor involve campus public safety officials. It is also inconceivable to think that many institutions of higher education have no civil defense program or plan in the event that a major disaster occurs. It is very conceivable that any university community, whether it has a population of 350 or 35,000, could be bit by a tornado, resulting in a total blackout, fires, widespread injuries, and loss of many lives because of a complete lack of emergency preparedness.

The campus public safety director should first understand and embrace the philosophy that a major disaster can occur on his/her campus and preparedness is essential. Since there is no way to predict when, how, or what kind of disaster could occur, the campus public safety director should develop an overall emergency response plan with a number of built-in options from which to apply to a given situation. All available resources such as federal, state, and local civil defense agencies and other emergency-response agencies should be included in this plan. The development of this plan should involve all agencies which might be needed in the event of a disaster on campus. Certainly, the local fire department, medical emergency rescue/ambulance service, hospitals, law enforcement agencies, national guard unit, and county and municipal civil defense agencies should be included both in the development and implementation stages.

The campus public safety director should assess the available resources on his/her campus in developing a disaster plan. Some colleges and universities have a commendable amount of emergency response equipment, supplies, facilities, and personnel. This is particularly true of institutions with hospitals and an ambulance service. Some campus public safety departments have fire suppression capabilities, ambulance services, and special equipment for use during major disasters. While other institutions have none of the above mentioned, they still have some resources which they must identify and include in their disaster-preparedness plan. For example, most campuses have suitable facilities which can be designated as shelters for use during severe weather or to temporarily accommodate mass injuries during any type of major disaster. Most institutions also have a health clinic or infirmary which is staffed by physicians and registered nurses. Most campus public safety departments have emergency warning devices such as vehicle lights, sirens, and public-address equipment with which to warn residents of impending danger.

There are some basic elements which should be included in any campus civil defense preparedness plan regardless of the size or location of the institution. These include:

1. The cooperation and inclusion of other emergency-response agencies in the development of a preparedness plan and in its implementation during exigent circumstances.

2. Identification of all available resources which may be needed in the event of a disaster to include outside resources and those on campus.
3. A campus-wide awareness and education program to include instructions to campus community members for their response in the event of a disaster.
4. Standing operating procedures for campus public safety personnel to follow to include communication to the campus community and to other emergency-response agencies.
5. An early warning system to alert the campus community of impending dangers (e.g. tornado or hurricane warning).
6. A well-developed and disseminated evacuation procedure for the campus population.
7. Predetermined shelters and locations for campus residents to go prior to and during exigent circumstances.
8. Coordinated emergency efforts outlined in a procedural format indicating areas of responsibilities, command and control, transportation arrangements, emergency facilities to be used, and alternate plans.

The campus public safety director should be ultimately responsible for planning, coordinating, and implementing a civil defense plan. Since the safety of all campus community members is his/her responsibility, he/she should direct and control all civil defense efforts while delegating appropriate functions to those capable to handle them. Emergency preparedness should not be a neglected area which might someday find the campus community and public safety officials totally unprepared to meet. Civil defense efforts should receive the full support from the president down and should be delivered in an accountable way by professional public safety officials.

SUMMARY

The delivery of security and safety services is a major undertaking for the campus public safety director who wishes to "cover all the bases." It is unfortunate that currently many institutions of higher education have not recognized their tremendous liability in these areas and, subsequently, have not acted accountably to ensure the safety of their campus community members. Some presidents and top administrative officials have contributed to this situation because of other more pressing needs and/or their lack of understanding of the significance of comprehending security and safety efforts and the resulting risks inherent in the absence of such efforts. In some cases, it is the campus public safety director who does not perceive these areas as important but is concerned with law enforcement activities and neglects the broad scope of his responsibilities. Administering an effective campus public safety program is not simple, nor is delivering services an easy task. It requires a knowledgeable, enthusiastic, and skilled public safety administrator to identify areas of need, develop meaningful approaches, and effectively communicate both to his/her superiors in such a way as to gain their confidence and support.

NOTES

1. John W. Powell, *Campus Security and Law Enforcement* (Boston, Massachusetts: Butterworth, Inc.), 1971, p. 151.

2. George Hess and Susan Stoner, "Emergency Radio Call Boxes—A Proven Tool," *Campus Law Enforcement Journal*, 11, 1981, pp. 28–29.

Chapter 10

SUPPORT SERVICES AND
EQUIPMENT/FACILITY CONSIDERATIONS

The age-old adage that "behind every successful man is a good woman" has some analogical application to the successful delivery of campus public safety services. Behind every successful campus public safety operation are quality support services which enhance the overall impact of campus public safety. The functions, tasks, and personnel involved in these services must have the support of the campus public safety program. Support services, from the communications operations to equipment inventory/maintenance, are often neglected areas of concern in many campus public safety departments. Campus public safety directors tend to emphasize patrol efforts through additional manpower, increased budgets, innovative techniques, and new programs while allowing support services to become obsolete in terms of their effectiveness.

In small departments many support functions are performed by full-time police or security officers or part-time student employees. In large departments these services may be more specialized into organizational units with well-trained, highly proficient personnel. Whatever the size of the department or organizational design, all campus public safety operations must utilize support services to their maximum potential and strive to develop innovative approaches to better serve the campus community.

COMMUNICATIONS

In order to provide effective law enforcement, security, and safety services to any campus community, an efficient and effective communications system is required. The size of the department and the scope of its responsibilities will determine the kind of communications system needed for a particular institution. While communications systems will differ substantially from campus to campus, basic principles of communications are common to all. The basis for any communication system is the receiving and transmitting of information. The efficient and accurate

178

communication of information is vital to any campus public safety operation. It should be of paramount concern of every campus public safety director to maintain such a system in order to stay informed of all his department's activities, to successfully perform routine functions, and to ensure accountability for all public safety operations. Failure to provide an adequate communication system can be debilitating to the smooth and effective delivery of services as well as constitute serious liability risks for the institution.

SYSTEMS AND EQUIPMENT

Public safety communications systems and equipment have undergone tremendous technological advances in the past two decades. Many campus police/security departments now have sophisticated communications systems, while others have lacked the resources to acquire state-of-the-art equipment. Unfortunately, many small colleges have no communications systems at all with which to support their security and safety functions. Certainly, computerized, high-tech communications equipment can make any communications system more efficient and effective. This is not to say that the campus public safety director cannot develop and maintain a highly effective communications system with basic equipment. In fact, for many smaller departments which have few incidents and activities a telephone, a two-way radio system, and well-trained communications personnel may be adequate to support the law enforcement, security, and safety services. It is important that the best and most feasible equipment be afforded for the campus public safety operation commensurate with the scope and type of its responsibilities.

The basic elements of a campus public safety communications system include: personnel, standard operating procedures, telephone system, two-way radio system, information recording, and monitoring equipment. While these may vary in type and be utilized in different ways and through a variety of approaches, they should be a part of every communications system.

PERSONNEL

A communications system is only as good as the personnel who operate it. Radio communications operators man the radio communications center, commonly known as the "radio room." They serve to receive and transmit all information by telephone, radio, and/or in person for the campus public safety department. The radio communications operator coordinates all police, security, and safety functions and ensures that assistance is provided where and when needed. Protection of officers in the field is the top priority of the communications operator. These individuals may be full-time employees or student employees. It is important that these operators be well trained and thoroughly oriented for performing all duties and responding to a wide variety of circumstances. They must have keen decision-making skills in getting complete and accurate information and translating it to officers in the field as they are dispatched to a complaint or incident. Radio communications operators should be provided on an around-the-clock basis. When feasible, it is suggested that these employees be dressed in a distinctive uniform with appropriate emblems and name tags. They should be expected to perform proficiently at all times. Figure 13 provides a typical job description for a radio communications operator. The campus public safety director must recognize the importance of communications personnel and their impact on the public safety operations. Often, these are the first individuals that a caller or visitor will encounter when contacting the campus police/security department. The impression left and the degree of efficiency with which service is communicated will certainly influence the public's perception of the campus public safety department. The quality of their performance will directly affect the officers on patrol and the integrity of the campus safety function.

STANDARD OPERATING PROCEDURES

It is essential that clear and concise communications methods and procedures be established and disseminated. Every circumstance possible should be included in order to give directions to the radio communications operator in appropriately handling such situations. A standard operating procedures (SOP) manual is recommended for the communications operation. The Florida State University Department of Public Safety has such a manual with which to assist the communications operations. The FSU Department of Public Safety's General Order 85-7 states:

> The intent of the Communications Operation Procedure Manual is to acquaint all communications personnel with the proper procedures regarding the effective and efficient operation of the Communications

FIGURE 13
JOB DESCRIPTION
RADIO COMMUNICATIONS OPERATOR

1. *Job Summary:*
Responsible for receiving and transmitting all communications by phone, two-way radio and/or in person for University Police Department and serving faculty, staff, students and visitors as a public relations/information person.

2. *Specific Duties and Responsibilities:*
Answers telephone and operates two-way radio and responds with appropriate information and/or actions.

Dispatches emergency aid as quickly as possible—such as police, fire department, rescue squad, ambulance or any other needed help—for all University personnel and/or visitors. Provides assistance to faculty, staff, students and visitors in locating buildings and/or persons on the University campus.

Keeps an accurate radio and telephone log of all calls from either police officers or public.

Monitors all pertinent two-way radio and emergency information (e.g. severe weather).

Coordinates emergency efforts during exigent situations.

Cooperates with city police and city radio operator on appropriate occasions.

Maintains adequate records related to Police/Information business.

Issues parking decals, maps and other material to faculty, staff, students and visitors when necessary.

Keep immediate work area neat, clean and well organized.

Assists University Police Officers with auxiliary services (i.e. typing, phone calls, and other minor duties) when called upon.

Provides training for new employees as necessary.

3. *Special Qualifications:*
Efficient in reading, writing and mathematical skills to perform necessary clerical duties.

Adequate proficiency in the English language.

Ability to communicate well with a variety of people and provide a good public relations image.

Potential ability to react calmly and intelligently in emergency circumstances.

Section. The C.O.P.M. is located in the Communications section. Consequently, all communications personnel should acquire a working knowledge of the C.O.P.M.[1]

Every campus public safety department should establish such an SOP manual and maintain it up to date. Especially essential for inclusion in this manual are communications procedures in the event of fire, severe weather, violent crime, complaints, officer assistance requests, etc. An orientation and training program is recommended for communications personnel to ensure their understanding of and competency with these procedures.

TELEPHONE SYSTEM

An adequate telephone system must be in place to handle all incoming and outgoing calls, especially during emergency situations. While one telephone line may be adequate for some small departments, a multi-line system is usually required. An emergency line separate from other lines is strongly recommended for all departments. This line should be restricted to emergency incoming calls and the number should be well advertized. Since the communications room is the nerve center for all public safety operations, the emergency line and other lines for department business should be located there. The campus public safety director should exercise care and be selective when determining the best kind of phone system and/or arrangement for his/her department. In many cases, his/her decision may be precluded by an existing system or decisions made by other officials. Nevertheless, the campus public safety director should offer recommendations regarding the kind of telephone system needed to serve the unique circumstances of his/her operation. It is suggested that a voice-activated recording device be installed on all incoming telephone lines. This serves to keep a record of all information transmitted over the telephone and may prove valuable when faced with litigation or when investigating a criminal incident.

TWO-WAY RADIOS

Two-way radio systems vary substantially in their performance and features. It is the campus public safety director's responsibility to assess his/her communications needs, research the best systems available, and determine which system is the most compatible and effective for his/her operation. Current and long-range needs must be considered lest the system become inadequate within four or five years. There are several system features to consider to include: size, frequency range, channels, monitoring capabilities, durability, service, parts availability, transmittal/reception range, and compatibility with other system(s) and/or equipment.

The base station should be located within the department's communications center. This radio must have sufficient range to communicate with officers in the field whether using their vehicle mobile radios or hand-held portable radios. In some cases, these base station radios must have adequate range to allow communication with surrounding law enforcement/emergency agencies. It is recommended that this radio have more than one channel and have scanning capability in order to monitor other surrounding agencies' radio traffic and communicate with these agencies when necessary for mutual assistance (e.g. local fire department, local police, hospital emergency room). It is important that the base station have a backup power supply to maintain its operation in the event of a power outage. In many departments, the communications system becomes inoperative when it is needed most (i.e. power outage during severe weather).

On the other end of the two-way radio system are various kinds of radios used by public safety officials. Patrol vehicles should be equipped with two-way radios which can effectively communicate from car to car and to the base station from any location within the jurisdictional boundaries. It is recommended that these radios be multi-channel units with scanning capabilities. Every campus public safety officer should be equipped with a hand-held portable radio, commonly known as a walkie-talkie. On many occasions officers are required to be out of their vehicles for various activities which may demand immediate communication with the base station or another patrol unit. It is recommended that every campus public safety department acquire enough hand-held radios to equip each officer with one while on duty. An adequate number should be on hand to accommodate special events when most officers are on duty.

INFORMATION RECORDING

It is of utmost importance that information be recorded and documented in some way so as to use for reference and to maintain an official record. Depending on the size of the department and the volume of information communicated, a number of information-recording methods are acceptable. Perhaps the most simple method is the handwritten log sheet. This method requires the radio communication operator to enter or log each significant radio transmission and reception as well as telephone calls on a log sheet with the time of the communication. This substantiates the call, the caller, the incident/activity, the information, and the date and time. In most cases, this type of information recording is considered reliable and even admissible as an accurate record in court.

Another method of recording and documenting information is the use of a date/time card system which utilizes a mechanical date/time device. With this method the radio communications operator fills out a preprinted form card with the basic information of the call or incident and inserts the card in the date/time device for recording and documentation. Then the card is placed in time sequence in a file box where it can be retrieved when needed.

With today's technological advances, sophisticated information recording systems have been developed which has streamlined public safety communications systems form large metropolitan police departments to relatively small campus security departments. Multi-track logging and recording devices can be installed, at a nominal cost, to record not only radio transmissions but telephone communications also. Such devices can be used to compile a record of all radio and telephone messages received and transmitted by the communications operator. These show the date and time of the message. These vary in style from highly complex reel-to-reel to more simple cassette, voice-activated systems. Some of these systems can be interfaced or included in a comprehensive computerized system which records all communication computer disks. This information can be easily stored and retrieved. When selecting an information recording system, the campus public safety director should consider the system more practical, cost effective, and efficient for his/her particular setting. Reasonableness should prevail.

MONITORING EQUIPMENT

An effective communications system should include certain monitoring devices with which to receive information. There are a variety of such devices and systems on the market. Some are built in to existing communications equipment (e.g. multi-channel radios). It is important that the communications operator be constantly aware of pertinent information from other agencies, especially emergency circumstances that might affect the campus community. Therefore, some arrangement should be made to monitor such agencies as the local fire department, local city or county police, ambulance service, civil defense agency, etc. Every campus public safety department, regardless of size, should maintain a weather monitoring device with which to monitor weather conditions and be informed of impending severe weather. It is also recommended that a CB radio be located in the communication center in order to monitor the designated emergency channel. Often, civilians who have

CB radios in their vehicles will turn to the emergency channel and call for assistance when they are confronted with or witness an accident or criminal incident. Any existing campus radio frequencies should be monitored (e.g. dormitory patrol, maintenance units, transient authority).

Another means of monitoring communications is the use of portible monitors and pagers. This is an excellent method of communicating one way to a wide variety of individuals and groups. A master encoder serves as the communications transmitter which sends designated tones and/or voice messages to individually monitored units, usually called pagers. The pagers are carried on the person of assigned individuals who may have designated tones to distinguish them from other pager carriers. It is recommended that the communication center be the hub or base for such transmissions. For example, all on-call, off-duty police/security supervisors should be afforded a pager to keep by which he/she can be contacted by tone and/or voice communicating a message or instructions. Another use of pagers might be for dormitory directors who may need to be on-call around the clock but, obviously, cannot sit by their phone constantly. When an emergency or urgent need exists, the campus public safety department can be called and, in turn, the radio communications operator can contact the dormitory director on his/her pager and relay the message. Other officials which may benefit from this type of monitoring system are student affairs directors, key maintenance personnel, campus physicians and nurses, and some administrative officials.

OFFICE OPERATIONS

An organized, well-managed, and adequately equipped office is an essential component of support services. It will enhance the effectiveness of all other functions. This is as true of the small security department with only five officers as it is with the large public safety division with eighty officers and several specialized sections. Each functional area should be identified and designated with its own specific objectives, procedures, and responsibilities. Officer support areas include communications, records, secretarial, clerical, and public relations. In some small campus police/security departments one secretary must perform all of the tasks for these areas. Other departments rely primarily on student employees for these functions. Larger departments often have full-time, specialized personnel in each of these areas.

It is recommended that an adequate number of office personnel be afforded for the campus public safety departments. This number will vary considerably depending on the size of the department and its responsibilities. However, the author recommends as a minimum for any public safety operation that a full-time secretary, around-the-clock radio communications operators (full-time or students), and sufficient clerical employee(s) be provided. As will be discussed in the next section, student employees can provide valuable assistance with many tasks including communications and clerical work.

Effective supervision and direction should be provided in order to ensure quality performance. In some larger campus public safety departments, each office support area may have a designated supervisor (e.g. sergeant of the communications section, records manager). This will assist the campus public safety director in maintaining accountability for all areas of the office operation. Even in small departments, an individual should be designated as the person "in charge" and responsible for office operations.

Every effort should be made by office personnel to project a positive and professional image to the public. Often, a visit to the campus public safety department's front office or desk may be the only encounter that some students and faculty may have with the department. Courteous and efficient service must be provided. This does not happen accidently or by chance. It requires an intentional and diligent effort by the director, his supervisors, and all employees. High-caliber employees must be selected and developed in order to perpetuate efficiency and a positive image.

Adequate equipment is a must for an effective office operator. For years, many small campus police/security departments sorely lacked enough good equipment and supplies with which to do their jobs. Second-hand typewriters, no paper reproduction capability, worn-out filing cabinets, and inadequate office supply budgets were common among many campus public safety departments. While progress has been made on many campuses in these areas, many such situations still exist. Every campus public safety department, regardless of its size, should be afforded as good equipment as any other office on campus. This includes technologically up-to-date typewriters, photocopying machines, computers, calculators, telephone system, dictaphones, and acceptable accessories to include quality office furnishings.

STUDENT EMPLOYEES

Campus public safety administrators are concerned with effectively providing adequate services to their clientele during times of budgetary constraints. As do other administrators, campus public safety directors have a broad range of services for which they are responsible. Some of these services require the use of professionally trained personnel (i.e. police patrol, answering complaints, effecting arrests, working traffic accidents). However, there are many services which campus police departments provide that may not require specially trained individuals. Since some chief administrators are experiencing a shortage of sufficient full-time sworn officers, one alternative has been the utilization of student employees in supporting the primary functions and accomplishing the mission of the department. This arrangement is more financially feasible, it affords employment for students, and it yields positive results for the campus public safety department. It also relieves the sworn officers from many "non-police" duties, thus allowing them more time for the traditional law enforcement functions which are important for the campus community.

The need for student employees is a reality. In some cases the number of auxiliary and special services added to the campus public safety department has exceeded the relative rate of employment of additional officers to meet the new demands. Subsequently, campus public safety administrators have looked to student employment as a reasonable solution to the program and have found help in time to need. While student employees are less expensive than full-time, trained officers, the quality of student performance can sometimes exceed that of regular employees. Responsibilities such as ticket writing, fire extinguisher inspections, radio communications, student escorts, building security, assisting motorists, security at special events, clerical, and others are all important to the goals and objectives of the campus police department. Competent students serve well to perform these kinds of duties.

Many campus police/security departments utilize student employees in several areas to support their department's efforts. On some campuses students man the telephones and two-way radio communications around the clock to provide emergency and general assistance to the campus community. This is a very strategic position, since the employee is responsible to some degree for the safety of the duty officers as well as the campus residents. Students also serve as an effective public relations person when assisting visitors to the police station and those who need help over the telephone. Students in many university police departments also serve as office clerks and file citation cards and other departmental reports. Typing is always a premium, and these student employees certainly help. A relatively new effort is the student patrol program. Under this program, students in uniform (with no weapons) can do a variety of duties which, in some instances, relieve the full-time sworn officers of "non-police" functions and afford them more time to patrol, investigate criminal incidents and respond to complaints. These students may be equipped with flashlights, handcuffs, two-way radios and in some cases "billy sticks." They will usually perform their tasks on "foot patrol." This enhances the public relations aspect of the student patrol program. One of the primary duties of a student patrol officer is to secure buildings at scheduled times and recheck them periodically. They may also be utilized to set electronic burglar alarm systems in campus buildings. A regular patrol officer is usually designated to supervise these student patrol officers and to ensure that their duties are carried out correctly. The student patrol officers may also assist regular officers with security at special events such as major athletic events, concerts, graduation ceremonies, etc. They can also serve to work traffic and parking at these events. Such student patrol officers may be uniformed, radio-equipped personnel and, when appropriately supervised, perform most of the duties of the regular officer except arrests. And when a small campus police/security department is stretched to the limit with personnel in meeting the many demands made by numerous campus activities, student patrol officers are a "welcomed site."

The student patrol program at Jacksonville State University in Jacksonville, Alabama is open to both student employees and student volunteers. The JSU College of Criminal Justice affords many students whose interests direct them toward active involvement with a police organization. This may be in the form of simply volunteering their services or as part of their internship requirement of their academic program. Usually, the shifts are set up as five-hour shifts during the late evening hours (7:00 P.M.–12:00 A.M.). These are the hours in which the building security functions and special events are usually scheduled.

The University of Alabama Police Department depends a great deal on UA students to assist their efforts in providing public safety services for the campus community. While their student employees are not uniformed, they are involved in almost every area of responsibility of the university police department. They serve as dormitory guards, issue parking tickets, perform building security duties, perform radio dispatch services, assist in fire inspections and assist other students with general aid (e.g. escorts, first aid). All of these student employees carry two-way radios.

There are other university police departments which utilize student employees to support their services. Student employees are an integral part of many campus public safety organizations across the country. While the method of style and the scope of these programs may vary from institution to institution, the need and dependence on the student employee is evident. The effectiveness of these programs is important, and if the full potential of these efforts are to be realized, some considerations must be made. A serious philosophy should be developed regarding the role, standards, and the scope of the students' position within the department. Selection of student employees is a major concern. Certain characteristics must be of priority in the selection of these students because of the responsibilities and privileges that may be part of their functions. Image should be of major importance when selecting students to represent the campus police department as well as the institution. Organization should be of utmost concern. A clear chain of command, supervision, job description, scheduling of shifts, leadership, and regular meetings are all part of a good organizational plan. Other considerations should be made such as uniforms (are they to be uniformed or not, and if so, what type?), equipment to be worn, limits of authority, training, etc. The key to a successful program is the progressive campus public safety administrator who has a clear understanding of the role his/her department must play within the institution's mission and, more specifically, the role of student employees as support personnel. He should be sensitive to the personnel, academic, social and career development of each student under his employ. Thereto, he should carefully consider those first-line supervisors and their influence on the students. He must also be alert to the importance of the safety of these student employees while in the performance of their duties and ensure that their responsibilities are of a safe nature.

The use of student employees in campus public safety departments has proven successful. The effectiveness and quality of services have been demonstrated while not being budgetarily prohibitive. As the scope of responsibilities seem to broaden for the campus public safety department and financial appropriations are reduced, the utilization of student employees provide the answer in meeting the increased demands. The positive impact on public relations these students make is a viable aspect of the philosophy and endeavors of the campus public safety department. They tend to "bridge the gap" between the police as the "law" and the college students. And when these student employees graduate and leave the department, they take with them valuable experience, a knowledge of the law enforcement profession and, hopefully, the ability to apply their training and skills to their new career. The advantages of student employee work programs are obvious and certainly beneficial to all concerned. Campus public safety directors who have not effectively utilized students within their department might do well to explore the possibilities and involve more students.

KEY CONTROL

Key control is a special area which should be placed within the campus public safety department to support security efforts. Many institutions assign this responsibility to the business manager, maintenance department, or some other department. Yet, it is the campus public safety department which is responsible for building security and its director that is held accountable for all security problems. Key control is logically a part of overall building security as a support service.

An effective key-control system has several requirements. First, it must be carefully supervised and controlled. A responsible manager should be assigned this responsibility and report directly to the director. Second, an accurate and well-organized recording system must be established and maintained in order to ensure the integrity of the key-control system. Third, strict rules and procedures must be established and adhered to when issuing keys or card keys. Also, a procedure should be included for revoking key privileges when violations of rules occur (e.g. duplicating keys, using keys at unauthorized times and/or places, or loaning keys). And fourth, keys and locking devices should be changed periodically where feasible to reduce security violations.

The campus public safety director should make efforts to educate the campus community about the importance of key control. Informing campus community members of security risks and their responsibilities should encourage them to use caution and consider key possession and use as important. A good working relationship with local businesses which have key-duplicating machines can be of value to the campus public safety director. Most institution keys have "Do Not Duplicate" engraved on them. It is helpful if local merchants will call campus public safety officials when an attempt to duplicate such a key is made.

FACILITIES AND EQUIPMENT

A well-organized and well-staffed campus public safety department must be complemented and supported with adequate facilities and good equipment in order to provide effective services to the campus community. The type and size of facility will depend on the size of the department and its scope of operation. The necessary equipment will be determined by the kinds of services provided and the areas of responsibility. On a number of campuses visited by the author, the campus police/security departments are located in a rear basement of an old building on the backside of campus! Often, the office space is very limited, with only two or three rooms. This important service unit of the institution should be afforded better treatment commensurate with its role and scope of influence. The main facility in which the campus police/security department is housed should be centrally located so as to be accessible to pedestrian and vehicular traffic. It should be adequate in size and designed to accommodate the operation comfortably to include the following: administrative/supervisory office space, lobby area, radio dispatch room, records room, supply room, squad room, kitchen, restrooms (to include showers), conference room, secretarial/clerical office(s), interview room(s), locker room for officers, and a storage area. Upon entering the front door of the facility, a visitor should immediately recognize the professional atmosphere and be greeted by a friendly, helpful public safety employee. This should be the case on a 24-hour basis. The facility should be attractive both externally and internally. Where possible, it should be a self-contained building rather than shared with another department. The facility should provide for ample parking for patrol vehicles and visitors.

Many campus public safety departments sorely lack for good equipment and, subsequently, fail to project a positive image and provide the kinds of services its campus community deserves. Many campus police cars are old, undependable, and, in fact, dangerous to operate. Some radio systems are antiquated and require excessive and frequent maintenance. Often, needed and requested equipment is not made available to improve the operation and expand much needed services. Campus police vehicles should be purchased on a predetermined schedule in order to preclude excessive "down time" and unsafe operation. It is recommended that regular patrol vehicles be taken out of service after 70,000 miles. Beyond this point, maintenance costs and down time make normal use prohibitive. Vehicles should be adequate in type and in number. The author recommends "police package" vehicles be used which are equipped with heavy-duty parts and devices designed for 24-hour patrol, inclement weather, and emergency response. The department should be afforded an adequate number of vehicles to provide effective patrol and backup vehicles when needed for special events and during maintenance down time on other patrol vehicles. Also, vehicles should be provided for investigative and supervisory purposes. Support vehicles (e.g., 4-wheel vehicles, pickup trucks, motorcycles, and bicycles) can also be important for some operations and should be kept updated for effective service. All vehicles should be equipped with the appropriated emergency or special equipment to include audiovisual devices.

Other equipment items of major importance to most campus public safety operations include but are not limited to the following: a two-way radio system (base station mobil units, and hand-held units), typewriter(s), computer(s), office machines, photography equipment, surveillance devices, speed-control devices, emergency lights, investigative equipment, etc. Personal equipment for officers should include weapons, batons, handcuffs, protective vests and other service items. Both adequate quantity and quality are essential for the smooth effective delivery of public safety services. It should be noted that the amount and type of equipment must be reasonably and practically determined based on the size and complexion of the institution, the role and scope of the public safety department, and the real needs of the department. Such determinations must be made after a careful and comprehensive assessment is conducted of the institution's needs and the subsequent needs of the public safety department. For example, while three patrol cars may be adequate for an institution with an enrollment of 4,000 students in a rural setting, six cars may be required for the same size institution in a downtown location.

Equipment and supplies maintenance and inventory is an important support component. Keeping all equipment operative is essential. Maintaining adequate equipment and supplies is necessary to support the line officers in the field. Flashlights, batteries, pens, raincoats, hats, notebooks, and all required forms (e.g. incident, offense report forms, accident report forms, citations) are some items which should always be available. Accurate inventory records must be kept to ensure all needed equipment and supplies are on hand as well as to prevent unauthorized inventory loss.

These facility and equipment considerations provide some basic guidelines and recommendations for the campus public safety administrator who has the responsibility of delivering law enforcement, security, and safety services. They are essential for the smooth and effective public safety operation.

SUMMARY

The quality of support services will determine the effectiveness of the delivery of public safety services. The campus public safety director must recognize the importance of support services and understand their proper role within the overall public safety operation. An ongoing assessment of support services and programs should be conducted to determine what operational/functional adjustments may be needed and to plan budget requests. Adding more uniformed officers may not be the panacea for improving public safety services. Increasing the number of security devices and full-time personnel may not be the solution to security problems. Instead, a better communications system, additional office personnel, student employees, and improved key control measures may better serve to enhance the efficiency and effectiveness of main line public safety functions. The wise campus public safety director should not equate "better" with "more" but consider special efforts to utilize existing support services and programs to their maximum potential by improving their quality. In the absence of adequate support services, it is the director's responsibility to make administrative officials aware of their need and justify their establishment by presenting the benefits gained by adding such services and programs. The entire campus community will benefit from quality support services and adequate facilities and equipment.

NOTES

1. William D. Tanner, General Order 85-7, Florida State University Department of Public Safety Manual, 1985.

Chapter 11

SPECIAL SERVICES AND PROGRAMS

INTRODUCTION

Leaving a vehicle parked in a parking lot while attending a basketball game on campus or trying to locate a convenient parking space just before history class all require the need for public safety special services. Without the convenience of parking, security at an athletic event, and crime prevention measures in parking lots and buildings, the campus community would be an unorganized, out-of-control, and unsafe environment. Special services and programs are integral parts of a comprehensive campus public safety operation. They complement the main line functions of law enforcement, security, and safety. It should be noted that "special" may be regarded as a primary functional area within some campus police/security departments. For example, traffic control may be designated as a special service on some larger campuses, while it is usually considered as a law enforcement function in the majority of campus public safety departments. Those special services and programs discussed in this chapter are: parking operations, special events, and crime prevention. Organizationally, these may be placed under one of several functional areas (e.g. crime prevention may come under safety or security services). Yet, conceptually and in practice, these are special programs which require special and unique efforts and approaches. They should be identified as "special" so as to focus on their special goals and objectives. It is encumbent on the campus public safety director to designate these services and programs as "special" and provide the necessary support to make them successful. These special services and programs should not be viewed as "extras" or "frills" but rather essential to providing a convenient and safe campus community environment.

PARKING OPERATION

The administration and control of a parking operation is perhaps the biggest problem for most campus public safety directors. Few campuses are immune to the many problems associated with parking. Most campuses were designed and constructed years before the tremendous increase in student-driven vehicles on campus. Consequently, the number of cars brought to campus at any given time may exceed the number of available parking spaces. While some institutions have increased the number of parking spaces to cope with this problem, they have neglected to address other parking-related problems and develop an effective plan to improve the overall parking situation. Other problems include control of designated parking areas, parking enforcement, habitual violators, record keeping, and collection of fines. Every campus has its own unique parking problems and approaches to those problems. A number of factors and characteristics of campus communities will dictate which approach is best. A large urban, commuter institution will certainly have different problems and approaches than a small rural, mostly residential institution. The institution's administrator's philosophy toward parking and the amount of support demonstrated will influence and determine parking policies and procedures.

The administration of the parking operation should be assigned to the campus public safety department. For most campuses, this means the campus police or security department will be responsible for all aspects of the parking operation. On some large campuses the parking operation is administered by a special section (e.g. parking management, parking and traffic division). On others, vehicle registration is handled by a separate department, while parking enforcement is carried out by the campus police. Whatever the organizational structure, the campus public safety director should still be responsible for the parking operation.

The campus public safety administrator should recognize that there are two basic organizational areas of a parking operation: (1) management operations and (2) field operations.[1] Management includes budget control, record keeping, policy-and-procedure formulation, parking decal acquisition and issuance collections and public relations/educational programs. Field operations encompasses equipment maintenance, information gathering, control security, and enforcement.

Management

While most institutions of higher education are not in the parking business for profit, some degree of budget and revenue accountability is expected. Wilbur J. Waterson, parking operations manager at Cleveland State University, points out that parking is essential to the attainment of an institution's educational goals. He contends that the cost of providing this convenience cannot be considered as educational overhead. He states: "The parking operation must pay for itself. . . . "[2] Some campus public safety directors have little or no control over this financial area. However, it is recommended that he/she be involved in the overall financial consideration of the parking operation and the revenue produced from decal sales and enforcement efforts (i.e. parking tickets). Most campus parking operations can be managed efficiently so as to pay their own way without excessive fees and fines. To do so requires planning support and cooperation from the president and other top administrative officials. Accurate information regarding all financial aspects of the parking operations should be compiled and analyzed on a regular basis. This facilitates decision making about problems and aids in planning new approaches. This information should include income sources and amounts, personnel costs, and equipment and supply expenditures.

Record keeping is another aspect of parking management which must be systematic and efficient. Records must be kept on all vehicles registered, income categorized by source, parking violation citations, tow-away information, special permits issued, and general information regarding parking patterns, special problems, and complaints. The use of computers has transformed this function to increase its completeness, accuracy, and flexibity. Whether a computerized or manual records systems is used, security and accessibility must be a concern for the campus public safety director. Accurate records will prove to be of tremendous value in supporting enforcement efforts and collections as well as for information to justify needs and changes.

Parking policies, regulations, and procedures are essential for any parking operation regardless of the type of program or size of the institution. These should be developed and continuously updated with input from various pertinent constituencies on campus such as the student government associations, faculty representatives, key administrative officials, outside consultants, and campus public safety officials. Those policies should be published in the form of brochures or pamphlets and should be disseminated to every individual who registers his/her vehicle. Included in this should be parking policies and regulations, definitions of terms, a campus map indicating parking areas, and fines for designated violations.

Most campuses use some form of parking decals or permits. These vary widely from institution to institution. The primary purpose for these is to identify vehicles which are properly registered as well as provide information about the driver. Most colleges and universities purchase these decals or permits from commercial sources and charge faculty, staff, and students for issuance in the form of vehicle registration fee. These permits or decals may be attached to various locations on the vehicle (e.g. bumper, rear window, front window, hanging on rear-view mirror). Usually, each decal is numbered and may be color-coded to indicate a designated parking location assignment.

Parking violation fine collection is a very important part of the parking operation. While there are several approaches to fine collection, an effective approach is essential to maintain the credibility of the enforcement efforts. Parking fines vary from $2 to $25 and higher. Accurate records must be kept assigning violations to violators to ensure proper identification for collection purposes. Fine collection must be equitable and applicable to faculty and staff as well as student. Most universities are now billing violators who do not pay within a prescribed time period. Some institutions use payroll deductions to collect fines from faculty and staff. Other institutions withhold student transcripts and/or do not allow them to register for the next semester until all fines are paid in full. Another approach to fine collection is revocation of parking privileges on campus until delinquent fines are paid.

In order to enhance the effectiveness of the parking program, a well-planned public relation/educational program should be implemented campus wide. This program's primary objective should be to inform and educate all campus members about parking on campus and solicit their cooperation in making the parking operation a success. The parking rules and regulations brochure is an excellent measure of disseminating this information. To complement this, campus public safety officials should speak to various campus groups, fraternities and sororities, etc. Posters can be designed and placed in strategic locations to encourage vehicle registration and proper parking. Public service spots on the campus radio station and the campus newspaper can be of value in making faculty, staff, and students aware of general parking policies and specific problem areas. There are as many ways to use public relations efforts to improve the parking operation as there are creative ideas.

Field Operation

The field operation for a parking system performs the "legwork" for the parking management operation by carrying out policies, procedures, programs, and enforcement functions. The field operation utilizes and maintains equipment (e.g. parking vehicles, mechanical control devices, meters, tire marking tools). It serves to monitor parking patterns and gather pertinent information as to parking problems, volume of vehicles, and number of spaces. Parking control is an important function of the field operation. This may be done by mechanical devices or attendants. Mechanical devices include electronic barriers which may be accessed by inserting a special card or money into a slot. Attendants may be posted at parking lot entrances to allow access only to authorized drivers. A combination of control approaches may be used. For example, an attendant may be stationed in a booth at the parking area's entrance and manually control a mechanical barrier to allow only authorized access.

A relatively new area of parking field operations is security. This function became necessary on many campuses due to an increase in crime, both personal and property. This is especially true on urban, downtown campuses. There are several approaches to parking lot security to include electronic surveillance, increased lighting, security patrols, and strict access-control measures. Some institutions with multi-level parking garages or decks utilize security surveillance cameras which monitor every area of each deck. This system is centrally controlled with a security officer viewing monitor screens. A number of institutions utilize shuttle buses as a security measure as well as for convenience purposes. Other campuses assign special parking security personnel to patrol parking areas on foot or in vehicles. Students are sometimes used for this. The University of Pennsylvania, with 46 parking areas, recognized the need to improve parking lot safety and security. Elevator intercoms were installed, garage access-restriction devices were utilized, and parking lot attendants' hours were increased in certain problem areas. Also, in-service training seminars were conducted for parking lot attendants to increase their effectiveness in preventing crime in parking areas.[3]

Perhaps the main function of most parking field operations is enforcement. In fact, parking enforcement is often considered as the most important aspect of an overall parking operation. However, with more effort directed toward better management and improved public relations and control approaches, enforcement efforts can be reduced significantly. Yet, enforcement continues to receive a great deal of emphasis and support as the primary means to maintain a successful parking operation.

Parking enforcement is usually done via the issuance of parking violation citations. These parking violations should be spelled out in a parking policies and regulations brochure. Common parking violations include: parking in the wrong zone, no parking decal, parking in a handicapped space, improper decal display, and blocking a fire hydrant. Parking enforcement may be performed by campus police officers, special parking enforcement officers, and/or student ticket writers. Parking citations should have certain specific information when issued (i.e. date and time of issuance, issuing officer's name, violation and corresponding fine, description of vehicle to include vehicle tag and/or parking decal numbers, and instructions for payment or appeal).

An innovative parking enforcement technique was recently invented by a young Southern Methodist University computer science student. This invention is a computerized ticket-writing program designed to make the enforcement process more efficient. The machine is a notebook-size minicomputer which uses a tiny information cassette. Covered with plastic for weather protection, the minicomputer is carried by the college or university parking enforcement officer. The computer prints parking tickets which resemble cash register tapes, which are placed under the vehicles windshield wiper just like the traditional parking ticket. The small cassette records all tickets and this information is transferred into the parking operation's main computer. Eliminating the need for manually transferring 25,000 to 30,000 carbon tickets into the main computer saved SMU $30,000.[4]

Every parking enforcement effort should include an appeals process. This should be clearly explained in the parking policies and regulations brochure. When a citation is issued, a date, time, and location for appeal should be stated. Some citations may simply instruct the alleged violator to go to the department of public safety for an appeals form and there is informed as to the date, time, and location of the next appeals hearing. The appeals hearing process may vary from institution to institution. It is recommended that the following basic elements be included: (1) a neutral site not associated with the enforcing agency; (2) an impartial appeals committee representing all major campus constituency groups (i.e. faculty, staff, and students); (3) the opportunity for the alleged violator to present his/her defense or be represented by legal counsel; (4) the written parking policies and regulations be used as the "law"; (5) a representative from the enforcing agency be available for information and clarification purposes; and (6) an immediate decision be made and informed to the defendant.

Some mention must be made of the importance of computer-aided parking management systems. This is a trend which will continue until virtually every institution will include its parking operation on computer. Since most institutions already have installed a computer system, this may mean simply adding a program for parking and placing a terminal in the campus public safety department. Others may see the benefit of installing an in-house computer or micro-computer which is not connected to the institution's system.

The University of Toledo is a good example of an institution which changed its parking records system from the manual filing method to a computerized system. Increased enrollment combined with tighter enforcement efforts created an unmanageable situation for the small vehicle-registration staff.[5]

Under the old manual system, many fines went uncollected due to the lack of identification of offenders and difficulty in collecting fines. A careful assessment and planning process by the director of campus security, the director of campus computer services, and an outside consultant resulted in the acquisition of a computerized data management system compatible with UT's particular needs. According the Frank J. Prizzulo, Jr., Director of Security at UT, "The computerized data management system has greatly increased the efficiency of the Vehicle Registration Office and has led to a higher percentage of accounts collected through timely notices and early identification of repeat offenders."[6] Many other college and university public safety departments have implemented computerized system which include the parking operation as well as law enforcement and security operations. While many campus public safety directors are computer illiterate, the time has come for them to realize the effectiveness and efficiency which can be accomplished with the proper computer system for their operation.

Administering a parking operation can be a frustrating and difficult task, or it can be a well-organized, effective operation. A commitment from the institution's administration, a comprehensive plan, an ongoing assessment and analysis of parking, good management, and a willingness to be innovative are key ingredients in administering a successful parking operation. Bringing all of these efforts together and gaining the support and cooperation of campus community members demands that the campus public safety director be a competent manager and be skilled in human relations. He/she must be willing to involve other campus constituency groups in planning and decision making and delegate authority to those capable of administering the various aspects of the parking operation. An improved parking system will be recognized and appreciated by all members of the campus community, as it supports the institution's commitment to provide a quality environment for the pursuit of educational goals.

SPECIAL EVENTS

Institutions of higher education serve as centers for many diverse special events from visiting renouned dignitaries to major collegiate athletic events. Academic freedom demands an open-door policy for the most controversial individuals and groups. Enthusiastic, fun-seeking students demand open-air rock concerts. Loyal alumni, money-minded presidents, and students demand strong athletic programs with large stadiums and coliseums. These are only a few of the many types of special events on college and university campuses across the country. Regardless of how large or small the institution, special events are the rule. Some special events are so routine that they are seldom thought of as "special," i.e. graduation exercises, lecture series, fraternity/sorority open parties, theatrical performances, summer-visiting high school groups, pep rallies, major continuing-education workshops and seminars, large banquets, etc. All too often college administrators plan special events with little thought of resulting traffic, parking and security problems. Often, the campus public safety director is the last person to be contacted or may discover the special event while it is in progress when calls for assistance flood the communication center.

The key to delivering services to any type of special event, major or minor, is planning. Sound planning techniques should be implemented when preparing for special events. Written policies and procedures should be formulated with a significant amount of flexibility built in. Almost every event is different and has its own peculiar characteristics and needs. Ironically, major events (e.g. football games, rock concerts) may be easier to plan for, since each event is relatively predictable in terms of the problem areas and manpower needs. This is not to say that these events are simple to work but that they are approached in a similar fashion. For example, most home football games are usually worked basically the same, and plans for the first game of the year can be used for all remaining games with a few variations. However, other special events (e.g. visiting controversial speakers) may require special consideration, planning, and response. John W. Powell, a noted campus public safety specialist, recommends that each special event be evaluated on an individual basis using the following criteria:

1. Type of event
2. Approximate number and general composition of those attending (students, outsiders, and so on)
3. Location (ability to control entrances)
4. Admissions charge or free admission
5. Access-control procedures (ticket sales and collection)
6. General rules regarding those participating and attending
7. History of similar events
8. Policies in regard to arrests, ejection from premises, and so forth.[7]

It is essential that the campus public safety director play a key role in all special events which may require assistance from his/her department. Advance written notification should be afforded the director with complete information regarding the event. When planning meetings are held by officials to make decisions regarding their event(s), the campus public safety director should be invited in order to have input on safety and security matters. He/she should determine what security requirements are appropriate for each particular event.

Major athletic events, large rock concerts, and other major special events usually require special considerations and preparation. Adequate manpower should be a concern and receive special attention. Staffing for special events has traditionally been arbitrarily determined by the campus public safety director based on a preview of the event, past experience, and some guesswork. Subsequently, his/her decisions are frequently secondguessed or disregarded. Phillip L. Mullendore, Director of College Safety at Pasadena City College, developed a formula to justify with specific numbers the staffing needs for special events. This formula involves an analysis of factors which adversely or positively affect the safety and security of an event. These factors are then given "point" ratings. These factors in this formula were developed after hundreds of events were reviewed and analyzed. The following factors tended to negatively influence an event and, therefore, the more points tabulated for the event, the more personnel needed to provide security.[8]

Factors
Time of event: Day = 5 points
                  Night = 20 points
Events occurring at night tend to create more problems
Attendance: 0–100 =   5 points
             101–500 = 10 points
           501–1,000 = 15 points
           1,001–up = 20 points
The more people attending an event, the greater likelihood of problems.
Age of people attending the event:
             0–14 = 5 points
           15–18 = 20 points
           19–25 = 15 points
           26–up = 5 points
Valuable property/large sums of money = 10 points

The points for adverse factors are subtotaled, and points are subtracted for factors that affect the event in a positive manner. The following are some positive factors with their "point" ratings:

Participants will be formally or semiformally dressed = 5 points
Three or more faculty members will act as chaperones = 5 points
Attendance by invitation only = 5 points

The total risk points are tabulated and personnel can then be assigned based upon the following formula:

Risk points	*Officers required*
0 – 15	0
16 – 25	1
26 – 35	2
34 – 45	3
46 – 55	4
56 – 65	5
66 – 75	6
76 + (Critical event)	8 or more

Mr. Mullendore points out that the above factors should serve as general guidelines, and each situation should be evaluated on its own unique circumstances.[9]

Another consideration for major events other than manpower needs is procedural guidelines. If arrests are made, who transports the prisoners? To what location are prisoners to be taken immediately? What special communications procedures are to be followed during the event? What procedures are to be followed in the event of an accident with serious injuries. Who is in charge? What arrangements are made for backup units from other agencies if needed? These and other procedural questions should be addressed before the event. It is important to ensure that all officers understand these guidelines and procedures. An officer's well-being could be at stake. Again, proper planning is the key. One or more planning sessions should be held by the campus public safety director to include his supervisors and other key individuals involved in sponsoring or working the event (e.g. stadium director, ambulance personnel, local law enforcement officials). An orientation session should be held just prior to the event to thoroughly inform and familiarize all officers of procedures and special circumstances.

Close working relations with local public safety agencies is a must when planning and working major special events. In many cases, the local municipality will be affected by having an increase in vehicular traffic, noise complaints, and disorderly conduct. Mutual planning and procedures with the local police, fire department, and ambulance service is recommended. It may be necessary to include one or more of these agencies in assisting with the event, either on a voluntary basis or prearranged pay basis. Such material cooperation of efforts is especially common for small institutions. Even large institutions must rely on assistance from local and state police, civil defense officers, and National Guard troops at major college football games.

A special event worthy of comment is a relatively recent concern for many campus public safety directors. This is the presence of visiting controversial figures or dignitaries on campus. Extremist, leaders of foreign countries, racially motivated speakers, certain politicians, and radicals are often targets of terrorists and/or protest groups. Special planning is essential. Efforts should be made to communicate with federal and state officials (e.g. FBI, Secret Service, state investigators) regarding vital information and special security requirements. The campus public safety director should be assertive in demanding to be informed and involved in these situations.

Planning for special events on campus is the responsibility of the campus public safety director. He/she should seek to be informed, develop plans, and utilize all available resources needed. Failure to properly plan and be prepared could result in tragedy and serious liability risks for the institution.

CRIME PREVENTION

The reality of crime on campus requires special attention and special efforts by campus public safety officials. There is no empirical research to support the myth that law enforcement efforts (e.g. patrol, apprehension of criminals, arrests) prevent crime. Certainly, it is also difficult to prove that crime prevention programs actually prevent crime, since predicting crimes that never occur is obviously impossible. Yet, it is the responsibility of institutions of higher education via the campus public safety department to attempt to reduce the likelihood and opportunities for criminal activity on campus. Subsequently, a pro-active crime prevention approach should be adopted which involves all constituencies within the campus community, embraces a comprehensive program approach, and is an ongoing, adaptable process.

Many campus public safety administrators have given little more than lip service to crime prevention efforts. Many of these directors actually think that patrol efforts, an increase in arrests, more manpower, and better equipment are the most effective crime prevention measures available. For years, campus police/security chiefs justified more personnel and equipment by attributing crime on campus to their deficiencies in these areas. Today, most university administrators recognize that effective crime prevention programs can be developed and implemented at reasonable costs by utilizing existing resources and creative ideas.

The flag bearer for any comprehensive campus crime prevention program should be the public safety director. As the chief law enforcement and security officer for the campus community, it is his/her responsibility to provide the leadership necessary to ensure that a well-planned, organized, and effective program is established. This will require his/her best leadership skills to articulate to the administration faculty/staff, students, and public safety personnel the importance of strong support and involvement from everyone. He/she must demonstrate sharp management skills in communicating, planning, directing, delegating, and evaluating every process of the overall program. The campus public safety department should serve as the safety and security consultant agency and make available its resources. In reality, other crime prevention program leaders and participants will look to the public safety department and its director for guidance and support in maintaining a consistent program from year to year. Where feasible, the director should appoint a crime prevention officer and establish a crime prevention unit.

It is recommended that an institution-wide standing committee be established to direct and coordinate the crime prevention program. Representatives on this committee should consist of high-level administrative officials, faculty members, staff members, students, and public safety officials. Specifically, this committee should include a physical plant administrator, faculty from different disciplines and/or departments, resident and commuter students, and the designated crime prevention officer. It is important that this committee be recognized by and receive the endorsement of the president of the institution. It should be the committee's responsibility to develop a comprehensive crime prevention plan to include practical approaches to implement the plan. The committee should monitor each special crime prevention program, continuously evaluate their effectiveness, and periodically report these findings to the public safety director. Each specially designated program coordinator or director (e.g. coordinator of bicycle registration, or coordinator or director of operation identification, etc.) should work closely with the committee and provide a periodic progress report to the committee.

It should be noted that certain crime prevention efforts may be handled primarily by the campus public safety department (e.g. dormitory security, personal safety/protection programs). However, these efforts should be coordinated with the crime prevention committee.

One of the first things the crime prevention committee should address is the setting of goals. Goals are usually general statements of purpose regarding crime prevention efforts. Realistic goals for an institution-wide crime prevention programs would include:

1. Identify crime problems and potential criminal activity.
2. Educate the campus community to the reality of potential crime on campus.
3. Make all campus community members aware of their responsibility in becoming involved to reduce the opportunities for crime.
4. Develop a comprehensive crime prevention plan involving all of the constituencies within the campus community.
5. Develop and implement specially targeted crime prevention programs.

Once goals are set, the task of developing a master plan for a crime prevention program is the next order of business. The basic elements of sound planning should be applied. A thorough assessment of existing criminal activity and situations which may lend themselves to opportunities of crime should be conducted. From this assessment, specific objectives should be developed for preventing and/or reducing the opportunities for crime. These will include specific programs, approaches, and resources needed for a successful crime prevention program. Timetables, organization, authority, and designated personnel should be determined. This plan should be developed so that a degree of flexibility and adaptability is built in for future needs and changes.

The crime prevention plan should include but not be limited to the following programs:

1. General crime awareness and public relations program. This would utilize a variety of media to make campus community members aware of potential crime while promoting a positive public image and encouraging better police-community relations.
2. Personal safety program. This includes sexual assault awareness, self-protection techniques, and sensible avoidance preventive measures.
3. Operation identification program. This encourages students as well as faculty and staff to mark all personal property and maintain an inventory.
4. Bicycle registration program. This establishes a procedure for students to register their bicycles with the campus public safety department, student government association, or other campus agency in order to prevent bike theft and assist in recovery efforts.
5. Campus watch programs. This is designated to encourage campus residents to be alert for suspicious persons and/or activities and report such activity to campus police officials.
6. Escort service programs. This provides nighttime escorts primarily for females in order to increase safety and create a feeling of security in campus community members.
7. Resident hall security task force programs. This is aimed at enhancing all dormitory security efforts through an organized, representative program. A number of mini-programs are usually developed by this task force.
8. Resident hall security guard program. This consists of guards stationed in dormitories to provide security by monitoring access, communicating with campus police, and being alert to any type of criminal activity or emergencies.
9. Call box/blue light station program. Call boxes or emergency

telephones/radios are located throughout the campus community for emergency use in contacting police/security officers.

10. Physical plant security analysis program. Regular checks of all campus buildings for the purpose of analyzing security to ensure a high degree of building security to prevent intrusion.

Each of the above programs should include an extensive public relations effort to inform and involve the campus community. Brochures, posters, leaflets, and other printed material should be utilized to disseminate crime prevention information. The campus newspaper, the campus or local radio/television station, and special bulletins are excellent means of reaching large numbers of campus community members. Perhaps one of the best information carriers is the campus public safety department. Its officers can share crime prevention tips and encourage safety and security awareness throughout their daily contacts with students and faculty/staff members. The student government association can lend tremendous support to crime prevention programs via its active participation and support. The housing office and student affairs division should be involved in crime prevention in terms of moral support, financial assistance, and active personal involvement. Simply put, a successful campus-wide crime prevention program requires broad support from campus community groups.

Do campus crime prevention programs work? Are they effective in reducing crime? Again, while these questions are often difficult to answer, many programs have been proclaimed as successes. In some cases, crime prevention measures proved to assist in preventing, or at least foiling, specific crimes. For example, at one southeastern state university the dormitory student guard program resulted in thwarting criminal activity and in the apprehension of the culprit on several occasions.

Stanford University provides a testimonial to the value of crime prevention programs. The Stanford University Department of Public Safety organized a Special Servicer Unit (SSU) aimed at crime prevention. The SSU consists of a full-time, non-deputized manager and approximately twelve students part time during the regular school year and approximately six working full time during the summer months. Students in the SSU, design and implement programs for crime prevention, personal safety, disaster planning, bicycle safety and security, and maintain a 90-person security force for special events. The SSU is also responsible for developing a neighborhood watch program, operation identification, and police emergency alarm boxes.[10]

The SSU is only one of several student-based safety organizations on campus. Two other student-organized programs, supported by student-fee assessments, have been successful. The escort service, Stanford United for Rape Elimination (SURE), was expanded to include nightly shuttles from libraries to dormitories. Another program, the Rape Education Project, offers presentations and discussions about rape on campus and seems to have considerably increased awareness about the threats and problems of sexual assault.[11]

Daniel A. Smith, manager of the SSU, attributes its success to a commitment by key university officials in initiating and supporting the effort. He also credits student participation in designing programs and carrying them out. He points out that it also requires patience in developing a comprehensive crime prevention program. He states: "It takes time to generate safety awareness."[12]

The University of South Florida provides another example of an institution which believes in its crime prevention effectiveness. FSU underscores the difficulty in measuring the effectiveness of crime prevention efforts. While statistics and data may often be misleading and meaningless, involvement by community members can be most evident and effective. FSU public safety officials can attest to the impact of community involvement. Their comprehensive public relations and crime awareness efforts have resulted in a significantly larger number of citizen-initiated complaint calls. Of 154 reported suspicious person/vehicle incidents, 65 were initiated by citizens. "Ultimately, the success of any crime prevention program or, for that matter, any university public safety department, is determined by the degree of community involvement/assistance and not strictly the number of crimes reported."[13]

SUMMARY

For years on many campuses special services were afforded little attention and effort. At best, they were provided as "necessary evils" and as an afterthought. Consequently, parking became unmanageable and congested, athletic events and rock concerts became seriously out of control resulting in injuries, and personal safety and property loss became problems. However, in recent years much more support has been given to specializing efforts and services directed at these types of areas.

Now on many campuses sophisticated plans and programs have been developed to deal with parking, special events, and crime prevention. Today, parking systems accommodate large volumes of vehicles in an organized, controlled manner. Adequate and sometimes elaborate security plans and trained personnel are provided to deal with most any type of problem which might occur at special events. Comprehensive campus crime prevention programs with broad community support and involvement are proclaimed as successes in reducing crime and making the campus community a safer place to live, work, and attend school.

It should be utmost concern to every campus public safety director to ensure that these special services are provided and that they are of top quality. He must understand the importance of gaining both administrative and community support in making special services effective. It is his responsibility to provide leadership in directing their programs and demonstrate the accountability for their efforts.

NOTES

1. Wilber J. Waterson, "Cleveland State Parking Director Emphasizes Planning, Credibility," *Campus Law Enforcement Journal*, 15, July/Aug-1985, pp. 28–30.

2. Ibid, p. 28.

3. William W. Wood, "University of Pennsylvania's Parking Lot Safety Program," *Campus Law Enforcement Journal*, 15, Nov./Dec., 1985, p. 11.

4. Joe M. Horn, "Computerized Ticket-Writing Program," *Campus Law Enforcement Journal*, 15, Nov./Dec. 1985, pp. 13–14.

5. Frank J. Pizzulo, "Computer aided management of parking usage system," *Campus Law Enforcement Journal*, 12, May/June 1982, p. 36.

6. Ibid., p. 36.

7. John W. Powell, *Campus Security and Law Enforcement* (Boston, Massachusetts: 51, 1982), p. 194.

8. Phillip L. Mullendore, "Staffing considerations for campus police managers," *Campus Law Enforcement Journal*, 15, Nov./Dec. 1985, pp. 26–27.

9. Ibid., p. 27.

10. Daniel A. Smith, "Crime prevention can work," *Campus Law Enforcement Journal*, 15, July/Aug. 1985, p. 12.

11. Ibid., p. 13.

12. Ibid., p. 13.

13. Max L. Bromley and Gonzalez, R.A. "Citizen Involvement in Crime Prevention: It Can Work," *Campus Law Enforcement Journal*, 14, 1984, pp. 17–18.

Part IV

THE ENHANCEMENT OF
CAMPUS PUBLIC SAFETY

The preponderant examples of sophisticated, progressive campus public safety operations across the country today serve as evidence that public safety in higher education has achieved a marked degree of success. Capable leadership and prudent management have brought campus public safety from non-existence to a viable role within the overall mission of higher education. Yet, there are mountains to climb. Being on the threshold of excellence, it is time for campus public safety administrators to focus on the enhancement of their operations. Extending their efforts beyond the campus community will yield meaningful benefits in terms of actual support as well as a certain amount of prestige and an improved image. Cooperation with other public safety agencies will establish positive relations, better communications, and a line of support in times of need. Involvement in local, state, and national associations affords the campus public safety officials with innovative ideas, relationships with fellow practitioners, and opportunities to contribute to their respective areas of public safety.

Perhaps the best way to enhance campus public safety is to assess the accomplishments which have been made and determine, as best possible, what challenges lie ahead. To a great extent, many of the accomplishments have better prepared campus public safety to meet current challenges and those of tomorrow. In any legitimate assessment process there will inevitably be areas identified as weaknesses or shortcomings. By looking at these, campus public safety administrators and other university officials will be able to more effectively achieve goals and provide quality services to the campus community.

Chapter 12

EXTERNAL RELATIONS:
COOPERATION AND INVOLVEMENT

PUBLIC SAFETY "TOWN AND GOWN" RELATIONS

Most small- and medium-sized colleges and universities across the country are located within the city limits of municipalities, thus a community within a community with both having similar objectives and responsibilities in meeting the needs of their residents. Both city and university officials recognize the importance of cooperation in all areas. The city fathers know well the benefits of having the institution of higher learning located in their community—more jobs, more money to buy goods and services, an enhanced educational, social and cultural environment, and a generally healthy economy. University administrators are aware of the university's dependence upon the city government to provide support essential to its operation such as public services (fuel, water, sewer), public safety (fire protection, emergency medical, and sometimes law enforcement) and other cooperative efforts (parking, recreational activities, facilities usage).

It is in an area of public safety that many of these unique "cocommunities" have learned to share their efforts to better serve the total population and, at the same time, reduce duplication of services and save tax dollars. While public safety is a major concern on college campuses, the city is usually expected to provide public safety services not already provided by the university. However, in recent years most universities have significantly increased and improved their public safety efforts and now not only more effectively serve the campus community but also afford assistance to the local community. Subsequently, we find these two communities interrelated in the area of public safety in terms of shared services, personnel, equipment, and goals. The campus public safety director must recognize the importance of establishing and maintaining close relations with local public safety officials. This may require

213

initiative on his/her part in opening lines of communications as well as special human relations skills.

LAW ENFORCEMENT

Law enforcement is the area of public safety that demonstrates more day-to-day cooperative efforts between municipal and campus agencies than any other. While law enforcement services are frequently duplicated within these communities, it seems to be the best approach in providing police services in each unique community environment and still afford mutual aid to both when needed. Here, it is important to note that a significant difference exists between private and public institutions with regard to law enforcement. In most states private institutions are permitted to have only security officers who are not sworn police officers and do not have the full arrest powers as do the law enforcement officers at public institutions. Usually, the local city police provide law enforcement functions (in terms of arrest and adjudication) for the private institution, while campus police handle most of their own law enforcement problems at the public institution. The University of Tulsa, Oklahoma; Vanderbilt University in Nashville, Tennessee; and Birmingham-Southern College in Birmingham, Alabama are examples of private institutions which provide most adequate security forces but must rely on the local police agencies to provide police authority in making arrests.

It is the small- to medium-sized public university within the small- to medium-sized city that we find the common setting in which both the city and the university benefit from cooperative law enforcement efforts. Here, cooperative efforts in areas of crime prevention, investigation of criminal activities, arrests, adjudication, incarceration, parking and traffic, radio communications, mutual aid and other activities are demonstrated routinely. Interrelated problems such as university students writing "bad checks," theft and trespass on campus by town "locals," off-campus fraternities within the city, major events resulting in civil disorders, and traffic problems are all reasons why the municipal and campus police officers find it important to work closely together toward common goals and objectives. A case in point is the University of Montevallo, located in Montevallo, Alabama. The university there has a student enrollment of approximately 2,800 with a police department of eight full-time officers. The city of Montevallo has a population of approximately 4,800 with a police department of six full-time officers. These two departments work very closely and harmoniously in providing law enforcement services for all residents, including the safety of persons, security of property, apprehension of violators, enforcement of parking and traffic laws, and solving mutual problems as they arise in this college town. The university relies on the city's court for adjudication of arrests and the city's jail for incarceration of prisoners. In turn, the city police frequently call for "backup" assistance when responding to exigent calls. The university police depend on the same mutual assistance with civil disorders at large athletic events as well as traffic and parking assistance at major concerts. Off-campus fraternity problems have been approached on a mutual basis and has had some good results. In this setting, both the university administration and the city council know the importance of these cooperative law enforcement efforts and have good feelings about the problems averted, the additional manpower (through mutual aid) and the sharing of expertise from both departments toward improving the quality and success of law enforcement for both communities.

It is not only the small campus and city that benefit from such a close working relationship, but any university and any city located together can better provide public safety services and do so more effectively and efficiently by sharing ideas, programs, personnel, equipment and services. In the area of parking and traffic, for example, the University of Alabama at Birmingham Police Department has an agreement with the city of Birmingham to enforce both parking and traffic on city streets that run through the university campus. This helps relieve enforcement in that area by the city police department and gives authority to the university police to handle such problems which directly affect its property and students. In the area of crime and investigation, Middle Tennessee State University (MTSU) in Murfreesboro, Tennessee provides a good example. Here, the city of Murfreesboro Police Department and the MTSU Police Department cooperate in investigating crimes of mutual concern. Information is passed between the two agencies in an effort to keep both informed and compare similar MO's (*modus operandi*). A direct private telephone line between these two departments assists in better communications on common cases. Also, a mutual two-way radio frequency allows individual officers to work closely together on investigations as well as other more routine calls. Both agencies benefit from these procedures, and the result is a higher quality of law enforcement than would be available by working solely independently.

In a 1985 workshop, entitled "University Police: An Extra Precinct

With Proven Resources," sponsored by the International Association of Chiefs of Police, Colonel Gerald L. Hough discussed some of the contributions made by the campus law enforcement agencies of the Michigan Department of State Police (MSP). Colonel Hough points to the benefits derived from Michigan State University (MSU). He makes it clear that the MSP–MSU relationship could easily be applied to the twenty other campuses in the state of Michigan. The rewards of having a university law enforcement agency as an "extral precinct" include: having access to records which are invaluable in investigations; utilizing campus police officers as investigative/information resources; having information on foreign nationals; and assisting with formulating and effecting more efficient traffic patterns on and around campus. In addition to the benefits of campus law enforcement, Colonel Hough mentions many other university resources that are available to local and state police (i.e. highway and traffic center, computers, language interpreters, criminal justice education and experts, and other specialists in various discipline areas which may be of assistance). He concludes by stating: "If you are not utilizing their (campus law enforcement agencies) resources and those they can access, you are shortchanging your officers as well as the community you serve. University police departments consistently deliver professional service in a demanding law enforcement role."[1]

FIRE SAFETY

Fire safety is a vital area of public safety that is of high priority on every campus and in every city. Fire prevention and fire protection are two aspects of a complete fire-safety program. While some universities are taking a more active role in fire safety for the campus, most still rely on the city for fire protection. One exception to this is Clemson University in Clemson, South Carolina, where the university there not only has its own fire department but also provides fire protection for the city of Clemson. Some universities have had a limited student volunteer fire department but usually depend on the local city fire department for assistance on major fires. An example of this type of fire service is found at Franklin Pierce College in Rindge, New Hampshire. The Franklin Pierce College Fire Department is run solely by seventeen student volunteers, and all of them are on call 24 hours a day. While most of their calls are routine false alarm, occasionally they do respond to a real fire. The students have one-way communication devices, called pagers, which alert them in the event of an alarm call. There is also a two-way radio communications procedure established with the Rindge Fire Department. The RFD can provide mutual aid when needed. A 1955 Ford front-end pumper is the only major piece of fire fighting equipment that the Franklin Pierce College FD has to provide fire fighting services for this small college.[2]

The vast majority of campuses receive fire protection services from the local city. However, more efforts are being directed by university officials toward better fire safety programs on the campus in conjunction with the city fire departments, thus resulting in a more complete fire safety program. The reality of negligence and liability must be reckoned with by top administrators of universities. City officials in whose jurisdiction the campus lies are also very concerned about fire safety on the campus.

Many small towns and cities have volunteer fire departments. It is interesting that in this area of public safety there is much interrelation of personnel among the campus community and the local volunteer fire department. This lends itself toward a more cooperative spirit of "togetherness" and better communications between the university and the city.

Important aspects of a fire safety program, as discussed in a previous chapter, are inspections, adequate written standard operating procedures, evacuation procedures, alarm system, water and hydrant information, and a good communications system. All of these are concerns of both city and university officials. It is strategic that cooperative efforts exist and that clear, open communication be maintained between both communities. The university needs effective fire protection from the city and the city needs knowledgeable contact persons to provide them with pertinent information regarding the campus. The inspection program is one area that can be a link between the city and campus. If the university maintains an adequate inspection system of all campus buildings and provides the city inspector with this information, it will both ensure the university of its own safety from fire hazards and assist the city in executing the inspections and keeping accurate records. The University of Alabama at Tuscaloosa, Alabama, Middle Tennessee State University at Murfreesboro, Tennessee, and Tuskegee Institute at Tuskegee, Alabama have full-time fire inspection personnel and ensure that fire extinguishers are kept in working condition. Written procedures will also be helpful to the university and fire department officials, especially in response to routine and/or questionable fire calls (false alarms). Through preplanned written procedures the local fire department may also be helpful with bomb threats on campus. Fire alarm systems and radio communications should be common concerns between the university and the city fire department. These can expedite the response, facilitate procedures and save lives.

Many universities are beginning to develop such fire safety programs and systems, while some have already proven theirs to be successful in saving property and lives. Jacksonville State University in Jacksonville, Alabama has begun developing and implementing a complete fire safety program. It actually begins with an emergency telephone sticker which is distributed to every resident student. The emergency number is directed to the JSU Police Department which will, in turn, radio the city fire department directly in the event of a fire on campus. In addition, an inspection program is under way by the University Police Department to inspect every building on campus for fire hazards to include the inspection of fire extinguishers. A city fire inspection form is used, in addition to the campus form, and is filed with the city fire department. A written SOP has been developed with mutual agreement of these procedures between the University Police Department and the Jacksonville Fire Department. Floor plans of all student residence halls are also on file with the fire department. The University of South Alabama in Mobile, Alabama has a more advanced program which includes a monitoring system located in a central location which monitors the local fire alarm system in every dormitory on campus. If an alarm is activated in any of these dormitories, a tone and red light will come on in the respective slot of the monitor panel to indicate exactly where the fire is located. The city fire department can then be contacted immediately.

EMERGENCY MEDICAL SERVICES

Emergency medical services is a relatively young area of public safety. Just a decade or two ago the primary concern and subsequent emphasis was on simply transporting the ill or injured to the nearest doctor or hospital emergency room. In the past ten to fifteen years, emergency medicine has come into its own, providing trained medical technicians and paramedics and advanced equipment with the ability to administer drugs and sustain life until transportation is available. Even smaller towns and cities are now feeling the responsibility to provide their citizens with this vital service. Most universities rely on the cities to share this service with their students. With thousands of students residing on the campus, it is probable that from time to time emergency medical problems will arise and university officials still feel enough of *in loco parentis* to exert efforts that ensure aid to these emergency circumstances. Some universities are hiring trained emergency medical technicians on their police or security forces to serve as "first responders" in medical emergencies.

The university's primary role (short of providing its own personnel, equipment and service) should be to cooperate with the local city's EMS. Good written procedures should be implemented and radio communications maintained with the service. Personal relations and contacts should be established. If the city's EMS is volunteer (as many are), it is a good idea to have some university personnel trained to assist in the city's efforts as well as afford a liaison between the two communities. The campus public safety department is the appropriate agency on campus with which to set up communications and procedures, since calls should come through the emergency telephone. The campus can further help the EMS by establishing "emergency call" procedures with each residence hall to negate non-emergency calls which could be handled by the school infirmary. In some cases, the university may feel obliged to donate pieces of equipment to the volunteer organization to demonstrate their support

Other Services

There are several other important public safety services which have been initiated between some cities and the universities therein. One such service is that of a severe weather alert system. The University of Montevallo utilizes an old steam-powered whistle that alerts both the campus and city residents of an announced tornado warning. The University of Alabama has a similar alert system for the campus which operates by activating the sirens of all the university police cars simultaneously. Another cooperative effort related to public safety is the providing of security for major controversial personalities and/or political figures who visit either the city or the campus. These can be times of serious incidents, and good communications and assistance are important. Still other crucial times for cooperative public safety efforts are during major crises and/or disasters such as tornados, employee strikes, disturbances on campus, major fires, etc. Preplanning for these situations is important. Confidence and good communications will prove to be literally a "lifesaver" during such exigent circumstances.

It is for certain that university administrators and city officials are committed to ensuring the safety of their residents. By working together, planning ahead and sharing resources, common goals and objectives can be more easily reached. The "co-communities" must adopt the "we're-all-in-this-together" philosophy if they are to efficiently and effectively provide the public safety services their people deserve. The innovative ideas and cooperative efforts are almost unlimited when there are clear and open communications between the two communities.

PROFESSIONAL ASSOCIATIONS/ORGANIZATIONS RELATIONS: BRIDGING THE GAP

For years, campus public safety departments have been perceived as "red-haired stepchildren" by other public safety agencies. Some city, county, and state law enforcement officials refused to recognize campus police as part of the law enforcement community. Fire department officials often placed little value in campus fire protection/safety efforts and failed to include campus safety officials in fire service organizations, programs, and endeavors. The newly emerging emergency medical profession of two decades ago did not initially consider campus public safety departments as participating agencies in providing emergency medical services. Moreover, the local, state, and national association and organizations which represent these public safety agencies did not readily recognize and accept campus public safety agencies as members. Many campus public safety departments did and, to some degree, still do suffer an identity problem. This is due, in part, by the perceptions of other public safety officials of the role and credibility of campus departments. Yet, part of this problem must be attributed to campus public safety directors themselves. Many campus public safety directors have not taken the initiative to establish lines of communication with outside agencies and become involved in professional organizations and associations. In fact, some chiefs and directors have not formed nor supported campus public safety associations. Subsequently, a gap has existed between campus public safety departments and other public safety organizations. This gap has left campus police, security, and safety officials isolated from the mainstream of professional public safety organizations and their programs, developments, and valuable information. Fortunately, there has been progress over the past ten years toward bridging this gap. More and more campus public safety directors have recognized the importance of participation in various professional organizations and associations. They have realized the rewards of becoming actively involved with these groups. The rewards are as follows:

Acceptance. By joining professional organizations and participating in their efforts, campus public safety departments achieve acceptance by these groups and become identified as a viable member in that particular field, i.e., law enforcement, security, fire service, emergency medical service, etc.

Communication. As a member of an organization, the campus public safety director has increased opportunities and avenues for communicating common problems, concerns, and ideas with other administrators. It is always easier to get assistance and solve problems if a relationship through association is established.

Information. Information is shared among group members both at meetings and via improved communications as indicated above. Also, many organizations disseminate information via newsletter, bulletins, journals, programs, workshops, etc. This information can be very helpful to the campus public safety director in administering an effective comprehensive program.

Credibility. As a member of a professional organization, the campus public safety director will find that the credibility and professional status of his/her department will be enhanced. This will be recognized by the university administration as well as by other public safety administrators. In essence, the "red-haired step child" perception will be diminished.

There are various organizations and associations with which campus public safety departments may become actively involved. Certainly, it should be pointed out that caution and reasonableness must be exercised in selecting which groups and how many should be participated in. Overextending professional participation can be both expensive and counterproductive. The reputation and relevancy of the organization should be considered. It should be determined if membership will yield worthwhile and meaningful benefits. It is the campus public safety director's responsibility to carefully choose those organizations and associations which would most benefit his/her department. Some organizations actually require no formal membership but are sponsored and funded by various government agencies. These types of organizations provide valuable information and training.

Since campus public safety departments vary in the scope of their responsibilities and functional areas, certain public safety organizations will be pertinent to some departments while irrelevant for others. For example, a campus security department with no fire protection/safety nor emergency medical responsibilities may find no reason to be associated with fire and emergency medical organizations.

Since there is a multiplicity of so-called professional public safety organizations and associations across the country, an attempt to present a complete listing will not be made here. What is presented are some common types of organizations with examples of the most respected and recognized of those which may be considered pertinent to the campus public safety department. The following types of organizations categorized by level provide an overview for campus administrators and public safety directors to consider for membership for their particular operation.

International/National Organizations

There are several public safety-related professional organizations worthy of consideration for the campus public safety department's participation. Perhaps the most relevant and most highly recommended by the author is the International Association of Campus Law Enforcement Administrators (IACLEA). The membership is composed of colleges and universities throughout the United States, Canada, and Mexico, as well as individual campus law enforcement directors and staff, criminal justice faculty members, municipal chiefs of police, companies offering campus law enforcement products and services, and individuals who support professionalism in campus law enforcement administration. IACLEA is dedicated to promoting professional ideals and standards in the administration of campus security and law enforcement. The association goal is to make campus security and law enforcement an integral part of the educational community and issue the safety and well-being of the campus. There are over a thousand members in IACLEA. The president is the elected officer whose term is for one year. In addition, there is a full-time executive director who handles business matters and serves as the editor in chief of the bi-monthly publication, *Campus Law Enforcement Journal.*

The International Association of Chiefs of Police (IACP) is another organization which may be relevant for many campus public safety departments having full police powers. Founded in 1893 this law enforcement organization represents 67 countries, with the majority of its members in the United States. It is composed of agencies large and small, local, state, and federal, with more than 480,000 officers in the United States alone. Many campus police chiefs are active members of IACP. The research, publications, and training produced by IACP provide a tremendous wealth of valuable information to all law enforcement agencies. Much of this information is directly applicable to the campus setting.

There are many universities across the country that have hospital facilities on their campus. Special security efforts must be afforded the facilities. It is encumbent on the campus public safety director who is responsible for hospital security to become knowledgeable about the special security needs which exist and stay informed as to current research findings and security approaches. The International Association for Hospital Security is a prominent organization established to develop, promote, and coordinate better security/safety systems in medical care facilities. There are in excess of 1,500 members which include primarily administrative and supervisory personnel in the field of hospital security and safety. The association sponsors seminars and workshops around the world and sends out five newsletters each year as well as a bi-yearly journal.

The Federal Emergency Management Agency (FEMA) was established in 1979 to focus federal effort on preparedness, mitigation, response, and recovery of emergencies encompassing the full range of natural and man-made disasters. FEMA's National Emergency Training Center in Emmitsburg, Maryland includes the National Fire Academy, the United States Fire Administration, and the Emergency Management Institute. To achieve the academy's legislated mandate (under Public Law 93-493, October 29, 1974) "to advance the professional development of fire service personnel and of other persons engaged in the fire prevention activities," the Field Programs Division developed an effective program linkage with established fire training systems that exists at the state and local levels. Academy field courses have been sponsored by the respective state fire training systems in every state. These programs range from two-day workshops to short courses designed for several weeks of instruction. They include both fire service and emergency medical service training. Since many campus public safety departments are engaged in both fire and emergency medical functions, many of the FEMA programs are relevant to campus needs.

Another organization which may be relevant to campus public safety efforts is the National Association of Emergency Medical Technicians (NAEMT). The NAEMT was found in 1975 by a representative group of nationally registered EMT's from existing state EMT organizations, national emergency medical service leaders, and the National Registry of EMT's to serve the needs of EMT's throughout the country. The association, which has a membership in excess of 20,000 in thirty-five affiliating EMT associations, is actively involved in all aspects of the profession. It publishes the *EMT Journal* and sponsors continuing education programs on a national, state, and local level. Many campus public safety departments encourage emergency medical training for their officers and, in fact, provide basic emergency medical training.

Certainly, there are many other public safety organizations and associations at the national level available to campus public safety departments and their personnel. Those mentioned here provide a few of the prominent groups. The campus public safety director should survey other potential organizations which may meet the needs of his/her department state organizations.

There is a multiplicity of state public safety organizations to include law enforcement, security, emergency medical, and fire services. Most states have active law enforcement associations to include state Fraternal Order of Police chapters, state police chiefs associations, campus police/ security associations, and various other peace officers' associations and organization. It is important for the campus public safety director to be involved in one or more of these groups, thus providing source(s) of information, training, and support to his/her department as well as for the benefit of the institution. It is always reassuring to know that a telephone call to a fellow police chief can provide much needed information and, often, assistance during time of crisis. The fellowship developed through state law enforcement associations builds relationships which yield real results when support is needed. Also, it should be pointed out that today's progressive campus public safety director can make meaningful contributions to these state organizations through his/her expertise, support, and resources.

Most states now have fire academies and professional associations for members of the fire service. While not many campus public safety departments are directly engaged in fire fighting functions, most are involved in fire safety efforts. Subsequently, participation in fire service organizations, associations, and/or programs provides a linkage with fire service officials and a source of information applicable to campus fire safety concerns. Such areas as fire safety education, fire inspection, fire safety standards, and fire safety equipment are vital to most any campus public safety program. As pointed out earlier, some colleges and universities are directly involved in fire protection services and can benefit from all aspects of fire service programs and associations.

Since emergency medical incidents will occur on every campus from time to time, it is important that the campus public safety director and/or his designate maintain open communication with emergency medical agencies and utilize all available information regarding emergency medical response. Most states have state and regional emergency medical associations. It is advisable for the campus public safety department to be represented in one or more of these associations to maintain close contact with those officials with whom training, licensing, and cooperative efforts must be coordinated. State emergency medical services (EMS) usually provide state-of-the-art training, equipment, and techniques which can directly benefit the college or university community. It is recommended that, where feasible, some campus public safety officers be trained as emergency medical technicians capable of providing at least basic life-support services to the campus community. Participation in state EMS organizations and associations is very important to receive current information, establish state relationships, and ensure mutual assistance when needed.

Local Organizations

While participation in national and state associations is important to keep the campus public safety departments abreast of new developments and maintain open lines of communications, it is the local organizations and associations with which involvement is the most strategic to everyday public safety operations. It is at this level that local problems and procedures need to be addressed and cooperative efforts developed.

Local law enforcement associations are of several types to include a local chiefs association, a law enforcement association, a local Fraternal Order of Police, and various local peace officers' organizations and unions. Participation by campus police and security officers in these types of organizations should be encouraged by the campus public safety director. It is also important that the director be actively involved in the local chiefs' association. In some counties the campus police or security force may be one of the largest, with as many or more community members to serve as local cities and towns. Mutual assistance is very often needed. Through relationships established through local associations, better procedures and cooperation can be developed. By the director's active participation, the campus public safety department will earn a degree of recognition and respect once considered unattainable.

Today, there are many campus public safety directors and their personnel actively involved in local law enforcement associations and organizations. In some cases, the campus public safety directors serve as president or other leadership positions with local law enforcement associations. Campus police officers are often actively involved in local chapters of Fraternal Order of Police. This was not the case twenty years ago and is evidence that campus law enforcement is being widely accepted among other more traditional law enforcement organizations.

Fire protection services for most universities are provided by local fire departments. It is very important the campus public safety directors associate with fire service officials and seek to become involved in local associations and organizations. Again, establishing close relationships will certainly facilitate cooperative efforts to provide the best possible fire protection for the campus community. The campus public safety director may be required to participate in local fire service organizations and associations as an associate member rather than a regular member, since he/she may not meet full membership requirements as a fire fighter. The most important consideration will be involvement. By becoming involved, the director will demonstrate his/her interest and appreciation for the fire service profession and its importance to the campus community.

As mentioned earlier, emergency medical crises will occur on the college campus. Since many universities rely on emergency medical response from local (city or county) medical rescue teams, it is vital to maintain good relations with those responsible for providing these services. One way of doing this it to become involved in local emergency medical service associations, either as a regular or auxiliary member, and to encourage campus public safety officers to become involved. This will help to bridge the gap between campus public safety personnel and emergency medical personnel. Cooperative efforts (e.g. emergency planning, emergency response procedures, budgetary concerns) will be enhanced by participation in their associations. In some cases, the campus public safety director may address local EMS groups on special needs and problems on campus as they relate to emergency medical response. On the other hand, EMS personnel can serve as resource persons to instruct campus police/security officers in CPR and other basic first-aid procedures needed for first responders.

There are many examples of positive relations between campus public safety officials and local fire and emergency medical services. Often, campus public safety officers serve as volunteers on local fire and emergency medical departments. In some situations, fire fighters and EMT's may work part-time as campus police or security officers. These kinds of arrangements and relationships are important in bridging the gap and sharing local public safety efforts. The campus public safety director should play a leadership role in encouraging involvement and demonstrate this philosophy by his/her active participation in local public safety organizations and associations.

CIVIC RESPONSIBILITIES

In many cities where universities are located, a common statement often heard is, "You never hear from those university people unless they need something." There may be a bit of truth in this statement in some situations. Many university officials isolate themselves from the local community and its civic affairs. Paying "civic dues" is as applicable to the campus public safety director as it is to anyone else. Certainly, the director can participate only in public safety-related concerns and stay quite busy. There is usually no pressure or obligation to become actively involved in civic affairs. Yet, this is an area often overlooked when focusing on improving public relations efforts. Involvement in civic affairs by the campus public safety director and his employees can enhance the recognition and credibility of the campus public safety department. This participation may be at the state, regional, or county level but is particularly important at the local level.

As a leader and a university administrator, the campus public safety director should be civic minded and extend his department's public relations efforts into the local community. Such involvement demonstrates his/her philosophy of "we're all in this together" and helps remove psychological/social barriers often evident in many "town and gown" situations. There are many opportunities to pay "civic dues" in a meaningful way in order to support worthwhile community efforts and, at the same time, serve to enhance the image of the campus public safety department. These include the following:

1. Active member of a civic group (e.g. Rotary Club, Jaycees, Lions Club, Exchange Club).
2. Participant in local schools through parent-teacher associations.
3. Support and participate in park and recreational activities (e.g. play softball, coach Little League baseball).
4. Serve on city boards and committees (e.g. water board, zoning board, park and recreation committee).
5. Assist with special civic fund-raising efforts (e.g. toys for tots, food for needy families, school playground equipment).
6. Serve as a volunteer fireman, EMT, or civil defense rescue member.

The campus public safety director should establish himself/herself as a respected community member willing to lend a hand and get involved to improve the local community in which the university is located. In the long run, this involvement will result in community support and improved relations with city officials and influential civic leaders. The director should also strongly encourage his/her personnel to become involved in civic affairs and do their share in "bridging the gap" between city and university interests and efforts.

SUMMARY

All organizations are influenced by external factors and, in fact, depend on other agencies, organizations, and individuals to sustain their existence. This is certainly true for campus public safety departments. The wise campus public safety director will recognize the importance of initiating and establishing positive relations with other agencies and organizations. The benefits derived from these relationships will prove significant to the image and programs of the campus public safety organization. By becoming involved in local, state and national associations, the recognition and credibility of campus public safety will be enhanced. The director who persists in operating in a vacuum, so to speak, will eventually find a dearth of support when support is needed the most. While involvement in some organizations and associations may require assertiveness by the campus public safety director, it will be worth the effort. In time, campus law enforcement/public safety will become more widely recognized and accepted among traditional public safety organizations. As a viable part of the higher education community, campus law enforcement/public safety can contribute significantly to their respective public safety efforts.

NOTES

1. Gerald L. Hough, "University Police: An Extra Precinct With Proven Resources," *Campus Law Enforcement Journal*, Mar./April, 1986, p. 35.

2. Thomas J. Meyer, "Franklin Pierce College's Fire Department: 17 Student Volunteers and a Vintage Engine," *The Chronicle of Higher Education*, October 16, 1985, pp. 33–34.

Chapter 13

ACCOMPLISHMENTS AND CHALLENGES:
AN ASSESSMENT

Campus public safety has made great strides since its early begin-nings when elderly watchmen strolled the campus shaking doors. While this form of security sufficed in those early years, the drastic changes experienced by the campus community in the decades of the sixties and seventies demanded a different kind of public safety service. Today, public safety is an integral part of higher education in America. It is as essential to most campus communities as maintenance service, telephones, and parking spaces. Campus public safety has established its own identity and gained a remarkable degree of respect among univer-sity officials as well as academicians. This is all due to significant accom-plishments made by campus public safety in just three decades. It is important to take a look at some of these accomplishments and assess their significance and practical value in meeting the challenges facing higher education.

Change continues to be a constant factor in higher education. As change continues to affect life within the campus community in, often, unpredictable ways, campus public safety officials must be prepared to respond effectively to the inherent challenges. New challenges already facing universities pose special problems for top administrators who must call on campus public safety officials to respond professionally and effectively in dealing with these problems. Many old problems still exist, with others reappearing from time to time. It is difficult to accurately forecast all of the problems and issues which lie ahead. However, it is beneficial to consider the current and potential challenges facing cam-pus public safety, to assess their impact on the community, and to develop effective approaches to deal with them.

ACCOMPLISHMENTS

There are campus public safety departments today which exemplify the most sophisticated law enforcement and/or safety/security organization in existence. Modern management approaches, technological advancements, and highly trained personnel have enhanced the quality of service provided by these organizations. However, it must be recognized that not all campus public safety organizations have attained this degree of sophistication, nor have some progressed far beyond those early days of the watchman. Yet, the great majority of campus public safety departments have achieved remarkable success and boast an impressive number of accomplishments. These accomplishments are best viewed within the following areas: (1) personnel, (2) services, (3) public relations, (4) role clarification, (5) and leadership.

Personnel

The quality of campus public safety personnel (in particular, uniformed officers) has improved tremendously since those early years. Perhaps no other accomplishment is more evident. Most campus public safety officers are now required to meet their state's police minimum standards training. This has afforded a level of training and preparedness for the campus uniformed officer equal to that of his municipal counterpart. It has given credibility to his/her authority and ability to respond to any circumstance within the campus community.

Beyond minimum standards training, impressive staff development programs have also contributed to the improved quality of campus public safety personnel. Even in those institutions and states where campus officers are not required to meet minimum standards training, many campus public safety directors ensure that their personnel receive training to include firearms training, special security techniques, self-defense, traffic control, and patrol techniques.

The educational level of campus public safety officers has risen dramatically on most campuses. It is not uncommon to find departments with more than half their officers holding bachelor's degrees, several with master's degrees and others working toward their degrees. This has had a positive effect on the quality of life within the campus community. Educated police and security officers relate well to the college students, since these officers have had the college experience. They are familiar with the campus setting and the academic process. Many campus public safety officers have academic training in criminal justice/law enforcement that specially prepares them for dealing with crime and the criminal justice system. The presence of these kinds of officers compliments the campus public safety department and enhances its effectiveness.

Services

The services and functions of campus safety have undergone major changes since the inception of campus security. Expansion and improvements in the quality of services entitle them to be listed near the top of the list of accomplishments.

The campus public safety department today better serves the campus community than ever before. The trend is toward continued expansion of services. Providing primarily building security three decades ago, the campus public safety department now effectively provides law enforcement, fire safety, parking and traffic maintenance, around-the-clock communications, crime prevention, safety education, and numerous special services and programs. The expansion of these service areas has enhanced the quality of life within the campus community.

Not only have services been expanded, they have experienced significant improvement in their quality. In recent years, campus public safety departments have become more service oriented in an effort to better meet the needs of the campus community. Consequently, the delivery of services has been done with a degree of difference from even a decade ago. With the emphasis in higher education on excellence, it follows that public safety services should follow suit. Enrollments have generally leveled and, in some cases, declined, shifting the emphasis in higher education from quantity to quality. Campus public safety has not been remiss in its mission to provide high-caliber services. Today, campus communities across the country are blessed with state-of-the-art law enforcement services. Fire safety programs often merit top ratings. Community relations programs and crime prevention efforts are second to none. Consequently, campus public safety has successfully accomplished remarkable progress toward excellence in service.

Public Relations

Campus public safety has, through its quality personnel, services, and leadership, established positive relations with many publics. This has been no easy accomplishment. Earning credibility and gaining acceptance has been a struggle at times. Yet, it appears in most cases that campus public safety, whether it be police or security in title, has overcome the hindrance of image problems. Today, campus public safety departments are viewed as professionally staffed organizations with the credentials and capabilities to handle most any circumstance that may arise. In more and more situations, the campus police department is considered by many to be a notch above the local police agency. Some campus public safety departments are more sophisticated and better staffed than local law enforcement departments and are actually depended on to assist the local agency on a regular basis. This kind of relationship strengthens public relations with the local community.

The most important public relations accomplishment has been the positive relations established within the campus community. Talented leadership, quality personnel, and the effective delivery of services have bridged the gap between campus public safety officials and the publics within the campus community. More top administrators today recognize the importance of the campus public safety department and the contributions it makes to the university. Faculty and staff appreciate the manner in which campus public safety personnel do their jobs. Students today consider these officers as their friends who respond to assist them and routinely patrol the campus for their protection.

All of these improved public relations have not been accomplished without effort. Special public relations programs to include crime prevention, PR brochures, safety lectures, and the provision of special services have brought about changes in perceptions by members of the campus community toward the public safety department. Most safety departments have well-planned and concerted efforts to improve public relations. They have been successful.

Role Clarification

There is evidence which points to a general consensus on the role of campus public safety. Certainly, this continues to be an issue on some campuses. However, most universities have developed a mission and goals for their campus public safety departments which serve to give direction for the role of these organizations. This has come in several stages, which, of course, vary from institution to institution. Initially, campus public safety's role was one of building security. This role prevailed until the late 1950s when campus officers were expected to eject trespassers. This stage considered officers to be quasi-police but with limited authority. The next stage saw the role shift to more law enforcement in nature. This was in response to demonstrations, violence, and crime during the 1960s and early 1970s. Beginning in the mid-seventies, the role of campus public safety began to develop toward a balance of law enforcement and service, with emphasis on quality in both. This continues to be the role of campus public safety on most campuses across the country.

This role clarification is a significant accomplishment. It affords the campus public safety leadership a better understanding of the mission of his/her organization and the expection of the institution's administration. It precludes some of the frustrations of officers. It provides a basis on which to plan programs, deliver services, and perform the daily function of the organization. The current role of campus public safety appears to best suit current needs of the campus community. It should be noted that the role may shift in the future to adjust to the changes which occur on the campus.

Leadership

Listed as last but certainly not least in importance is leadership as a major accomplishment of campus public safety. In fact, high-quality leadership must be credited with the selection of top-notch personnel which effectively exemplifies the quality of campus public safety. These leaders have, in many cases, educated university administrators to the special public safety needs of the campus community. They are responsible for enhancing the image of campus public safety and promoting its philosophy of professionalism and service, both on and off campus. Campus public safety directors frequently serve on prestigious university committees. Some directors hold the title of vice-president. They have introduced and implemented modern police techniques and management approaches. Many of these individuals are highly qualified, hold advanced degrees, have extensive law enforcement experience, and are often graduates of the FBI National Academy.

This is in contrast to the campus public safety director of twenty years ago which was often relegated to a supervisor within the physical plant department. More often than not this individual was a retired municipal or county officer with very little understanding of the campus community and less ability to articulate effectively with the various publics he served. Slowly but surely these individuals were replaced with more competent leaders who's perceptions and philosophies were more compatible with those of higher education.

With this high-quality leadership in campus public safety, institutions of higher education will be well prepared to meet the challenges that lie ahead. Of a truth, campus public safety leadership is both an accomplishment and a reason for accomplishments.

CHALLENGES

In assessing the challenges facing campus public safety, it will be necessary to address past and present issues and problems, since many of these will impact on future challenges. This discussion will not provide an exhaustive list of the many ongoing challenges and problems. It will, however, present some of the problem areas for which those responsible for administering campus public safety services should plan. Unlike the 1960s, perhaps institutions of higher education will be prepared to effectively respond to problems and crises.

Crime

Crime is a challenge that has past, present, and future significance. It is an interesting phenomenon as it relates to the campus community. It is a complex issue for several reasons. Prior to the 1960s, crime on campus was not considered a significant problem for most institutions. However, this is not to say that it did not exist. It is difficult to measure just how much crime occurred on campus, since most existing police/security departments, if they existed, either kept no records at all or did not accurately identify and report them. Another problem related to assessing crime on campus before 1960 was that many, or perhaps most, university administrators ignored the crime problem and/or denied its existence. Since *in loco parentis* was in effect, many criminal acts committed by students were considered pranks and acts of misconduct by university

officials. Consequently, many actual criminal incidents were not classified as such.

Increasing enrollments, building expansion, the demise of *in loco parentis* and student protests during the 1960s and early 1970s yielded more crime. This time, university officials could not ignore its impact, its effect on student life, liability risks and public image concerns. Crime became a recognized problem and a challenge for campus public safety officials. Improved campus public safety management kept better records and began to accurately report crime. For the first time, a more realistic assessment of crime on campus could be developed.

From the late 1970s through the mid-1980s the crime rate on campus remained relatively consistent, usually paralleling national trends. There are no indications that the crime rate within campus communities is on the decline. Therefore, crime remains a very formidable challenge to campus public safety officials.

While many of the traditional types of crime (e.g. assault, theft, rape, disorderly conduct) are destined to plague campus communities in the future, there are indications that some criminal activities will emerge to pose special challenges to campus public safety officials. Some of these are old problems, while others are relatively new. Drugs, and specifically narcotics abuse, may well be one of the greatest challenges ahead. While the use of marijuana and some other illicit drugs has steadily dropped in the past five years, the use of cocaine by college students has increased. One study found that as many as one-third of America's college students try cocaine by the time they graduate.[1] The abuse of narcotics in the United States seems to be spreading in numbers and throughout the various social classes.[2] There is no reason to think that the campus community will be exempt.

Technology has obviously affected the academic community. Consequently, the new crimes of data manipulation, software piracy, and computer-related violations are crimes to be reckoned with. This is an exceptional challenge, since it will require special expertise to deal with these problems. This will, in turn, require new investigative techniques and specialized training.[3]

As discussed in an earlier chapter, terrorism may well become a real threat to institutions of higher education. Education and preparedness will be essential for campus public safety personnel.

Alcohol

Recent federal legislation aimed at raising the age for alcohol purchase and consumption will have a very real effect on the campus community. Since the majority of undergraduate college students are between the ages of 18 and 22, most students will be prohibited from indulging in what has become college students' favorite form of entertainment: drinking and partying. Most college students consider themselves as adults. Moreover, most of the athletic and social activities encourage the use of alcohol. Fraternity activities will pose particular problems, both on and off campus, since many of them include alcoholic beverages and students under 21 at the same functions.

The enforcement of these new state laws will be a monumental challenge for campus law enforcement officials. Policies and procedures will have to be formulated in response to this problem. Many of the enforcement difficulties experienced during Prohibition years may be old problems revisited.

Athletics

Athletic-related problems seem to be on the rise and may stay around for several years to come. Problems of drugs among athletes and fan violence present formidable challenges to campus public safety officials. More and more news releases contain information about intercollegiate athletes using narcotics and other types of drugs. While at first glance this may appear to be a problem for athletic officials, it is a crime-related problem that should concern every campus public safety administrator. These specific cases that become public are often only the tip of the iceberg and may involve other students and non-students. Campus public safety officials should not look the other way or be discouraged in their efforts to investigate drug cases among athletes.

Major athletic events on many of our campuses draw large enthusiastic crowds. The competitive spirit, the crowd, the excitement, and often the alcohol all combine to create an atmosphere conducive to violence. Certainly, affrays among competitive players are common but are usually controlled by game officials. The most explosive and potentially dangerous problem is fan violence. This has been on the increase in the past two years. There have been instances where hostile words developed into fights and fights into brawls, with serious injuries being the result.

In some cases, fan violence has escalated beyond the control of security personnel. Crowd control then becomes a real problem. A case in point is a recent incident of fan violence which occurred at Auburn University following an intercollegiate football game. Some fans ran onto the field and began destroying the turf. Officials used the field sprinkler system to disperse the turbulent crowd.

Fan violence is a challenge to campus public safety officials. It must be approached before the incident occurs through planning and preparation. As collegiate spectator sports become ever more popular and fans become more intense, campus public safety officials in cooperation with athletic officials must cooperatively meet the challenge with effective methods.

Student Protests

As the pendulum swings, it appears that student protests and demonstrations are on the way back. As discussed earlier, there has been a resurgence of these activities at several institutions from coast to coast. With increased student interest in such issues as apartheid in South Africa, U.S. military activism, abortion, gay rights, and nuclear testing, it is very possible that the passivism experienced on campus for the past twenty years may be ending. If the current trend continues, it will behoove campus public safety officials to be well prepared to deal with student protest and the ramifications thereof. Hopefully, lessons can be learned from the sixties and the challenge can be met with effectiveness by campus public safety officials. The accomplishments made by campus public safety organizations since these unforgettable years (i.e. better-trained personnel, better leadership, effective communications, and improved public relations) should serve to prepare for times of crisis ahead. In this sense, the accomplishments should meet the challenge.

Role Clarification

Listed as an accomplishment, role clarification is also a challenge for many campus public safety organizations. This problem exists especially on many small campuses and in many private institutions who have not been mandated to train their officers under police minimum standards. This is also true at some large public institutions. Consequently, some of these institutions continue to relegate their security to watchmen while neglecting liability risks. Public safety functions in these institutions continue to be fragmented or, even worse, neglected. Fire safety, civil defense, and crime prevention efforts may be non-existent. In such situations, the challenge is clear: a comprehensive public safety approach is needed. Toward that end, campus public safety leaders must provide research and information that justifies the improvement of public safety services. When the challenge is met and the mission accomplished, the campus community and university administrators will be recipients.

Liability

Campus public safety officials, university presidents, and boards of trustees are increasingly becoming the defendants in lawsuits resulting from actions or negligence pertaining to some area of public safety. While this was once considered a problem for local law enforcement officials, campus public safety directors have increasingly been faced with the reality of liability risks. It is, therefore, encumbent of campus public safety leaders to be accountable in all areas under their responsibilities. They must ensure that their officers are properly trained, adequately equipped, and sufficiently supervised. They must exert every effort to provide crime prevention programs, adequate lighting, approved fire safety equipment, and proficient response. Department policies and procedures should be developed and followed whether dealing with department personnel or in the delivery of services to the public. Keeping the bases covered is of utmost importance. This, in itself, is a challenge that may well become a greater one in the years ahead.

SUMMARY

The accomplishments of campus public safety have contributed to the quality of life within the campus community. They have also served to establish campus public safety as a vital component of higher education. These accomplishments have further enabled institutions of higher education to achieve their goals and fulfill their principal missions of teaching, research, and service. This progress has not been easy nor is it complete. Campus public safety is still developing and making accomplishments on campuses across the country. As more university administrators recognize the importance of comprehensive public safety programs on their campuses, they will be better able to provide their clientele with a safe environment and a wide range of services.

The accomplishments made by campus public safety organizations have better prepared institutions of higher education for the challenges of today and tomorrow. Most university administrators now have highly qualified law enforcement, security, and safety personnel on their staffs capable of providing public safety services and responding to exigent circumstances. Whatever the challenges ahead, campus public safety exists to deal with them effectively and professionally. While it is impossible to forecast all of the challenges which campus public safety may encounter, it is a tenable claim that progressive campus public safety administrators will stay atuned to the changing climate within higher education and capably meet each challenge with affirmative response.

A prudent assessment of campus public safety's accomplishments and its challenges reveals the aforementioned significant progress along with a few shortcomings. One of these is the failure of many college and university administrators to recognize the need for effective public safety programs for their institutions. Despite the remarkable accomplishments discussed in this chapter, there are far too many institutions which lack any semblance of an effective, accountable public safety department.

Another area which has not experienced sufficient progress on many campuses is that of full police authority for campus public safety officers. This is especially true for many private institutions which have the same problems as do public institutions which provide full police authority for their officers. This severely limits the effectiveness of the officers, jeopardizes safety on campus, and restricts the institution's decision-making authority involving crisis situations.

Another shortcoming as mentioned in an earlier discussion relates to the failure of many institutions' administrations to recognize all of the public safety needs and to adopt a comprehensive approach for campus public safety. The result is fragmentation of public safety functions and, consequently, reduced effectiveness in the delivery of services. There is evidence to indicate positive development in this area.

Perhaps the shortcoming which is the greatest hindrance to many campus public safety operations, yet most often overlooked, is the negligence or inability of campus public safety directors to inform their superiors of public safety needs and acquaint them with state-of-the-art methods with which to better provide public safety services. While the campus public safety director may be a highly qualified, knowledgeable public safety administrator, his/her supervisor may know virtually nothing about the proper role, the goals, the functions, and the procedures of the campus public safety department. In many cases, campus public safety is only one of a number of areas of responsibilities reporting to a vice-president. This vice-president may not have the time or take the time to be familiar with the real needs of public safety on his/her campus. It should be the campus public safety director's responsibility to educate, so to speak, his/her superiors about campus public safety to include its needs, problems, opportunities, and accomplishments.

Despite these shortcomings, campus public safety today has made exceptional progress and, in fact, has achieved success in providing an effective, essential public safety service for the campus community. Campus public safety has certainly earned its recognition and its important place in higher education. With strong leadership, it can achieve excellence.

NOTES

1. Thomas J. Meyer, "One in Three College Students Tries Cocaine, Study Finds; Bennett Urges Presidents to Crack Down on Drugs," *Chronicle of Higher Education,* Vol. 32, No. 20, July 16, 1986, p. 1.

2. Edward J. Tully, "The Near Future-Implications for Law Enforcement," *The FBI Bulletin,* Vol. 55, No. 7, July 1986, p. 3.

INDEX